MAD
FOR IT

ANDY MITTEN

MAD FOR IT

FROM BLACKPOOL TO BARCELONA
FOOTBALL'S GREATEST RIVALRIES

HarperSport
An Imprint of HarperCollins*Publishers*

HarperSport
An Imprint of HarperCollins*Publishers*
77–85 Fulham Palace Road,
Hammersmith, London W6 8JB

HarperCollins' website address is: www.harpercollins.co.uk

First published 2008

1

© FourFourTwo 2008

A catalogue record of this book is
available from the British Library

ISBN-13 978-0-00-728080-3
ISBN-10 0-00-728080-7

Printed and bound in Great Britain by
Clays Ltd, St Ives plc

This book is dedicated to the people I met along the way and their incredible passion for a game called football. And to my dad Charlie, who lit the spark by taking me to watch him play in the Irlam v Urmston cup derby in 1984.

Contents

'By the 1980s, the rivalry had become vicious, with United's Scouse manager Ron Atkinson describing a trip to Anfield as like going into Vietnam. Big Ron's experience fighting the Viet Cong has not been fully substantiated, but he can be forgiven for exaggerating – he had just been tear gassed.' *Liverpool v Manchester United*

'Ian Ramsey began supporting The Shire "to be different from my mates. I wanted to support the least fashionable club." He didn't have to look far … to a club that gave 32-year-old Alex Ferguson his first managerial job in 1974. There were only eight registered players when Ferguson arrived. "They were the worst senior club in the country," Ferguson later wrote.' *Elgin City v East Stirlingshire*

'Tyres are set ablaze, telephone booths vandalised, windows smashed, and anti-regime chants are heard across Tehran and Iran's other cities … in a country where boys and girls fear holding hands in case the special morality police take them in or, worse, send them to a moral correction unit, football may not be enough to contain their passions.' *Iran v Iraq*

Introduction

It was not a day too soon. When Manchester United took on Manchester City away in October 1986, I pestered my dad to take me. I was 12 years old. Dad wasn't a lover of watching football, always preferring to play, but he finally relented and acquired three tickets for the main stand at Maine Road.

I devoured the pre-match hype in the *Evening News* and knew every player of both sides. It wasn't a golden age for Manchester football and the attendance of 32,440 was then the lowest post-war for a derby, partly because the game was the first Manchester derby to be televised 'live'. Before we left the house, mum again warned us to be careful as we went off to watch players like Graeme Hogg, Terry Gibson, John Sivebaek and Chris Turner. So much for United having the big name stars.

Dad parked the car near the stadium in Moss Side's tight terraced streets. I was impressed, as he seemed to know all the ticket touts loitering outside the ground looking to do business. Most were black lads whom he'd played football with and against, a lot of them City fans who ribbed him about 'being United' and told him to watch his back as we were in a City section. They were joking, but the atmosphere was vicious outside Maine Road as fans scurried towards the relative safety of the turnstiles, the police moving everyone along to stop trouble erupting. Unlike our local home-town semi-professional derby involving Irlam and Urmston, the antagonism expressed in this derby was not born from social and economic differences but was generated by football. Both laid claim to be the top club in Manchester. City had for a long time been the most successful club; United's first league and cup victories were achieved, according to City fans, through subterfuge when United took advantage of City's misfortune to poach their best players for a pittance. And the list of United's crimes against their neighbours went on from there. United fans gloried in their club's far greater glamour and worldwide fame.

The game had an interesting twist as John Gidman, the Liverpudlian fullback, had left United days earlier. 'I had bought a sports shop in Liverpool and honestly thought that I was going to run that for the rest of my life as I drove back to Liverpool,' he recalls. Almost immediately, he received a phone call from Jimmy Frizzell, Manchester City's manager.

'Frizzell wanted to sign me. He said, "We're playing United on television this weekend and I want you to play." So I signed and I marked Peter Barnes. He told me to go easy, but you can't do that. He was a great lad but a bit of a softie and I said: 'I'm going to kick f**k out of you for 90 minutes.' They took him off. It was nice for a Scouser to make an impact in the Manchester derby, although when I played at United we always considered Liverpool to be our biggest game.'

It still is, mainly because United's players and supporters began to measure themselves, not against their 'lowly' Mancunian neighbour, but against the Scouse juggernaut which dominated English football and swaggered across Europe until Heysel. Derby rivalries often defy logic. Although Mancunians will tell you they despise Scousers for a whole set of other reasons, historical economic rivalries between the two cities being one, Everton versus Manchester United is rarely described as a derby, neither is Liverpool versus Manchester City.

When United scored, City hooligans stood upright like meerkats to spot any stray celebrating Reds. Dad told us to keep quiet. I couldn't work out why people from the same city hated each other so much, but the buzz was indescribable. My fascination with derby games would only grow.

Twenty-one years later, I'm sitting opposite the Newcastle manager Kevin Keegan, who has just seen his side win the Tyne–Wear derby against rivals Sunderland. The vanquished visiting manager Roy Keane has just faced the press, but he doesn't go for the sentimental, populist, touch. Unlike King Kev.

'You don't get an atmosphere like that anywhere else in the world,' he says proudly. 'You can go round the world twice and you won't get that. Not in Liverpool, the Nepstadion, Budapest, the Maracana or at Boca Juniors. The derby match up here is very, very special.'

He's playing the role of local hero well, but part of me wants to disagree. That's because I'd been travelling to derby games around Europe for *FourFourTwo* magazine and this book for six years. I'd seen derbies where the atmosphere far exceeded that of the Tyne–Wear contest. I'd watched Corinthians play Sao Paulo in the Maracana and wanted to assure Keegan that the atmosphere was far more intense than St James' Park. But I was there to listen, not speak.

Paulo Di Canio, who has played in five derbies, has his own candidates. 'The Juventus–Torino rivalry has deep historical roots, while the Milan derby, Inter verses AC Milan, is probably the best in the world in terms of evenly-matched sides and sheer quality on the pitch,' says Di Canio. 'At West Ham, we played four or five local derbies a year, so perhaps it's less of an event, but you knew when we played Arsenal, Chelsea or Spurs that we were totally fired up.'

Di Canio was adamant which two derbies stood out. 'Apart from the Old Firm (Glasgow) which is far and away the biggest rivalry in all of sport, nothing compares to the Rome derby (between his former club Lazio and Roma). People begin talking about it six weeks in advance, the preparations being made with weeks to spare. The build up is huge, nothing else matters. Roma and Lazio fans care more about winning the derby than where they finish in the league.'

Di Canio, a one time Lazio Ultra, progressed from terrace to pitch, where he scored in the Rome derby. It's a major reason why he is still revered today by the fans he once stood alongside.

Sir Alex Ferguson, though, begs to differ. 'I have been to derby games all over the world ... in Milan, Madrid, Rome, Liverpool and in London, plus, of course, from my old playing days I know all about the fierce rivalry between Rangers and Celtic. However it's our fixtures against Liverpool that get my pulse racing and they are the games I look forward to more than any others. I regard our fixtures with Liverpool as more of a derby than our all-Manchester matches against City.'

Opinions differ widely on which derbies have the most meaning for supporters. Ask Blackpool fans and they'll tell you that there is no game like when they meet Preston, just as I thought that my local Irlam v Urmston was a game of the utmost importance all those years ago.

Despite often loathing their enemies, fans talk proudly of their derby game – often because their appreciation of its importance is so subjective. While a trophy haul is tangible, the atmosphere at a game isn't. Scientists don't measure the noise levels and record the flag displays at games, leaving their impact and size open to exaggeration and debate. Fans of Barca and Madrid consider their clash to be the biggest in the world, yet fans at much smaller derby games deem 'their' derby much more authentic because it is more parochial and intense. 'How can a Madrid player from South America possibly hate Barcelona with the same intensity as a Wrexham born player hates Chester?' one Wrexham fan told me. 'We've seen the posh tennis playing twats take our girls and our jobs. We've got genuine reasons to hate them.'

So while Cristiano Ronaldo may be a superior athlete to any player plying his trade in the Israeli league, Manchester United's fans are not necessarily superior beings. Derbies give the fans of Hapoel Tel Aviv and Maccabi Tel Aviv a chance to demonstrate that they are more committed, more loyal because of the colour, noise and fervour they generate.

'We are not as big as some of the European clubs,' one Hapoel devotee told me in a bar next to Tel Aviv's frequently bombed bus station, 'but we have a much tighter and better organised fan culture. We are better fans and we demonstrate that against [our main rivals] Maccabi.'

Geography, history, sectarianism, class, religion and economics each play their part in shaping the unique nature of derby matches. Nor is there only one type of derby. The term needs some clarification, as it is used to widely different types of rivalries. Some wrongly assume that a derby was originally a cross-city match, the term originating in the East Midlands city of Derby, yet Derby County haven't played a true derby since 1891 when they merged with the city's only other major team, Derby Midland.

Derby fans consider the fixture with Nottingham Forest, who are based 15 miles away, their biggest game. And while Forest have their own cross-city derby with Notts County, they consider the game against Derby to be their main, well, derby.

The origins of the word 'derby' are derived from the horse race known as the Derby Stakes, which was first run in 1780 and named after Edward Stanley, the 12th Earl of Derby. It became established as the high point of the racing season as part of the meeting at Epsom in Surrey in early June. Such was its importance, other classic races were named after it, such as the Kentucky Derby.

Derby day, the day of the race – always a Wednesday until recently – became a hugely popular event, not just for the toffs but as a big day out for all Londoners, a public holiday in all but name. Great numbers of people drove or took the train down to Epsom, making a day of it with picnics and lots to drink. In 1906, George R. Sims wrote: 'With the arrival of Derby Day we have touched the greatest day of all in London; it may almost be said to be the Londoners' greatest holiday – their outing or saturnalia.'

Around the time George Sims was writing, the word moved into more general use to describe any highly popular and well-attended event. In particular, it came to be applied to a fixture between two local sides, first called a local Derby and then abbreviated. But it is used to describe football games between teams which may be situated far further apart, regional rather than local rivals.

The 28 games featured here are by no means definitive, but they are chosen because they demonstrate the incredible diversity of derbies, as well as the common elements they share. The Faroes was the only place on my travels where I was unable to find a fan with a bad word about their rivals, for instance. In Glasgow, it wasn't difficult.

Some games are omitted because we only wanted each team to feature once. The cross-city derbies in Madrid and Barcelona are fascinating, but they don't compare to the Barca–Madrid game.

I tried to spend at least 48 hours in a city to write a feature. It irritated me as a Mancunian and United fan when writers were parachuted into Manchester for the day and returned to write lazy features full of stereotypes, which often missed the point. And while I spoke to the usual suspects like players and local journalists, I tried to talk to as many fans as possible. Fans often have a far greater feeling for a rivalry than any player could have. Because of my background editing the *United We Stand* fanzine, I've always felt comfortable around fans and understand the nuances and hierarchy of fan culture. When I went to Anfield or Ajax Amsterdam, I didn't do what television cameras tend to do and collar the fan desperate to perform for the cameras for his or her opinion.

Instead I sought out the views of the most hard-core supporters. Sometimes they were hooligans; sometimes they were old men who hadn't missed a game for half a century. But they were always people who cared deeply about their club.

I tried to be objective. I always knew I was going to be in a no-win situation the minute I agreed to write the piece on Cliftonville–Linfield in Belfast. In fact, I turned down the assignment many times. I finally agreed when Mat Snow, then editor of *FourFourTwo* told me, 'You either write it or I'm commissioning someone else.' I couldn't let the opportunity slip and loved my time in Belfast. I produced a positive and passionate piece to reflect that enjoyment. I tried my best to be fair and the initial feedback on the message board populated by fans of football in Northern Ireland was very encouraging. Then the bigotry started to seep in and extremist cyber warriors took over. One wrote that I had been so fervently anti-Linfield (had I?) because I'd stayed at the house of a Glentoran fan, their hated enemy, on my sojourn in Belfast. Actually, I'd lodged with a Linfield fan.

That's football fans, though. When Hugh Sleight took over Mat Snow's job at *FourFourTwo*, he encouraged me to cover as many derbies as possible. I was happy to oblige. Of the pieces that have appeared previously in the magazine, I've already been able to gauge reactions. I've been accused of bias, yet been informed that I never need to buy another pint should I return to Wrexham or Rotterdam. I remained in contact with the fans at many clubs, while I've no wish to speak to the official of East Stirlingshire who was possibly the rudest person I came across on all my travels.

As in politics, a week is a long time in football: for example, when the Southampton–Portsmouth chapter was written Southampton were in the ascendancy. Now, for the time being, Portsmouth have turned the tables and are the Premiership side, as well as celebrating a long overdue FA Cup win. For rivalries that go back in time, it was decided to retain the flavour and relevance of those particular clashes rather than update to more recent matches, which would dilute the impact of the originals.

Of the games included here, I have covered 14. It would have been impossible for one writer to cover them all, nor am I necessarily the best qualified person to do so. The other writers are listed and credited with their biographies elsewhere. I am thankful to all. Each one of us has tried to convey why these games are, as *FourFourTwo* entitles its regular feature on derby games of all shades and on all continents, 'More Than A Game'. From the high theatrical drama of Rome's Il Derbi Capitale and el gran classico in Madrid to the infinitely more parochial Caledonian tussle for supremacy between the Shire and Elgin on Scotland's windswept north east coast, football's most intense encounters are laid bare in these pages.

Andy Mitten
Barcelona, June 2008

Seeing Red
Liverpool v Manchester United, March 2007

One of the most eagerly-awaited games of the season, between
two teams whose cultural influence extends far beyond their
city boundaries.

My head feels like it's going to explode. Barely ten yards in front of me,
John O'Shea is wheeling away in celebration and the stunned Scouse
silence means the joyous screams of the Manchester United players are
audible. We've beaten arch-rivals Liverpool in dramatic and, many
will say, undeserved circumstances: one-nil, at Anfield, with a killer
late goal after defending for much of the game. As a result, we're now
twelve points clear in the race for a Premiership title most fans considered out of reach last August.

As the players shout at lung-bursting volume and frenziedly hug
each other, I have to contain the euphoria of this perfect, body-tingling
buzz, not showing the slightest sign of pleasure. I'm standing on the
Kop, a lone Mancunian in a mass of 12,000 fuming Liverpool fans.

After glancing one last time at the ecstatic United players and 3,000
delirious travelling fans in the Anfield Road stand, I jog back to the car
through the streets of dilapidated and boarded-up Victorian terraces
which surround Anfield. Past pubs, the ones closest to the ground
teeming with fans from Bergen and Basingstoke with their painted

SIX CLASSIC GAMES

United 3 Liverpool 4
League, February 1910

United's new Old Trafford home, resplendent with an 80,000 capacity, earned the club the 'Moneybags United' tag. The stadium's grand opening was going well as United led 3–1 after seventy-four minutes. Then the visitors scored three times …

faces, jester hats, and replica kits. It reminds me of Old Trafford. Finally, in the relative safety of the car I let my emotions go and punch the air repeatedly, before looking out to see a man staring at me from his front room window. He raises his two fingers. It's no 'V' for victory and I don't need assistance from a lip reader to know what he's saying. It's time to get on the East Lancashire Road and back to Manchester.

My mood had been so very different before the match as I queued to get onto the Kop for the first time in my life. I'd not seen a United fan all day, save for the Mancunian ticket touts working the streets alongside their Scouse counterparts behind the Kop. 'We're in the same game and we all know each other,' explained one. Whether you're at the Winter Olympics in Japan or Glastonbury Festival, the vast majority of spivs will be Mancunian or Scouse, an unholy alliance of wily, streetwise grafters.

Like me, 95 per cent of the United fans at Anfield wore no colours, but paranoia gripped me as I reached my seat. It would take just one person to suss I wasn't a Liverpool fan and I'd be in serious trouble. I wasn't going to attempt to fit in by trying a Scouse accent, mutilating words like 'chicken' to a nasal 'shickin' or calling people 'la', 'soft lad', or 'wack', but I wasn't aiming to advertise my allegiances either.

'Alright mate,' said the lad next to me in a North Wales accent as I found my seat.

'Alright mate,' I replied, cagily. They were the last words I spoke all game.

When Liverpool's fans sang 'You'll Never Walk Alone' I focused firmly on events on the field. I did the same when they chanted, 'You've won it two times, just like Nottingham Forest,' in reference to United's two European Cups compared with Liverpool's five.

I ignored the continual anti-Gary Neville abuse, was surprised that Cristiano Ronaldo wasn't booed once – 'We don't go for all that "little Englander" nonsense,' a Scouser explained later – and stunned that the Kop applauded Edwin van der Sar as he took to his goal. The Dutchman applauded back warmly.

All around me, Liverpool's flags continue the European theme: 'Paisley 3 Ferguson 1' reads one. Liverpool are obsessed with flags. One piece of cloth even has its own website; others try hard to be examples of the famed Scouse wit.

At half-time, I met Peter Hooton, former lead singer of The Farm and lifelong Liverpool fan in front of the Kop's refreshment kiosks where the Polish catering staff struggle to decipher the Scouse brogue.

'What are you going to do when we score?' he asked.

'When?'

'When.'

But Liverpool don't score and United have taken six points from Liverpool this season.

It is commonly agreed that there is rising tension between fans of Liverpool and Manchester United. At Old

SIX CLASSIC GAMES

United 2 Liverpool 1
FA Cup Final, 1977

With the League Championship in the bag and a European Cup final to follow, rampant Liverpool were clear favourites – even among some United players. 'We were not too confident,' admits striker Stuart Pearson. 'We knew we'd give Liverpool a game but they were so good you could never say: "We're going to beat these".' United won a thriller, thus denying Liverpool the Treble.

Trafford last October, both clubs sought to defuse the increasingly fraught atmosphere. During an FA Cup game at Anfield in February 2006, a Liverpool fan had hurled a cup of excrement into the 6,000 United fans on the lower tier of the Anfield Road, hitting one on the head. After the game, Liverpool fans rocked the ambulance carrying injured United striker Alan Smith to hospital – though Smith later received hundreds of cards from well-wishing Liverpool supporters, keen to stress that this was something which made them ashamed.

At Old Trafford, past greats like Bobby Charlton, Ian Callaghan, Denis Law, and Roger Hunt were paraded on the pitch before the game and a penalty competition was held between rival fans. It didn't work. Not that anyone was too surprised given the levels of animosity. Liverpool fans approaching Manchester that day had been greeted with freshly-painted 'Hillsborough '89' graffiti on a bridge over the M602 in the gritty United heartland of Salford. Closer to the stadium, another sprayed message bore the legend: 'Welcome to Old Trafford, you murdering Scouse bastards.'

The teams were led out by Gary Neville, punished for the heinous crime of celebrating a goal in front of Liverpool fans the previous season, and Steven Gerrard. Both understand the United v Liverpool rivalry acutely given their lifelong affinity with the clubs they captain. Both would rather stick pins in their eyes than join the enemy. Both were subject to dog's abuse in the songs which rang round the stadium, which also rehearsed some enduring stereotypes and prejudices about the two clubs and the inhabitants of their cities.

United fans: 'Gary Neville is a red, he hates Scousers.'
Liverpool: 'USA! USA!'
United: 'Michael Shields gets bummed by queers.' (Referencing
    Liverpool fan Shields, who was jailed in Bulgaria for an attack on
    a waiter before Liverpool's 2005 European Cup victory, a charge
    which he denies.)

Liverpool: 'Walk on, walk on, with hope in your heart, you'll never walk alone.'

United: 'Sign on, sign on, with hope in your heart, you'll never get a job.'

Liverpool: 'We won it five times in Istanbul, we won it five times.' (*Liverpool fans hold up placards bearing the number five.*)

United: 'Steve Gerrard, Gerrard, he kisses the badge on his chest ... then puts in a transfer request, Steve Gerrard, Gerrard.'

Liverpool: 'All around the fields of Anfield Road, where once we saw the king Kenny play – and could he play. Stevie Heighway on the wing, we have tales and songs to sing, now its glory around the fields of Anfield Road.'

United: 'Murderers, murderers.'

Liverpool: 'Shit on the Cockneys, shit on the Cockneys tonight.' (*A surprising reference to United's perceived out of town support – United are usually loathed by Scousers precisely because they are Mancunian*).

United: 'If you all hate Scousers clap your hands.' (*More people join in this than any other chant.*)

Liverpool: 'We all hate Mancs and Mancs and Mancs.'

United: 'Park, Park wherever you may be, you eat dog in your own country. But it could be worse, you could be Scouse, eating rat in your council house.'

Liverpool: 'Once a blue, always a Manc.' (*For Wayne Rooney*)

United: 'Once a blue, always a Red.' (*For Rooney*)

Liverpool: 'You fat bastard.' (*To Rooney – a Scouser who has contributed financially to the 'Free Michael Shields' campaign*).

United: 'City of culture, you're having a laugh.'

Liverpool: 'Oh Manchester, is full of shit ...'

United: 'Does the social know you're here?'

Like all the greatest rivalries, it's the common ground that divides the most. Manchester United and Liverpool both hail from largely

SIX CLASSIC GAMES

Liverpool 2 United 1
Milk Cup Final, 1983

An Alan Kennedy equaliser ten minutes from time cancelled out Norman Whiteside's twelfth minute opener and extra-time followed. With 100 minutes played, Ronnie Whelan curled a shot around the United defence to score the winner and seal Liverpool's third consecutive League Cup.

working-class, immigrant cities with huge Irish populations. Just thirty-five miles apart in England's North West, both were economic powerhouses that enjoyed a friend/foe relationship by the 19th century. Liverpool considered itself the greatest port in the world, gateway to North America for millions, and a key trading post for the Empire. Manchester was 'Cottonopolis', the first city of the industrial revolution – hence the phrase 'Manchester made and Liverpool trade'.

Civic co-operation in anticipation of greater wealth ensured that the world's first passenger railway was opened between the cities in 1830, but by late 1878, the year Manchester United were formed as Newton Heath, a worldwide trade depression left Manchester grappling with economic stagnation and labour migration. Liverpool was blamed for charging excessively high rates for importing the raw cotton spun in Lancastrian mills and Manchester's solution was to give the city direct access to the sea to export its manufactured goods, thus cutting out the middle man of Liverpool.

A canal big enough to carry ships was proposed, which infuriated Liverpudlians. They tried to ridicule the plans out of existence and Liverpool-based backlash against the ship canal ranged from music hall songs and pantomime references to reasoned economic argument. None of it prevented the Manchester Ship Canal being built and the city became Britain's third busiest port, despite being forty miles inland. This is why the United crest has a ship on it. But this was only a temporary respite for Manchester.

With the end of the British colonies and the introduction of container ships, Liverpool's port became less viable, while the disintegration of the textile industry hit Manchester and both cities suffered generations of economic decline and depopulation. Extreme deindustrialisation and suburbanisation was coupled with growing unemployment and poverty among the proletariat. The nadir was marked in 1981 by violent riots in Manchester's Moss Side and Liverpool's Toxteth districts.

Yet when it came to football and music, both cities punched well above their respective demographic weights, making them special to millions around the globe, but also reinforcing and extending the rivalry.

On the pitch, enmities were not clear cut. Manchester City were the bigger Mancunian club until World War Two, while Everton were often the pre-eminent Merseyside force. Indeed, the rivalry between United and Liverpool was respectful until the 1960s with some Manchester United players even going to watch Liverpool when United didn't have a game.

'We'd stand on the Kop,' recalls Pat Crerand, a former hard-tackling United midfielder turned pundit. 'The Scousers would have a word with us, but it was good humoured.' Bill Shankly used to call Crerand at home every Sunday morning for a friendly football chat. Shankly and the United manager Matt Busby, who both hailed from Lanarkshire mining stock in Scotland, were also close and Busby had played for Liverpool.

'I always had great respect for Liverpool Football Club and Bill Shankly,' adds Crerand (though that didn't stop him, in his early-'70s role as United's assistant manager, from snaring Lou Macari in the Anfield main stand just as he was about to sign for Liverpool). 'When I go to Anfield now, I speak to long-standing Liverpool fans who can't put up with what the rivalry has become, with the hooliganism and the nastiness between the fans. Liverpool and Manchester are both working-class cities that have produced two of the greatest football clubs in the world. People should be proud of that, but they're not.'

United had the hegemony in the 1960s – twice league champions and the first English team to win the European Cup. Not since that decade has a player left United for Liverpool or vice-versa (Phil Chisnall was the last, in April 1964). Liverpool were far superior to United in the 1970s and '80s, winning four European Cups and eleven league titles as United endured twenty-six title-free years, but United were usually the better supported club and matched Liverpool in head-to-head encounters. And even as Liverpool had the success, United enjoyed a reputation and allure which rankled Liverpool supporters who thought it undeserved.

By the 1980s, the rivalry had become vicious, with United's Scouse manager Ron Atkinson describing a trip to Anfield as like going into Vietnam. Big Ron's experience fighting the Viet Cong has not been fully substantiated, but he can be forgiven for exaggerating – he had just been tear gassed.

'We got off the coach and all of a sudden something hit us and everyone's eyes went,' Atkinson recalls. 'I thought it was fumes off new paint or something, but it was tear gas. In our dressing room before the game there were a lot of fans, Liverpool fans too, kids, all sorts, eyes streaming. Clayton Blackmore was so bad he wasn't able to play. I was in an awful state. I'd run in and there'd been two blokes standing in front of the dressing room door and I couldn't see who they were. I was blinded and I'd pushed one of them up against the wall. Afterwards, [assistant manager] Mick Brown said, "What you done to Johnny Sivebaek?" I said, "What are you on about?" It turned out that Sivebaek, who we'd signed the week before, didn't speak much English and in his first game, against the European champions, he was gassed as he got off the coach and then got hurled against the wall by his new team manager. No wonder he didn't perform that day!'

Liverpool fans frequently sang songs about the 1958 Munich air crash, but stopped for a time after the 1989 Hillsborough disaster.

United fans barely sang about Hillsborough until a minority changed that in recent years. Yet for every United fan who stoops so low, you'll find one who respects the continued boycott of *The Sun* on Merseyside and the continuing campaign for justice for the ninety-six who perished.

For United fans, no matter how dangerous the trip to Anfield became, it remained one of the most eagerly-awaited of the season because it contained all the edge, passion, and vitriol that you'd expect from a long-standing cultural and social enmity between two teams whose cultural influence extends far beyond their city boundaries.

SIX CLASSIC GAMES

Liverpool 3 United 3
League, April 1988

First v Second, but Liverpool's substantial lead made them clear title favourites. Reduced to ten men and trailing 3–1 with thirty minutes left, United were on the ropes until goals from Bryan Robson and Gordon Strachan levelled the scores. The latter celebrated by smoking an imaginary cigar in front of an outraged Kop.

In the 1990s, Liverpool's demise coincided with United's ascendancy under Alex Ferguson. Asked to list his greatest achievement at United, Fergie once replied: 'Knocking Liverpool off their fucking perch. And you can print that.' That wasn't quite how Scousers intended it to be when they unleashed their 'Form is temporary, class is permanent' banner in 1992 as United squandered a league title at Anfield.

In contrast to the hooligan-blighted '70s and '80s when Liverpool were on top, the Sky-led football boom allowed United to capitalise on their success and the Mancunians accelerated into a different financial league by regularly expanding Old Trafford; meanwhile Liverpool were hampered by Anfield's limited capacity. United were so commercially successful that many fans objected to the 2005 Glazer takeover principally on the grounds that they were not needed, while Liverpool fans welcomed their new American owners in 2007 because they are.

Both clubs fill their grounds but Old Trafford has over 30,000 more seats than Anfield, allowing United to make more than £1.4 million per home match than Liverpool. Liverpool only have to look east for the justification for building a new stadium.

It's three hours before kick-off at Anfield and I'm sitting in a pub full of Liverpool fans in Liverpool city centre. Among them is the novelist Kevin Sampson, author of seminal tomes like *Away Days* and *Powder*. Reading *Powder* and knowing that Sampson was a Liverpool fan, I interviewed him for the *United We Stand* fanzine in 1999.

I met him at Lime Street and it went well – it remains the most popular interview in the fanzine's eighteen-year history, although we received three letters from readers appalled about 'fraternising with the enemy'. Our conversation should have been over a lunchtime pint, but extended to an overnight stay as Sampson introduced me as a curiosity figure to assorted Liverpool characters who claimed they'd never met a Mancunian United fan before.

Some didn't want to socialise; they didn't want to *like* what they had spent a lifetime loathing. They were content with the status quo that Liverpool and United despised each other and wouldn't have it any other way: happy to reinforce stereotypes, exaggerate prejudices, and ignore the evidence that the two clubs are almost too alike to admit it. United fans were the same, perpetuating the clichés of Scousers as employment-shy thieves and passing over the statistic that you are almost twice as likely to get your house burgled in Manchester (which has burglary rates three times the national average) than Liverpool.

It's the same in the pub today but there are signs of grudging respect.

'Is there *anything* you respect about Manchester United?' I ask a table of hardcore Liverpool fans.

'Paul Scholes', comes one reply.

'Ryan Giggs', another.

'I don't like Gary Neville, but I respect the way he signs contract after contract at United. We'd love a player who celebrated a goal so passionately against his main rivals.'

'Why are United fans obsessed with Liverpool?' asks another. 'All your songs are about Liverpool. Ours are too, but we support Liverpool.'

One thing we do all agree on

SIX CLASSIC GAMES

Liverpool 3 United 3
League, January 1994

After winning the league for the first time in twenty-six years, United went to Anfield and were 3–0 up in twenty-four minutes. But Liverpool refused to be humbled and Nigel Clough pulled two goals back before half-time. United searched for another goal, but Neil Ruddock equalised with eleven minutes left. A classic.

---

is a decline in the atmosphere inside both grounds. Sampson is now behind a campaign to 'Reclaim the Kop'. In October 2006, he wrote an impassioned plea on a Liverpool website regarding his club's support. It came after Liverpool had played Bordeaux, when sections of the Anfield crowd taunted 3,000 Frenchmen with chants of 'Who are ya?', 'Eas-eh' and 'You're not singing anymore'.

'Seasoned heads were shook,' reads the website. 'It was embarrassing. These fans had welcomed travelling Reds for our away game, and here, at Anfield, we were ridiculing them. This is NOT the Liverpool Way. We led from the front. We never followed. Be it pop music, terrace chanting, fashions; we were pioneers in the British game. The "Reclaim the Kop" aims are to promote The Kop's traditional values, its behaviour, and its songs. It aims to encourage fair play and respect towards the opposition; to promote The Kop's traditional songs and chants; to encourage wit and creativity; and it aims to rebuild the camaraderie and individuality of football's greatest terrace.'

'Our support needs sorting out before the quilts [the antithesis of the streetwise fan] have watered us down to nothing,' added Sampson.

It would be easy to attempt to score cheap points at the very idea of organised spontaneity, but United fans have gone through exactly the same. Despite great success on the pitch, the atmosphere inside an increasingly commercialised Old Trafford withered throughout the 1990s. The 'singing section' in Old Trafford's Stretford End is contrived, but it was needed to kick-start a lame atmosphere which still pales alongside past decades.

Like Liverpool fans, long-standing United fans cringe at elements of the club's glory-hunting support. There is tension and in-fighting within both fan bases – hardly surprising given that they are so big. Like Liverpool fans, United fans hate the way opposing clubs bump up the price of tickets for away fans – a rich club doesn't mean rich fans. Both sets of fans are regular visitors to Europe and have similar tales of police brutality. Many on both sides are indifferent to the fortunes of the England national team, preferring pride in their own city and team. The laddish fan elements dress in a similar way, listen to the same music, and note the same cultural influences. When news filtered through recently that the Salfordian 'Mr Madchester' Anthony H Wilson had cancer, there was as much respect on Liverpool websites as on any United one – despite Wilson once presenting Granada's regional news wearing an FC Bruges rosette on the eve of Liverpool's 1978 European Cup Final against the Belgians.

Both fans talk with pride about the renaissance brought by new developments in their cities after decades of decline. Yet for all the similarities, there are stark differences between Liverpool and Manchester.

'Liverpool has a very small middle class,' explains one Anfield season-ticket holder who lives in Manchester. 'As soon as people get money they leave, moving to the north of the city or to the Wirral. Or else they move to Manchester or London to further their professional ambitions.'

Several Liverpool and Everton players live in Manchester's suburbs and regularly shop and socialise in the city, no United players live near Merseyside. You don't see neon signs offering 'quality perms' in Manchester.

Liverpudlians seem more maudlin, with the popularity of the deceased measured by the number of tributes taken out in the bulging obituary column of the *Liverpool Echo*. Mancunians are more inclined to adopt a harder exterior – and

> ## SIX CLASSIC GAMES
>
> ### United 2 Liverpool 1
> ### FA Cup, 1999
>
> ---
>
> The treble seemed a long way off as Liverpool led an off-the-boil United with barely a minute to go. Then Dwight Yorke equalised and Ole Gunnar Solskjaer scored the winner in injury-time. In an uncanny rehearsal of what would follow in Barcelona, a gleeful Stretford End demanded to know: 'Who put the ball in the Scousers' net?'

not just to the thousands of Scousers who flood the incongruous Trafford Centre, Manchester's superior concert venues (the Liverpool team booked their Take That tickets for the *Manchester Evening News* Arena on the day they came out) or Manchester Airport, now that Scousers look beyond North Wales for their holidays.

Three days after the game at Anfield I received a text from the Liverpool fan who sorted me with a ticket for the Kop.

'The lad next to you knew who you were,' he writes. 'He couldn't think where he had seen you but he clicked after the game. He'd seen you covering the Wrexham vs Chester game for *FourFourTwo* last year and knew you were a Manc. He told the others after you had gone.'

It wasn't just Manchester United who got lucky.

'Get Ready for a War'
River Plate v Boca Juniors, April 2001

They know each other as 'the chickens' and 'the shits'. Seventy-nine arrests is considered a quiet day at the office. River Plate v Boca Juniors is more than just another game …

Autumn in Argentina and it's warm and sunny without being uncomfortably hot, but in Buenos Aires the mercury is beginning to rise. It's midday and around 2,000 fans are gathered outside *El Monumental* ('the Monument'), the 70,000 capacity home of reigning Argentine champions River Plate, and the stadium which witnessed Argentina lifting the World Cup in 1978 beneath a shower of ticker tape and toilet roll. Suited and booted middle-aged men, briefcases in hand, stand toe to toe with the young, replica shirt-wearing riffraff, a stark contrast in their scuffed trainers and ripped jeans as they queue along the edge of the stadium's perimeter fence.

As the queue bottlenecks towards the pitifully inadequate number of open ticket booths, the crowd surges forward *en masse*, forcing dozens of armed police into action with their shields. As the jubilant River fans emerge from the scrum, one by one they kiss their tickets before holding them aloft like trophies and exchanging high fives and celebratory hugs with others. It's as though they've already won the match in question, even though it's still two days away and it's not being played here but at on the other side of town at *La Bombonera* ('the Chocolate Box'), home of River's bitter rivals Boca Juniors. But this, you see, is no ordinary match. This is *El Superclassico* ('the super derby') and River's allocation of 11,000 tickets will be snapped up in next to no time.

So big is *El Superclassico* that to the media this week's anti-capitalist demonstrations in Buenos Aires, sparked by an impending free-trade convention in the city, is a mere side show in comparison to the main event. Television chat shows and radio phone-ins are dominated by Boca-River this week and for the next few days, Argentina's top sports newspaper *Olé* will dedicate ten pages of editorial to the clash each day. Also, on every wall around the city is a poster published by Argentina's weekly football magazine *El Graphico* bearing the red and white shirt of River, the yellow and blue shirt of Boca, and the words *Se Viene* – 'It's Coming.'

Argentina's two biggest and most successful clubs have met 166 times before this week – Boca winning sixty-one, River fifty-five – and have been fierce rivals since 1923 when River moved from La Boca, a cosmopolitan, working-class neighbourhood where both teams then resided. Since 1944, River have played in Nuñez, also known as *Barrio River* ('Neighbourhood River'), a middle-class neighbourhood some ten kilometres north west of La Boca, up the River Plate from which the club takes its name. They have since been dubbed the middle-class team.

Although most people will tell you this class divide no longer applies, the rivalry remains just as intense. For example, River's kit manufacturers are sportswear giants Adidas, with their biggest rivals Nike doing the honours for Boca, so you'll rarely see River fans wearing Nike gear, nor Boca fans donning the Adidas logo. As for wearing the colours of your rival team, well that's totally out of the question. The only apparent contradiction in the rivalry is the fact that both teams are sponsored by *Quilmes*, Argentina's most popular beer.

So deep do emotions run between these two that we've barely stepped off the plane when my translator Pablo, an ardent River fan, greets us with some words of warning: 'Get ready for a war.' Sadly, 'war' is an all too accurate description of some of the scenes that have marred Boca–River fixtures in the past. In June 1968, seventy-four fans were killed at *El Monumental* when Boca supporters caused panic by throwing burning paper onto the home fans beneath them. More recently, in 1994, a busload of River fans was ambushed several miles away from the ground, resulting in two of them being shot dead. River had won the game 2–0 and for days afterwards graffiti appeared around Buenos Aires reading 'River 2 Boca 2.'

These crimes of passion are committed by the *Barra Bravas* ('tough gangs'), Argentina's notorious hooligan groups. River's *Barras*, *Los Borrachos del Tablón* ('The Drunks from the Board,' a name derived from the days when the terraces were wooden planks on which the fans bounced up and down), have succeeded the Boca hooligans, *La Doce* ('The Twelve', so called because the fans believe they are the team's 12th player), as Argentina's most feared gang.

For both sets of *Barras*, *El Superclassico* is the season's most important game. 'On balance, most fans would rather beat La Boca than win the championship,' says Matias, a 24-year-old River *Barra*, motorcycle courier, and trainee lawyer, who was brought up in Palermo, a middle-class neighbourhood not far from *El Monumental*. 'It is more important to beat Boca on their own turf,' he explains. And this week, they'll get the chance.

Down at *La Bombonera* in the newly opened Boca Juniors museum I ask an assistant whether Boca fans share the same sentiments when it comes to beating River. 'Are you kidding?' he replies. 'There was a party round here when River lost on Wednesday [in the Copa de Libertores to Uruguayan side The Strongest]. I'd rather Boca beat River and ruin their chances of winning the championship than Boca lose to River and win the championship ourselves.' With River five points clear at the top of the table and Boca loitering near the bottom, he would say that, wouldn't he?

As the fans gear themselves up for what is their cup final the players are trying to keep some sense of perspective. The River players, in particular, are doing their level best not to get caught up in the hysteria. 'I know this game means a lot to both the fans and the players,' says River's diminutive playmaker Ariel Ortega, known as *El Burrito* ('the Little Donkey, because he hails from Ledesma in the north of Argentina where there are no horses, only donkeys). 'But I want to make it clear that I would never trade a championship for a single victory against Boca.'

With only a day to go, the whole of Buenos Aires is consumed by the game, which is staggering given that twelve of Argentina's nineteen top division clubs play in the capital and its surrounding area. 'River-Boca is a national derby, there are fans of both clubs all over the country,' explains Juan Sasturain, a journalist and author – Argentina's answer to Nick Hornby, according to Pablo. 'When River play Boca you can bet your life there will be a fan of each team, up in the north of Argentina near the Bolivian border, stood in their replica shirts fighting,' adds Sasturain.

'In general, if you are not a Boca fan, you are anti-Boca. Boca have something socially irritating about them, I don't know why. Maybe it's because they have fans from so far and wide.' A bit like Manchester United then.

So, Boca are widely recognised as the country's best supported club. But which of the two clubs is the biggest? 'I cannot say because they're both very different in terms of history and image,' says Sasturain. 'Historically, River is stylish and offensive; Boca is the opposite – heart and strength. River is money and the middle classes; Boca is popularity and the working classes.'

As the game draws ever closer even Ortega, who was admirably circumspect only yesterday, gets caught up in the media hyperbole. In a bet with celebrity broadcaster and Boca fan Alejandro Fantino, Ortega has agreed to dye his hair green if River lose. In turn, Fantino will dye his hair bright red if Boca lose. Worried he might lose the bet,

Fantino asks Boca midfielder Antonio Barijho, who regularly dyes his hair (blond being the current colour of choice), which brand of dye he should buy. 'Don't bother buying any, you won't need it,' says a confident Barijho, who instead insists Fantino should tell Ortega to dye his hair in the blue and yellow of Boca if River lose.

'Ortega would have no hair left if he'd made the same bet over the past few seasons,' says Barijho, and it's a valid point. River have lost six of the previous ten meetings between the two, winning only one. Has Ortega bitten off more than he can chew?

Certainly Boca's is the more relaxed camp on the eve of the game. Whereas their training sessions at *La Bombonera* are open to both press and public, up at *El Monumental* we have to rely on sneaking through an unguarded gate to watch the River players being put through their paces. That is until an angry security guard boots us out.

On leaving *La Bombonera* the evening before the game, having collected our tickets, a security guard calls us over; our pale skin, short trousers, and cameras are dead give-aways that we are not from round these parts. 'Tell them to be careful,' he says to Pablo. 'There is a strange atmosphere around this week.'

So tense is the mood now that with the game imminent, Pablo says he feels uncomfortable being in enemy territory, even though he's not wearing River colours. He's in far less danger than one misfit we see ducking into a house, wearing River's red and white replica shirt. 'He's a brave man,' says Pablo, who has thus far been ferrying me around in his wife's car. 'Tomorrow I will bring my car to the game. It is not so good so it doesn't matter as much if it gets vandalised.'

As we drive through the dusty streets of La Boca, with its mixture of crumbling, derelict buildings and bright pastel-coloured houses, we pull up outside San Salessiano, a Catholic school. On the wall outside is a magnificent mural, painted in 1969, depicting Buenos Aires at the time. On the left of the picture some workers stand beneath the industrial backdrop of La Boca and on the right stands a businessman and a tango dancer depicting the city's middle classes. In the middle is a priest, stood next to two children, one wearing a Boca shirt, the other wearing a River shirt. This is the church's ideal of Buenos Aires: harmonious. Tomorrow's game will be anything but.

Within minutes of arriving at *La Bombonera* news filters through that the River team bus has been ambushed by Boca fans on the way to the ground. The windows were stoned, River's club president took a blow to the head and two others were injured. At the ground a 1,200 strong, armed police unit (three times the usual size) prepare themselves for more outbreaks of violence. But security is tight, with every fan being searched and stripped of anything that might be deemed offensive, even empty plastic bottles. Apart from ticket-less fans trying to storm the gates there are few signs of serious trouble, but as an outsider, you still fear for your safety.

At the other end of the ground – the River end – however, there are knife fights breaking out and one *Barra* completely loses it with a concrete paving slab when it refuses to break under the pressure of him stamping on it (he wants to throw the broken pieces at Boca fans). Twice we hear the sound of gunfire. Whether the police or the fans are responsible nobody knows.

La Bombonera is a purpose-built football stadium – no athletics or dog-racing tracks here – so the crowd are very close to the pitch and almost on top of it. Three sides of the ground (one side and two ends) form an extremely steep concrete, three-tiered C-shape, with the area behind each goal standing only.

Away to our right, anything from coins to urine rains down on the Boca fans as River's travelling support, fuelled by alcohol, marijuana, cocaine, and pure adrenalin, make their presence felt from the two tiers above. Strangest of all though, amid the sea of red and white many of the River mob are wearing handkerchiefs and surgical masks over their faces. This, Pablo informs me, is because River's nickname for Boca and their fans is *El Bosteros*, roughly translated into English as 'The Shits', in reference to the unpleasant smell that wafts over La

Boca, a remnant of the area's industrial past. If you go down to the port and smell the water you'll know what they're on about.

To Boca's fans, River are know as *Las Gallinas* ('The Chickens'). This goes back to 1966 when River played Penarol of Uruguay in the final of the Intercontinental Cup in Montevideo. River were 2–0 up and cruising in the second half when their keeper caught the ball on his chest – puffed out like a chicken's if you will – and proceeded to mock the opposition, who became so enraged that they lifted their game and ended up winning 4–2 after extra time. Boca have never let the River fans live it down.

Inside the ground the only people missing from the 52,000 crowds are the two sets of *Barras*. They prefer to make a late entrance so the other fans reserve a space for them at the centre of the middle tier. Once inside, the two sets of fans exchange taunts and sing songs – nothing new there then – but the real craze in Argentina is to jump up and down on the spot. And I mean everybody. Both sets of fans at the same time. Now Boca's is not the most state-of-the-art ground and as the stadium shakes under the weight on 52,000 lunatics pogoing simultaneously, you wonder if it's going to crash to the ground.

Amid the sea of yellow and blue away to our left are a surprising number of women and children, some of whom are so young they nestle in their dad's arms as he screams his support, blood-vessels near to bursting in his forehead. As if the crowd is not fired up enough, the reserve teams of both clubs play their fixture immediately prior to the first team game. It keeps everybody entertained at least. Not that they need it.

When the fist teams finally appear they do so through an inflated tunnel, which stretches out into the centre of the pitch to prevent the players, especially those of River, being pelted with whatever the fans can get their hands on. A few bottles make their way over the tall perimeter fencing but all of them miss their targets.

As ticker tape pours down from the sky, children appear on the pitch carrying two giant flags bearing the words *no mas violencia: un mensaje de Dios* ('no more violence: a message from God'). 'It won't be enough,' says Pablo, as the 'boos' reverberate around the ground, drowning out the sound of 'We are the World' and 'Imagine', which are playing over the stadium's public address system.

An appalling, goalless first half is lifted only by the appearance of Maradona, a former Boca star, of course, who emerges on the balcony of his box to the delight of Boca's fans and the derision of River's. At half time he even puts on a juggling show using a ball thrown up to him by one of the cheerleaders.

In the second half the referee, who was the best performer on the pitch in the first half, loses control of the game under intense pressure from the home crowd. He'd agreed to meet me for an interview over breakfast tomorrow morning, depending on how the game went. Needless to say, we never get the phone call. Boca, who are the better side anyway, win 3–0 after River have two men sent off. After each goal, the Boca fans, Maradona included, take off their shirts and lasso them round their heads. They'll be going home happy and will be able to hold their heads high. At least until the two teams meet again.

In the back of Pablo's car another River fan – also called Pablo – and a friend of *Los Barrochos* (though not one himself) is inconsolable. 'I am always without hope when I come to see River play Boca, because I always feel like we're gonna get fucked,' he says, unable to comprehend River's recent poor record against Boca. 'I don't understand it. Against teams who play good football we play beautifully and win. Then we go and lose to Boca and their shitty, ugly football.'

Still, at least nobody was killed. And with only seventy-nine arrests at the stadium, today's Buenos Aires derby was one of the quietest.

Buenos Aires – A tale of two teams
Boca Juniors

Boca were founded in La Boca district of Buenos Aires in 1905 by Irishman Paddy McCarthy, newly arrived Italian immigrants, Pedro and Juan Feranga, and three students from the National School of Commerce – hence the name 'Juniors'. They chose to play in the colours on the flag of the next ship to sail into port. It was a Swedish vessel – hence the yellow and blue.

Their most successful periods were the early 1930s and the late 1970s and early 1980s, when, inspired by Diego Maradona, they reached the South America Club Championship final three years in a row. Controversially, though, no Boca players were included in Argentina's 1978 World Cup-winning squad, because of their rugged style under then manager Juan Carlos Lorenzo.

Boca have a history of bigger, more robust players, such as Gabriel Batistuta and Argentina's 1966 World Cup captain Antonio Rattin. Even Boca's skilful players, such as ex-stars Diego Maradona and Juan Sebastian Veron and Barcelona-bound Juan Roman Riquelme are powerfully built.

River Plate

Also founded in 1905, River were formed in La Boca when two local English teams, Santa Rosa and Rosales, joined forces after playing against each other in a friendly. Both teams played in white, which caused confusion until River had the bright idea of sewing red patches on to their shirts to distinguish themselves – hence River's colours.

The 1940s saw River and their famous forward line *La Maquina* ('The Machine') dominate the domestic game and this success continued into the 1950s with Alfredo Di Stefano to the fore. More great players followed, including Daniel Passarella and Mario Kempes.

In contrast to Boca, River have a reputation for producing stylish teams and players who fit within that framework. Current stars Ariel Ortega and Barcelona-bound starlet Javier Saviola as well as Valencia's Pablo Aimar are classic River players.

The Ultimate Showdown
Iran v Iraq, October 2001

More than a million people died when the two nations fought in the 1980s. Today, the only battle that counts lasts for just ninety minutes …

Tehran's thoroughfares buzz with anticipation, the streets seeming to move as one in a westwards direction towards the Azadi national stadium. Here Iran will today take on their bitter rivals Iraq in a win-at-all-costs World Cup qualifier.

The pace is glacially slow, but there is a harmony that is rare in Iran these days. The atmosphere is charged, but the fans smile and salute each other. Flags are draped over every tree and lamp-post, and Iranians lose themselves in a nationalistic fervour which is usually denied them.

'This is what it used to be like, when the Shah was in charge,' a 73-year-old university lecturer turned shoe-shiner tells me. 'Then we were told it was all right to be proud of being Iranian. Now we are told that our nationality doesn't matter, that Islam is all that matters. But whoever says that should go and look at all the historical sites that litter Iran. We are an ancient land and our spirit is strong. We will prevail over anyone who tries to dampen our national spirit.'

Inside the stadium, their team emerges to the thunderous acclaim of 110,000 Iranians packed like pilchards in a tin. There are no Iraqi fans here, only the few officials who have travelled with the team. The Iraqi national anthem is played out to a stony silence but there are no jeers. When the Iranian anthem begins, though, the mood changes; the crowd boos, and the players, who mouth the words, look embarrassed. 'They hate anything that reminds them of the State,' a photographer from one of Iran's leading daily newspapers tells me. 'This isn't their national anthem, this is the State's ...'

In 1979, a year after reaching their first World Cup finals in Argentina, Iran underwent a dramatic change. The Shah, an absolute monarch who favoured Western values, was overthrown. By nature protective of their culture, Iranians had felt increasingly threatened by the Shah's policies. In his place, the *Mullahs* (Muslim clerics), led by Ayatollah Khomeini, came to power. The Islamic Revolution of that year transformed Iran from one of the most cosmopolitan and diverse cultures in the Middle East into the most introspective.

Ironically, those same Iranians who wanted to preserve their national identity now found their country dominated by Islam, a religion that does not recognise borders. Far from being encouraged to be proud Iranians, they found themselves pushed, first and foremost, to be dutiful, obedient Muslims.

Worse still, a year later, in 1980, Iran and Iraq went to war. The first Gulf War, actually a dispute over territorial control of the shipping lanes of the Shatt-al-Arab waterways, lasted for eight years. In Iran, it was given the spin variously of Jihad (or Holy War) and 'The Imposed War' and proved a useful propaganda tool for Khomeini. According to the Islamic Republic of Iran, Iraq was the pawn of Western influence, armed by the USA and France. Those who died fighting them were exalted as martyrs. It became one of the bloodiest conflicts on record. In the second year of the war, Iraq made moves towards a peace settlement, but Khomeini rejected them, saying that Iran would 'fight until the last drop of blood'. An estimated 1.2 million people died on both sides, yet thirteen years after the final drop of blood was spilled the government still celebrates the beginning of the fighting, with 'Holy Defence Week'.

The young (under-30s) who form 70 per cent of the population don't remember much about the war. They care little either, brushing it aside and trying to keep themselves entertained. In Iran today, entertainment is mostly of the home variety. Although banned, many homes have satellites. The Internet, which is not banned but under heavy surveillance, allows the young another entry point to the outside world.

They see what the world has to offer, but can rarely interact. Football offers an outlet to vent their frustration at this debilitating state of affairs. The fact that Iran has a strong team helps. 'We want the sort of freedom that young people have everywhere else; the freedom to laugh, the freedom to dance, the freedom to celebrate our successes. When we watch Iran play football we feel these freedoms,' says Amir Mahdian, a 21-year old receptionist and devoted follower of the national side.

The passion that this has generated means football personalities in Iran are bigger than pop stars elsewhere. Ali Daei, the national team captain is a UNICEF ambassador like Geri Halliwell. 'Daei is a legend to us; he has achieved what every Iranian dreams of, he has accomplished success abroad [with Bayern Munich and Hertha Berlin in the Bundesliga], and he represents his country with pride,' says Mohammad Heydari, 15, from Tehransar.

Reaching the World Cup finals in 1998 meant that Iran came into contact not only with host nation France, but with the rest of the world. Much more than the chance to score a political point by beating the USA (or rather 'The Great Satan'), this was an opportunity, and one which the nation and national team grabbed with both hands.

Qualifying for Korea and Japan in 2002 and renewing those tentative contacts with the outside world quickly became an obsession for

Iranians. 'Iran must go to the World Cup, it is necessary; no one can imagine anything else,' Dariush Kabiri told me in the days leading up to the first qualifier against Saudi Arabia, a game that would give me my first taste of football in Iran.

Walking away from the stadium after that match, I felt a glow of satisfaction I had never felt anywhere else. It was strange, because the Azadi is not a glorious venue, but there was something there. It wasn't the huge crowd – officially 100,000, but probably closer to 115,000 with all the standing tickets that are illegally sold at the turnstiles – or the propaganda slogans that are plastered between the upper and lower tiers. I just felt proud of 'our' boys, and their 2–0 win over a team they had not beaten for five years. Suddenly I, like so many other football fans before, had become absorbed into the throng.

Dreaming in that schoolboy kind of way, about all the possible permutations involved, the one name that kept cropping up was Iraq. Iraq, our most bitter rivals, Iraq the perennial party poopers, Iraq our foe. What surprised me was how laid back most Iranians were about the Iraqis. I thought I'd hear frenzied bouts of expletives and censure. Instead, to a man and woman I heard that 'the war is the past', that 'the Iraqis aren't so bad', and that 'it is only a game after all'. Still, they didn't hide the fact that beating the Iraqis would be sweeter than beating most other opponents.

Iraq is an Arab country. Iraqis speak Arabic, a language with its roots in Hebrew. Iranians are not Arabs and most do not want to be. Their language is Farsi, derived from northern India over 7,000 years ago. Now, though, twenty-two years after the Shah was overthrown, many Iranians again fear that their national identity is being eroded. This time the threat comes not from the west, but from the Arabisation of Iran favoured by its religious leaders.

Those leaders have become increasingly aware of the strength of feeling the country's football team generates. When Iran visited Iraq to play the first of the two World Cup qualifiers between the countries, the Islamic Republic of Iran saw an opportunity. These are heroes representing Islam, they wanted to say, figureheads not for Iran, but for Islam.

Because, ironically, the most significant shrines to Shia Muslim (the dominant religion in Iran) are in Iraq, the Iranian national team were sent to visit them – and state TV barely stopped showing the footage. So far as the regime in Tehran was concerned, football was of secondary concern – this was a propaganda tour. So when the team came back with a 2–1 win, having gone a goal down, it was all down to providence. On their return, the players were treated like heroes. They appeared on chat shows, and were asked what it felt like to have 'conquered' Iraq.

The process of qualification ticked on. The win against Iraq had given Iran a comfortable three-point cushion over second-placed Bahrain, and four over Saudi Arabia, who were beginning to show some form. Indifferent performances against Thailand and Bahrain resulted in a pair of draws though, and with the Saudis registering significant wins against the same opponents, Iran suddenly trailed by two points. The saving grace was that they had a game in hand.

A heroic display in Jeddah against the Saudis earned Iran a 2–2 draw and kept them on course for automatic qualification, but the return game against the Iraqis now took on a completely new dimension and importance. It was make or break, ninety minutes in which Iran's fate might be decided. A defeat or a draw and the Saudis would be in the driving seat. The game in hand would be wasted and the two-point deficit might not be bridgeable.

Suddenly the level of rhetoric increased. True the Iraqis had lost to the Saudis the previous week and would now only be playing for pride, but most Iranians felt this would make them even more dangerous. The ambivalence of previous weeks turned into a tangible hostility. Iran has no fewer than eight dedicated sports dailies and their polemic tone put into shade anything the tabloids in England have ever been guilty of. No 'Achtung, For You Ze War Is Over'; instead, 'Now the War Begins in Earnest' was the calmest headline any of the papers managed in the days leading up to this crucial match.

The fans were no less reluctant about letting their feelings be known. Masood Zamani, a farmer, had left his land two days prior to the game to come to Tehran and soak up the atmosphere. 'I have been watching them for a long time. This is the best team we've had since the one that went to Argentina [in 1978]. When I watch them I feel proud to be Iranian. It is important for us to be successful, because we need to find a place for ourselves in the world. Most other ways are closed to us.'

Women are not allowed to attend football matches but Saeedeh and Samira Shojaiepour, students from the city of Karaj, just outside Tehran, would be there in spirit. 'We will pray for a good game and we will pray that the manager makes good choices and most of all we will pray that Iran win and go to the World Cup.'

Again and again I heard how essential Iran reaching the World Cup finals was, how young people loved football so passionately because it allowed them to express feelings about their national identity that in so many other walks of life had become taboo. 'The older generation do not understand our need to be different from them,' said Saeedeh and Samira. If we hate the Iraqis it's only because they can stop us from getting to Japan, not because our parents fought a war against them.'

Miroslav Blazevic, most famous for leading Croatia to third place at France 98 – losing out narrowly to the French themselves in the semi-finals – is the man in charge of Iran. He has an abundance of confidence that goes beyond sheer enthusiasm. It is almost intimidating. He is the master of his own mind, and his tactical awareness is noted in the game. Blazevic has published two books on tactics, but the Iranian press, who for the most part seem to dislike him with a passion equal to his confidence, continually question his tactical awareness. For each game in the campaign Blazevic has changed his formation or tweaked his tactics, and this has given Iran an extra edge.

I meet Blazevic and his ever-present translator Mr Challangar shortly before the match against Iraq. They seem poised and confident about what lies ahead. How has he changed Iran's psychological attitude? 'That's a question I haven't been asked since I've been here,' he says. 'They keep asking me about tactics, tactics, tactics, but the attitude of the players has changed completely and that is what I'm most proud of. This team didn't have the highest morale before, but today I can say that they are a solid outfit. Now when we fall behind, as we did to the Iraqis and the Saudis twice, we never say die. These are new Iranians.

'I can tell you, that I know the winning formula, without considering the technical merits of a team. I know that stability and unity can bring success, and that this squad is like a family. There are no internal divisions. They will be ready to take on the world.'

The day before the game I catch up with one of Blazevic's stars, Mehdi Mahdavikia, the 24-year-old German-based Iranian right wing-back, at his mother's house in Tehran for a meal. 'First we need three points,' he says. 'But I'd be foolish to say I don't recognise that it has an added significance for the people. With the special circumstances around it, and the sensitivity that people have towards the war, we know there's a lot at stake, but we're not going to let that distract us.

'We only think about the sport. There is no hatred on our part towards the Iraqis. When we visited Iraq, we received a very warm reception from the people. However, we can never forget the unique sacrifice that our martyrs made in the war we had and we honour their memories.

'We'll win. But it's going to be a tough game. We don't expect any favours, least of all from the Iraqis. They're going to give everything they have. They have a lot of pride.'

And so, finally, the day of reckoning arrives. As I set out to the Azadi, my mind drifts back to the Saudi Arabia match. Then the crowds had begun to swarm around Iran's national stadium by 6 a.m. The demand for tickets was tremendous. 'I must see this game, I have travelled for sixteen hours to be here,' Masood Sistani from Zahedan had told me.

By 7 a.m. riot police were in evidence, and by 8 a.m. they had delivered the first of a series of routine beatings. The reason for these never became altogether clear, but as I nursed my own police-sponsored bruises, a young fan told me that these security forces were drafted in from the provinces and had a chip on their shoulders about Tehran's citizens.

For the visit of Iraq though, the pre-match beatings are few and far between. Instead there is a feeling of dark foreboding, a tension that suggests everything is being bottled up for later. At every significant square and junction, the security forces stand at the fringes, a menacing presence and an ill-omen for the rest of the day.

Standing at pitch side and looking up at the faces of the colourful masses, it is impossible not to be taken over by the sheer drama of the occasion. Behind the grease-painted faces of the young there is a desire, a real vehemence that today they will taste victory.

The war is never allowed to be too far from people's thoughts. Even now, its allegorical symbols are a fixture in Iranian society. So on the day that Iraq visits Iran, when they are once again the enemy, it is obligatory to wheel out the war wounded. As the Iraqis warm up, alone in front of 110,000 Iranians, the home team's players embrace the veterans and present them with flowers. The reaction of the crowd is mute, the cynicism of the whole ceremony obvious to everyone. For most fans, the only war that really matters is the one that will last for the next ninety minutes.

It is a real cup-tie from the first kick to the last. Iran have all the possession, they make all the running, and they take the risks. The Iraqis play like demons. They are here to be the spoilers. They have no chance of going to the World Cup themselves, but if they can stop Iran, if they can take away Iran's unbeaten record in qualification, then it will make up for all of that. They are also playing for their futures.

When the Iraqis lost to Iran in Baghdad, Saddam Hussein's son Uday, who runs the Iraqi Football Federation, sacked eight of the team. There is a real fear in the faces of the Iraqis. They dare not lose.

For twenty-seven minutes, they defend with their lives. Then comes the breakthrough. Mahdavikia serenely passes the ball from the right edge of the eighteen-yard box past the despairing Iraqi keeper Saad Jameel. The crowd, merely frenzied up until now, lose all control. They leap as one, and in the scrum that follows, fights break out over lost seats. The Iraqis try to chase the game, and the tension goes up another notch, but Iran stay in charge.

Half-time and Blazevic is pleased. 'More goals lads,' he tells Mr Challangar to tell his boys. But the second half comes too soon for the Iranians. They are still playing the first half in their heads. They create a great chance, but miss and the Iraqis counter-attack quickly. Qathan Drain converts a well-worked move to bring the scores level.

The fans turn up the volume, and Iran respond. They show all the spirit, all the unity that Blazevic had told me about. The game is at their mercy. Chances come and chances go. The anxiety level reaches fever pitch... and then the dam bursts. Iran's latest pin-up Ali Karimi scores. With seventy minutes gone, it's 2–1. For the remaining twenty minutes the Iraqis pour forward, desperately chasing the game and, when it comes, the final whistle is like the mercury bursting on a thermometer. The relief is tangible. The crowd cheer, cry, hug each other. Iraq, the old foe, has been defeated. But much more importantly, the World Cup finals are a step nearer.

But after the joy comes the release of pent-up anger. The Iranian footballers have become symbols of national pride, that rare thing in Iran, a totem around which to gather, a lightning rod for dissent against the unhappiness that people feel in their otherwise humdrum lives. Here were ninety minutes of exultation for the masses, but what is there for them now?

In the wake of the victory, the crowds take to the streets. Their delight turns into a violent reaction to the harsh circumstances they face. Tyres are set ablaze, telephone booths vandalised, windows smashed, and anti-regime chants are heard across Tehran and Iran's other cities. Some claim this is a spontaneous reaction and to some extent they are right. But in a country where boys and girls fear holding hands in case the special morality police take them in or, worse, send them to a moral correction unit, football may not be enough to contain their passions.

Tomorrow La Scala
AC Milan v Inter, November 2002

The world's capital of fashion and opera, Milan was never going to stage just any old footballing derby. This is the story of the nine-decade duet between two very different teams.

On a damp Saturday night 80,000 expectant fans flock to the leafy, well-heeled western outskirts of Milan, Italy's football and fashion capital. From the outside, the three-tiered San Siro stadium resembles a giant Hallowe'en pumpkin, shafts of white light beaming out through the slits of the six huge spiralling walkways around its perimeter.

Once inside, each end suddenly explodes ten minutes before kick-off into huge, perfectly choreographed displays of banners, slogans, and colour-coded placards. The whole vibrant spectacle is down to the dedicated work of hundreds of members of the much-maligned *ultras*, the organised supporters groups only some of whose members engage in violence. But tonight they compete in an artistic battle orchestrated with a synchronisation worthy of La Scala, the city's other famous theatre a few kilometres away to the east in Milan's cobble-stoned city centre.

The second tier of the *curva sud* – south bank – of the 'home' side disappears under a red-and-black sea of placards. In a seamless scene-change, an enormous banner unrolls above the crowd, forty metres by thirty, depicting a cartoon scene of Milan stars with the slogan, *La Storia Infinita* – the never-ending story. The 7,300 'visiting' Inter contingent respond by making the *curva nord* shimmer with hundreds of shiny blue-and-black placards, dotted with the famous bright yellow stars, sported only by teams who have won at least ten titles.

Then they too unfurl above their heads a huge banner featuring Giuseppe 'Peppino' Prisco, one of the club's most popular directors, who died last season. Much loved for his mischievous media comments, the elderly lawyer is shown with his trademark wicked grin and making a vulgar hand gesture. His message 'to the worms in Hell' is not lost on Milan's *diavoli rossi*, the red devils. From the Milan end, fireworks shoot into the night sky from the front of the second tier. The whole show is carried off with style and humour, provoking gasps and applause from around the packed stadium, and will lead the evening TV sports bulletins.

Tonight's derby – in Italy the English term is used – has an importance beyond its usual city confines. For the first time in a decade Milan's two teams are simultaneously tilting for the Serie A title. Just one week before they had found themselves sharing the very top spot in the table, an event not seen for an astonishing thirty years. The line-ups feature a string of top Italians – Christian Vieri of Inter and his best friend Filippo 'Pippo' Inzaghi of Milan, Gigi di Biaggio, Francesco Toldo, Paolo Maldini and his defensive sidekick of fifteen years, Alessandro 'Billy' Costacurta – but on the night this 253rd Milanese derby is won for Milan by a 12th-minute display of Brazilian football geometry.

The gangly Rivaldo threads a flat diagonal pass from the centre circle towards wide player Serginho on the left edge of the Inter box. Inter's Argentinian defender Nelson Vivas, standing in for country-man Javier Zanetti after the latter's midweek international duties, desperately stretches but can't cut out the inch-perfect ball. With one deft touch the spidery Serginho takes the ball sharply square inside, wrong-footing keeper Francesco Toldo who is shaping to anticipate a burst towards the left byline. The move ends with a hard grass-cutting shot into the gaping Inter net, and the San Siro erupts with an ear-ringing roar. It is AC Milan's 97th derby win, now ten more than Inter. Gate receipts are around €1.4m. The worldwide TV audience runs into tens of millions.

It wasn't always thus.

In the very last days of the final year of the 19th century, a small group of enthusiasts met one evening to establish the Milan Cricket and Football Club. Most football historians quote the date as 16 December 1899, but in reality the original document of the club's founding statute was lost, so the gathering could have been any time between the 9th and the 17th of the month. There is also doubt over its location. Some accounts refer to the Hotel du Nord in Piazza Repubblica, others locate it at the nearby Bar Fiaschetteria in Via Berchet, which certainly became the regular meeting place. No exact figures exist for the numbers in attendance.

But what is not in doubt is the club's English roots. Half a dozen English names featured in the association's original membership and the driving force behind that inaugural meeting of what would later become the mighty Associazione Calcio Milan – AC Milan – was an English textile worker, one Herbert Kilpin.

A keen striker, Kilpin – the 29-year-old son of a Nottingham butcher – was the team's first captain, its first club president being one Alfred Edwards. So it was that the final letter 'o' was dropped from Milano to adopt the English spelling. The club's original pitch was on the site of what is now Stazione Centrale, Milan's main railway station, a huge marble masterpiece of Italy's Fascist era of public works of the 1920s and 1930s.

But the history of the Milan derby is the history of a sporting divorce. The two parties separated over a point of principle without ever coming to blows, then ended up sharing the same home without ever quite kissing and making up. They are football's odd couple.

The separation came just a little over eight years after that original gathering. A splinter group led by artist Giorgio Muggiani, broke away because it wanted to permit foreigners to play for the side, contrary to Federation regulations. On 9 March 1908 a group of like-minded rebels gathered together at the L'Orologio restaurant in Via Orefici just a goalkeeper's kick away from the city's famous landmark, the giant Duomo cathedral. And thus was born Internazionale Milano, the new name proudly reflecting the reasons for the divorce.

'The colours they chose for their new kit reflected these early romantic leanings,' says Fabio Monti, Inter expert at the Milan-based *Il Corriere della Sera*, Italy's leading daily newspaper. 'The black was to represent the night, blue for the sky.' It was an idealistic gesture towards the nascent internationalism of the turbulent European politics of the early 20th century. Ironically, after winning their first *scudetto* – (literally, 'little shield') – in 1910, Inter's first captain Virgilio Fossati was himself later to fall victim to the nationalistic carnage of World War I. Meanwhile, the design of the club crest produced by those early artistic founders is today ridiculed by *Interisti* as illegible.

Italian football fans are notoriously superstitious. And the birth of Inter produced what must be one of the most eerie ghosts at any football feast. Barbara Ballardini, 29, who compiled an entire academic thesis on the fans of Inter and Milan, explains: 'Historically, AC Milan have experienced lots of ups and downs, with long periods without winning anything. Before the schism that created Inter they had already won three *scudetti* with the latest coming the year before the breakaway. But then they entered their longest ever barren period. AC Milan had to wait another forty-four years before they won their next *scudetto*. And that inaugural Inter meeting was attended by forty-four founding members.' Woo, spooky.

For many years the Internazionale splitters were dismissed as a bunch of upper class intellectuals, while AC Milan remained associated more with the working classes. Indeed, Milanese dialect gave early nicknames of *Casciavit* for Milan and *Bàuscia* for Inter – roughly translated as 'spanners' and 'braggers'. But, these original socio-economic differences are now well outdated. A recent survey also found little difference between the fans' political affiliations, with the traditionally left-leaning Milan fans shifting towards the centre since the arrival in 1986 of club president Silvio Berlusconi, the media billionaire and current Prime Minister of Italy's centre-right governing coalition. Like the rest of Italy, club nicknames derive from team colours, hence *nerazzurri* (black-blues) for Inter, and *rossoneri* for Milan's red-and-black.

The very first meeting of the two Milan formations was, perhaps uniquely in the history of footballing derbies, not actually staged in the home city – nor even in the country. The two sides came head to head on a football pitch for the first time in Chiasso, some fifty miles north of Milan just over the border in Switzerland. 'Nobody really knows why,' admits Fabio Monti. And if the affable Monti doesn't know, you suspect nobody does.

The result of the match, reported at the time as a 'Chiasso Cup' tie, was a 2–1 victory for the Milan Football and Cricket Club. Goalscorer Lana, Milan's number seven, went on to score the Italian national side's first ever goal two years later.

The renegade Inter's early history was peripatetic, shifting from one location to another until 1930 when they settled at the roofless Arena stadium just outside the city's inner ring of ancient gates which date back before Napoleon. Evocative of an ancient Roman amphitheatre, the Arena still hosts Serie D games.

Meanwhile Milan, with the big money backing of the Pirelli tyre-manufacturing family – nowadays one of Inter's main sponsors – built a stadium on the then city periphery, in the San Siro area, in 1926. They sold it to the city authorities in 1935. An enlarged version was inaugurated in 1939 with a 2–2 draw against England in a friendly international just four months before the outbreak of World War II. In Italy, not even global conflagrations tend to stop football matches, and the following year Inter obtained permission to shift their title-winning end-of-season fixture against Bologna to the larger San Siro to accommodate the crowds.

The odd couple were back living under the same roof. Or at least Inter had cheekily brought its toothbrush to stay the night. The domestic arrangement was to be made permanent from 1947.

'Yes, it's a peculiar history,' admits Barbara Ballardini, the thesis-writing *rossoneri*. 'Two huge teams with huge fan bases that share the same ground and don't really have any strong ties to any particular part of the city. They are devoid of religious or political rivalries, save for the '70s when some *ultra* groupings reflected the violent political environment in Italy at the time.'

But one of the most curious features of Milanese footballing culture is that nobody can explain why they chose one team or the other. 'As a little girl I just always liked wearing red. I'd dress up as a *Milanista* at carnival,' laughs Barbara Ballardini. It's about as good a response as you get. When asked by a sociological survey why they chose Inter, one third quoted family allegiance. Yet an astonishing 18 per cent said they couldn't remember. Thirty-five year-old financial advisor Andrea di Cola is an Inter season-ticket holder: 'When I was a kid they were a legendary club. Now, even though we haven't won anything for years, I like the fans. They are notoriously critical, yes, but there is a lot of self-irony in it all. It's good fun.'

The derby's passion on the pitch comes without the surrounding air of menace sometimes associated with such confrontations. 'There certainly isn't the aggression that you get back home,' says Linda McCanna, a 30-year-old Manchester United fan from Cheshire now living in Italy with Massimo, her AC Milan season ticket-holding boyfriend. 'If a City fan – or a Liverpool fan, for that matter – wandered into a United pub they'd be likely to find a bit of bother, especially on a matchday. Here, they sing songs against each other at the match, but then afterwards they're in the bar sharing a drink. They know each other, work in the same places, live in the same areas.'

Perhaps surprisingly, the absence of violence also derives from the network of *ultras*. 'There did used to be trouble between the opposing *ultras*,' Barbara Ballardini explains. 'But back in 1983, when a particularly nasty derby confrontation outside the San Siro got out of hand – an Inter fan died – the *ultra* leaders got together and agreed a kind of non-belligerence pact between themselves.' It has held to this day.

'I'd say, if anything, Milan fans dislike Inter more than they dislike us,' admits Max, a *rossoneri* season ticket-holder. 'We have to share "our" stadium with them, and we've won more than they have. The Milan *curva sud* sings songs against Inter at every game, not only when we are playing against them.' The chant 'July and August' ridicules *Interisti* pre-season boasting which often comes to nothing by season's end. Given Inter's lack of a *scudetto* since 1989, it hits home. 'But they seem more bothered about beating Juve,' says Max. 'At least that's what they pretend.'

'It is true. For Inter the derby is a very important game. But historically, it's against Juventus that feelings ran highest,' says no less an authority than Mario Corso, legendary left-winger of the 'Grande Inter' side that swept all before them in the early-'60s. Under coach Helenio Herrera, regarded as the inventor of the notorious *catenaccio* defensive style, Inter won four *scudetti*, two European Cups, and two Intercontinental Cups.

Corso, who notched up 414 league appearances for Inter, recalls: 'In '65 we won 2–0 and overtook Milan to win the league. And I scored. That is a special memory. But against Juve there was an angry feeling, it always felt worse being beaten by Juve. It was almost a derby.' Indeed the Juventus–Internazionale fixture is classically known as *il derby d'Italia*, being the only ever-present Serie A fixture and because of the Inter and Juventus supporters clubs spread around the country.

But across town at the Milan club headquarters in Via Turati, Cesare Maldini, whose captaincy included lifting the European Cup at Wembley after defeating Benfica 2–1 in 1963, dismisses any suggestion that Milan's city derby is anything less than a charged-up affair. 'No, no, the players really felt it,' recalls the ex-*rossoneri* leader, and father of current captain Paolo. 'The derby was always the most important game – it meant being supreme, for the fans to say they were the top team in the city, for a few months. When Milan won 6–0 a couple of years ago, and at "their place" too,' he chuckles, 'it was a terrific shock. It really meant something.' From his own playing days he can't pick out one particular derby game, 'but in those days the winning fans would go out celebrating in the streets, and carry mock funeral wreaths to the other club. Admittedly, you don't see that any more.'

The lack of animosity between the clubs increasingly extends to the transfer of players. Last season saw Dutch midfielder Clarence Seedorf, Croatian defender Dario Simic and much talked about *trequartista* (playmaker) Andrea Pirlo switch to Milan, following midfielder Cristiano Brocchi the season before. 'I could never have changed from *nerazzurri* to Milan, no never,' affirms the 61-year-old Corso. 'I had the opportunity,' reveals Maldini, 'back before Paolo was born. Moratti (Angelo, father of current Inter president, Massimo) wanted me but it didn't come off. In those days it was almost unthinkable to change colours. The players had certain bars and places we went to. Really, it was unthinkable.'

But Alberto Costa, Milan correspondent at the *Corriere della Sera*, insists switching shirts is not solely a modern phenomenon. 'There are precedents. When Milan were relegated to Serie B in 1982 they were in a very bad way financially. Inter helped them out by lending them three players, Aldo Serena, Canuti, and Pasinato. They came straight back up into Serie A.'

A modern echo of that camaraderie came last November. Inter's Christian Vieri sent a congratulatory text message to Andriy Shevchenko when the back-from-injury Milan striker scored the vital

Champions League winner against Real Madrid. A week later the gesture was reciprocated when 'Bobo' Vieri himself ended a goal drought by blasting all four against Brescia.

The *Corriere della Sera* man sums up the relations between the Milan giants: 'On the pitch, between the players, there is great rivalry. But it's very, let's say, very "English": it's hard competition between professionals, it means a lot, but it's all done with fair play.' He makes a telling point: 'When they changed the name of the San Siro it wasn't by accident that they re-named it the Giuseppe Meazza stadium.' Meazza was an Inter hero whose career spanned twenty years until 1947, scoring 283 goals in 408 matches. 'But he actually played the last two seasons of his career with the *rossoneri*', says Costa. 'He represents both clubs.' The new San Siro museum has memorabilia and trophies of both teams exhibited together.

The derby may well serve to emphasise the original closeness of the Milanese clubs, but it also points up the peculiar differences in club 'culture'. The old delineation of working class reds and aristocratic blues may be long gone. But Inter still hang on to that old patina of prestige, the first of the two to win the yellow star. Nowadays, however, without a title win since 1989, it is an illustrious history that weighs ever heavier. 'Two different realities,' is how the two institutions are summed up by Federica Zangalli, whose role as football reporter for TeleLombardia, the leading regional TV station, gives her a unique insight. 'As a club Inter are still very much run like a family firm, dominated by Massimo Moratti. He is a fan, he loves the club. The criticism is that he loves it too much. There is no "wall" dividing the owner from the management who run the club, the team. If he sees a player he likes, he buys him.' This is why only Inter could have tolerated for so long the Ronaldo saga. Juventus, for example would have cut their losses and offloaded the troublesome star much sooner, as they did with Zidane. 'Moratti is a lovely man, a romantic, which football needs. But perhaps he is too nice a person for this modern business of football.'

'The arrival of Berlusconi in 1986 revolutionised Milan. They are now run like a multi-national company. Unlike Inter everyone knows their specific role and little things don't blow up into great big problems.' The enormous Berlusconi-era successes – six Serie A titles, three European Cups, three European Super Cups, and two Intercontinental cups – reversed the imbalance in silverware with their neighbours. The *rossoneri* now have sixteen *scudetto* to Inter's thirteen.

'Whereas at Milan there's an upbeat approach, at Inter there is this culture of suffering,' observes Zangalli. 'It is almost as though it's in their DNA to suffer. The more they miss out on winning something, the more anxious they become, the fans, the club, so the more pressure there is to win something. It's a classic vicious circle.'

But former player Corso denies Inter's is a culture of pessimism. 'There is a lot of irony, very self-deprecating. It's always been like that.' It is perhaps no coincidence that many comics and literary figures are numbered among Inter's celebrity fans. Away from the ultra-dominated *curva*, Inter supporters in the costlier seats are notoriously the most impatient in Serie A. 'Yes, it's true, they are very negative,' says Fabio Monti, *Il Corriere*'s Inter-watcher. 'If at half-time they are not winning they start to whistle against their own players every time they make a mistake.' Zangalli agrees: 'That, of course, makes the players more nervous still. Several players have moved from Inter to Milan in recent seasons, and they all notice the difference arriving at AC.' Is it just that success breeds success so the *Milanisti* are more relaxed and patient? 'No, Inter fans have always been like that,' bemoans Monti. 'Even before this barren period they were always more negative, more critical of their side. Perhaps it comes from having such great expectations because of their history, it's difficult to say,' he admits with an exasperated shake of the head.

Milan and Inter, the odd couple indeed. If AC are now the laid-back slightly devilish Walter Matthau, then Inter are the neurotic Jack Lemmon, trying too hard and beset by self-doubt. Simplistically speaking, AC Milan's game classically is founded on a patient passing approach, dubbed by detractors as *gioco orrizontale* – the square ball. Inter's is traditionally built around one outstanding world-beater – Sandro Mazzola in the 1960s, Ronaldo in the late-1990s, Vieri now – exploiting the *gioco verticale*, the direct long ball. Peppino Prisco, the rascally former Inter vice president, once defended the team's style by referring to the famous 1949 derby victory: 'square ball five, long ball six.'

Milan sold more than 53,000 season tickets for this current season. Inter, despite not having lifted that championship shield since 1989, and despite having inexplicably thrown it away by losing to Lazio on the final day of last season, sold only a shade fewer. The odd couple look destined to share domestic life for some time yet.

The Mother of All Battles
Al Ahly v Zamalek, January 2003

In the land of the Pharaohs, behold a ritual as immense as the pyramids yet mysterious as the Sphinx: this is the Al Ahly–Zamalek derby.

In a city as crowded and polluted as modern day Cairo it is easy to lose any sensation that you are in the midst of the world's oldest civilisation. Cairo houses a quarter of Egypt's seventy million people alongside the only surviving Wonder of the Ancient World, the Great Pyramids, still standing after four and half millennia.

Cairo is a Middle Eastern city where Christian and Muslim live together in something close to harmony. A city that can be seen from space – not because of any mammoth feat of human ingenuity but thanks to the enormous cloud of pollution that pinpoints it on satellite pictures. Cairo's exploding population has already engulfed a dozen towns that were once a desert away from the capital, and within twenty years the Great Pyramids will no longer be a coach ride from the city but in the heart of downtown.

While the unrivalled chaos of the last century has left a city coming to grips with its collapsing economy, a youth culture trying to drag its elders into the 21st century, and all the inherent issues that having Libya and Israel as your immediate neighbours brings, one thing has remained a constant – a footballing rivalry that can genuinely claim to dwarf Real v Barça and Boca v River Plate.

Al Ahly v Zamalek goes beyond fanatical. It is part football match, part political rally, part history lesson and generally a good excuse for the locals to hurl rocks at each other. Throughout most of the Egyptian league calendar Al Ahly and Zamalek appear to be no more than successful teams in an average league. Neither club have a huge home ground. Zamalek's Hassan Helmi stadium holds a shade under 40,000 while the larger club, Al Ahly, paradoxically hosts less than 20,000 in their Mokhtar el Tetch. Yet come derby day the supporters abandon their homes to descend upon Cairo's 100,000-seater national stadium for Likaa El Kemma – 'the Meeting of the Best'. What the contest may lack in technical quality and international superstars, it makes up for with unbridled obsession.

For fifty weeks a year, Cairo's tour guides, cab drivers, strangers in the street, hawkers selling plastic pyramids do little but regurgitate tales about pharaohs and mummies, but for two weeks surrounding the match, any excuse to talk about football is seized. Here, as in many places around the world, English football is an international language, 'ah... Beckman, Manchesta Uniteed'. But get Egyptians onto the subject of Ahly v Zamalek and you see them as they were decades ago as wide-eyed children.

When no less an expert than Scotland's World Cup referee and Ahly v Zamalek veteran Hugh Dallas refers to the game as 'bigger than the Old Firm,' you know that it has to be a wee bit special. 'You just don't realise quite how big it is until you see it for yourself,' he enthuses. 'I've done 14 or 15 Old Firm matches and even they don't come close to this. I genuinely believe that this is as big as it gets...'

Football arrived in Egypt during British rule a century ago. Although none of the English clubs survive from that era, Zamalek was formed to represent the expatriates of the time. Originally founded in 1911 as Kaser-el-nil (Place on the Nile), in 1923 the club was renamed Al Mukhatalat, meaning 'Mixed', signifying Egyptians and Europeans playing together, representing the ideal of Egypt as a conduit between Europe and Arabia. Meanwhile, Al Ahly was founded in 1909, their name meaning 'national', the club coming to represent students and the rising nationalist movement that craved an independent Egyptian republic.

In World War II, tensions were rising to unprecedented levels. Although both clubs had tried to retain an apolitical veneer, when King Farouk, who all too frequently used football as his PR tool, leant his considerable patronage to Mukhatalat there could be no denying the club's political allegiances. When Farouk was deposed in 1952, the league was suspended and the club was forced to change its name once again – reflecting its affluent roots, to Zamalek, after Cairo's wealthy island district in the Nile. The political seesaw having tipped its way, Ahly appointed the newly founded Republic of Egypt's new ruler General Gamal Abdal Nasser as club president in 1954.

Years of bitter struggle followed. As Zamalek strived to keep up with Ahly's dominance, the rivalry became less a sporting contest and more about politics. And just to sharpen things up, Ahly established a permanent home for themselves – in the heart of the Zamalek district. The enemies were now sharing an island less than three miles square.

Events reached crisis point in 1966 when a game between the two was halted as the army stormed the stadium. In the ensuing riot over 300 people were injured and an unspecified number killed. Just a few months later the Arab–Israeli Six-Day War broke out and the league was suspended.

Normal service wouldn't be resumed until well after 1973's Yom Kippur War, Ahly immediately re-establishing their superiority, winning seven of the next eight titles. In fact, when Ismaily sneaked the title last year it was only the fourth time since the Yom Kippur War that one of the Cairo giants hadn't been crowned champions. During this time Ahly had not only won eighteen out of twenty-seven league titles, but had also secured three African Champions Leagues and four African Cup Winners' Cups. As the century closed, Ahly received almost unanimous support across the continent when they were voted African Team of the Century. No guesses as to which was the only club to challenge the vote.

But who supports which club and why? Perhaps surprisingly, religion has no place in this rivalry. Even veteran fans claim not to be able to see an obvious divide between Muslims and Christians. Walid Darwish, a regular Egyptian football observer and key figure in Ibrahim Said's transfer to Everton, is stuck to find a real pattern in club loyalties over the last twenty-five years. 'The '50s, '60s, and '70s were about politics, not sport. Back then families had a clear choice – Nationalist or Royalist, and so Ahly or Zamalek, but it was never religious. Today's interest is purely sporting. Traditional family loyalties certainly go back to the politics, and the tradition is for children to grow up supporting the team of their parents, regardless of where they live.

'The older generation has moved on from the hatred that divided our country. Egypt is a liberal society by Middle Eastern standards and even those that were in the middle of the political fighting are enjoying the relative stability, so they don't want to live in the past. The only people that still contribute to any political divisions are the press, because for the last forty years almost each and every one of the papers has had a visible loyalty to one of the camps. These days young Egyptians are deprived of any proper political orientation, so the historic meaning to the Ahly–Zamalek rivalry is likely to be forgotten. They cheer their team and hate the others, because that is what they do. It is a tradition embedded in the Egyptian consciousness that makes us classify everyone in the simplest terms: man–woman, Muslim–Christian, northern–southern, Ahlawy–Zamalkawy. My guess is that we will soon have this club classification on our national ID.'

While today's fans enjoy a relative truce in hostilities, two players have proved an exception to the rule: Hossam and Ibrahim Hassan. The twins have dominated Egyptian football for nearly fifteen years.

Hossam is the most celebrated player in Egypt's history, a 157-cap and 76-goal international, inspirational leader, immense physical presence and supreme poacher, while the less prolific Ibrahim, a full-back, has on numerous occasions provoked the ire of the Egyptian FA. Two years ago they became the first players for a generation to cross the great divide when they quit Ahly for Zamalek. The transfer started when Ahly offered Hossam just a one-year contract extension, while pressing Ibrahim to retire altogether. With both out of contract, there wasn't even a fee involved when Zamalek came knocking. The double move provoked a reaction in the red half of Cairo compared to which Sol Campbell and Luis Figo both got off lightly. Death threats are taken seriously in this part of the world, and the twins still have to be accompanied by armed guards to this day.

In El-Fishawi (the cafe that claims not to have closed once since opening 300 years ago) waiter Kareem still takes it personally. 'We loved them. We would have done anything for them. They moved to Europe – we were happy for them; they returned – we were happy for them. If they had wanted to retire we would have given them a party and lined the streets. But to move to Zamalek? Unforgivable. Like selling the Sphinx. Even for money you do not betray your mother like that,' he says.

'People started talking about the old rivalries of politics and nationalism for the first time in years,' comments EgyptianSoccer.com's founding editor, Mohammad Safi. 'In footballing terms it was such a waste of time. Ibrahim is past his best and Hossam's touch has gone. Besides they have always been too much trouble.

'A few years ago in Morocco, Ibrahim tried to incite the home fans by giving them the finger. It may not seem much to a European, but with North African tensions the way they are, that is just plain crazy. He also stormed Ahly's directors box a while back. When they crossed the divide things got even worse. During last year's 6–1 victory for Al Ahly, it was madness out there. The Ahly fans had really turned on them. I mean really vicious, but the twins didn't care. After the game Hossam waved his shoes at them, which is a huge insult over here.'

One person better placed than most to judge the defection is former Ahly hero now of Everton, Ibrahim Said. 'I can't say I was happy, but to me it was a professional decision and I understood. Good players will always be in demand and some will end up making such moves for personal reasons. You can't change it, but you can beat them to show them the error of their ways!'

Things have spilled over on the pitch for years. In 1996 local referee Kadry Azeem caused chaos by not disallowing a legitimate Ahly goal – after a quick conference Zamalek walked off in a huff, just the latest in a long line of player walkouts, the most serious being in the early '70s when an Ahly exit resulted in the most destructive football-related violence since 1958. Today, with no Egyptian referee daft enough to want to stand in the middle, a who's who of Europe's top whistle-blowers have been drafted in for the occasion. Not that the players seem any more respectful of imported officials. In 1998 France's Mark Bata made his mark when, five minutes into the game, Ayman Abdel Aziz hacked down the then-Ahly hero Ibrahim Hassan from behind. Bata didn't hesitate to show Ayman a red card, and he left the pitch after a few minutes. The trouble was that, yet again, the entire Zamalek squad and management followed him. Ahly were awarded the match 2–0 and Zamalek received the heaviest punishment in the league's history – a nine-point deduction, a two-year ban for their coach and bans for players Sabry and Khaled of a year and three months respectively.

One man though has managed the improbable task of not upsetting anyone: Hugh Dallas. 'The first time I refereed the match was a bit spicy,' he recalls. 'It was the first match since the brothers (Hossam and Ibrahim Hassan) had made the move and I walked straight into it. The players were fine, but the fans were a little more lively. I did have to stop the game a couple of times to remove rocks from the pitch. Fortunately the field is quite a way from the crowd so I wasn't too concerned for my own safety and I'd had a good game, which helps.' It did: the Egyptians loved him. 'He was a credit to referees everywhere,' says Walid Darwish. 'He is the only one that we have actively sought to bring back. Coming into this atmosphere is so tough, but he looked after both matches almost perfectly. After every derby, players and coaches give interviews complaining about the officials, but after Mr Dallas's games no one could find a bad word to say about him.'

This year our very own ninja-ref Uriah Rennie has been given his chance. When his appointment was announced the Cairo media pounced on his reputation, portraying him as a cross between Wyatt Earp and Bruce Lee. The papers ran pictures of him manhandling Roy Keane, and TV pundits revelled in his status as a karate blackbelt. It all adds to the excitement of the build-up.

It is difficult to imagine an event with a heavier police presence. Three hours before kick-off a double ring of policemen in full riot gear surrounds the stadium. Once inside, at the end of every row sits a policeman with helmet, baton and shield. Soldiers guard every exit and half a dozen dog teams patrol the running-track separating the fenced-in crowd from the pitch. But as a show of strength it's deceptive: most of the uniforms seem more concerned with smiling for the camera, smoking and watching the game than getting stuck into crowd control. Only when I try to take a photograph of a teenager with blood gushing from his head do they intervene in an attempt to prevent such an image reaching the world's media.

This year's event is apparently a little quieter than usual. Many Zamalek fans evidently feel too humiliated to show up following last season's historic 6–1 defeat. Given that Zamalek won the African Champions League in December it seems incredible that they carry such a defeatist air. When the teams emerge their body language mirrors their fans. Ahly players and supporters strut into the match as if the result is a foregone conclusion. When Zamalek trot out they look like they believe it too.

'You have to understand that winning the league is the only thing that counts in Egypt,' Nile TV's Mohammad Rahim explains. 'The Champions League is a bonus, cups are good, derby wins are important, but if a coach wants to keep his job, it is the league or he's out. Ahly have won all twelve games this season and with just fourteen to go most people feel the league is already over. If Zamalek look like they are beaten it is because as far as the league is concerned, they probably are.'

As the game approaches it is bedlam in the red half, and the noise is near deafening. You would have thought that not having a roof on the stadium would lessen the atmosphere, but such is the incessant din of the Cairo traffic that the crowd has to give its all to be heard. 'You stand in the tunnel and are deafened by the noise,' Ibrahim Said recalls. 'You get goose-pimples and a sickening nervous feeling through anticipation, knowing that for the fans and players nothing else matters or exists in the world. It's wonderful! Even as a child I have never missed a derby. There were times when my father would not let me go, but I would sneak out and go anyway. You are in awe of the event and its atmosphere. It is impossible for impartial observers to understand what it means to be a part of it and to play in front of 100,000 people. I have been fortunate to score in these games, and the feeling is indescribable. There are very few better feelings. I've got the taste for derbies now, so I hope I get the chance to play in April's Merseyside derby.'

Right from kick-off it is evident that despite instructions from their Brazilian coach to play something close to a natural game, the Zamalek players' priority is to avoid at all costs a repeat of last year. Despite their apparent inferiority complex, Zamalek somehow manage to score after five minutes when El Hady finishes off a counter attack. But within a matter of minutes Rennie seals his fate as the Zamalkawy's new voodoo figure by awarding an obvious yet still frenziedly-contested penalty to Ahly. After a flurry of yellow cards for dissent, Gouda's penalty sends El Sayed the wrong way.

With both sides surrendering possession with a frequency that would make England's Euro 2000 side blush, no real pattern emerges. Individuals display odd flashes of skill but nothing sustained. Belal and Gilberto continue to squander chance after chance in front of the Zamalek goal and are duly punished when another counter allows Abdelwahed to restore the lead.

It is unseasonably cool and the match is played at high tempo, but even as Ahly make it 2–2 you wonder if they can keep it up. Sadly the answer is no. From here on the crowd provide the most entertainment. Both sides waste far too many chances to report, making Rennie's performance arguably the best of the match. Managing to keep control as players writhe around on the floor and dive for penalties is remarkable given his notorious hair-trigger in the Premiership.

After the game several people approach me – the only European journalist in the press box – to apologise for the match. They offer excuses such as both sides were missing key players. Zamalek are without the out-of-favour Hassans and 'the Egyptian Zidane', Emam, while Ahly lack Bebo, who scored four in last year's match.

But few big games ever live up to the billing and no doubt by the time the next Likaa El Kemma comes round, tonight's will have gone down in legend as another classic. After all, who would ever doubt the claims of a nation with 5,000 years of storytelling history, or a referee from Motherwell?

The One That Got Away
Southampton v Portsmouth, March 2004

It's the South Coast Derby that hardly ever happens. And when it does, ancient maritime rivalries get out of hand ...

Portsmouth fan Steve Woodhead grimaces at the map hanging in the hallway of his home, little more than a decent defensive punt from Fratton Park. Dated 1829, it shows the town and surrounding area. In a spidery, old-world hand are scrawled the following words: County of Southampton. 'I sent off for that,' says Woodhead contemptuously, as if he's been palmed off with something contravening the Trade Descriptions Act. 'I only keep it because it matches the wallpaper.'

It may be a throwaway remark, but the devil is in the detail. Scratch the surface and this snapshot illuminates a deep-seated set of local grievances, existing not only geographically, but on cultural, social, and economic grounds. For many Portsmouth fans, the insularity resulting from the city's island status and their perception of a raw deal from Hampshire down the centuries have driven a wedge between themselves and neighbouring Southampton – or 'skates' and 'scummers', to give them their disrespective sobriquets.

Skate, slang for sailor, supposedly has its roots in the fevered imaginings of how naval types might take the concept of fisherman's friend to the nth degree as they whiled away lonely months at sea. Slightly less far-fetched is the derivation of the term Scummers. While details may be sketchy, the most popular version centres on a dock strike across the two cities by workers from the same firm. As the Portsmouth faction stuck to its guns, the 'Southampton Company Union men' swallowed their pride and went back to work – one acronym later and their brothers in arms had become the Scum. However fishy these tales, the schism between these old maritime towns – one Royal Navy, the other merchant – just seventeen miles apart, has become, for Pompey fans in particular, a chasm when it comes to football.

In the Artillery Arms, favoured watering hole for many of Portsmouth's 600-strong Internet supporters' group, the Pompey Anorak Brigade, Woodhead, a founding editor of the now-defunct fanzine *Frattonise*, takes a deep breath and lets me have it with both barrels. 'The rest of Hampshire repudiates Portsmouth,' he says. 'Southampton might as well be the county town, even though it's officially Winchester. The rivalry predates football by a couple of hundred years. Portsmouth has always been subsidiary to Southampton – until 1835, they owned the docks – and there's always been that thing of the navy having bred Portsmouth. The rise of the town from a collection of villages was at odds with the tenor of the rest of the area.'

Woodhead believes the city's history of 'breeding people for war – with the blessing of the Crown for the most part' is almost woven into the DNA of anyone born on Portsea Island. Its status as an island club makes Pompey unique in the English game. He admits to being simultaneously 'proud and horrified' of the more vociferous side of Portsmouth's resolutely working-class support, and he's not alone.

'Aesthetically, there's not much to the place. I wish it were more cultural. I can't stress that insularity and tribalism enough. But there's affection, big-arsed shaven-headed blokes will cuddle you. It's cheerful and violent. It's the end of the line – us against the world, out on our own little limb. It's a Portsmouth attitude. You trust your family, the people you went to school with and grew up with in your own little area, and no one else. There are a lot of parallels with the East End.'

Attempts are being made to gentrify the area. On the seafront, the Gunwharf Quays development has a cinema multiplex, retail outlets, bars and restaurants galore – to be capped off by the £8 million Spinnaker Tower project. But for all the facelifts, the inescapable feeling is of a city with a distinct edge. Rough-and-ready Paulsgrove, to which many Pomponians moved following the huge swathe of post-war slum clearance, made the headlines in August 2000 for the residents' week-long protest against 'paedophils' (sic) in the wake of the Sarah Payne name-and-shame campaign in the *News of the World*.

Crime writer Graham Hurley is a former producer of TV's *The Big Match*, a resident of Portsmouth since 1977, who worked in Southampton for twenty years. The hero of his books, DI Joe Faraday, is based at Fratton nick. Hurley describes Portsmouth as 'a gift' to the novelist, a diamond in the rough. 'Southampton is much less distinctive,' he says. 'It's wealthier and has, by and large, attracted a better quality of business. Portsmouth's lack of wealth has led to a particular kind of culture – it has no side. It doesn't matter what you do, if you're a brain surgeon, judge, novelist. People are not impressed. You're judged on what you are, and I think that's increasingly rare.'

Pride is not peculiar to the eastern end of the M27, however, as Nick Illingsworth, editor of Southampton fanzine *The Ugly Inside*, explains. 'Southampton has had its bad years. The city was built on the shipping industry, and because of that it has a very cosmopolitan feel. But it went into steep decline in the 1970s as the great liners slumped. Throughout the '80s, there was desolation, but the spirit of Southampton shone through, a spirit born in the days after the *Titanic* went down with the loss of so many local lives, and cemented in the Blitz as the town was flattened. That spirit resurfaced in the 1990s. We have a very open outlook on life. We don't go for the insular mentality of our neighbours, but we are fiercely loyal and willing to stand up and be counted.'

Dave King, the deputy editor of the Southampton-based *Southern Daily Echo* and one-time sports editor of the *Portsmouth News*, recalls his arrival on the south coast. 'I was shocked when I came down here, hearing about fans with such vitriol for each other that they claim they wouldn't even visit the other's city. That's astonishing compared to places like Nottingham and Merseyside, where family members support both teams. You'd be hard-pushed to find that here. Depending on which side of the River Hamble you live, you're Saints or Pompey.'

Martin Hopkins, match commentator for Portsmouth radio station, The Quay, laughs at the ridiculousness of it all, but cheerfully admits boycotting anything Southampton-based. 'I wouldn't dream of buying screwdrivers from Draper Tools, Sanderson Paints, or anything from their sponsors.' He can still recall his first visit to the training ground in the early-1990s. 'Mark Chamberlain turned up without a jacket. It got progressively colder, so he went to his car to get an extra layer. He came back wearing a Southampton training top. He'd been at their academy. When Alan Knight and Andy Awford saw it, they tried to wrestle him out of the car park. They were only half-joking.'

Hopkins' colleague, Sam Matterface, has been equally struck by the passion and is now a committed fan. 'You don't have any choice. I'd liken it to the Mafia. It takes a while to get in, but once you're in you can't get out. It's a working-class town and football's a working-class game. Look at Southampton and its, "When are we going to Cowes?" Portsmouth's built on its naval base and, "We're off to sail the world in a five-tonne warship", Southampton's about yachting.'

Across the Solent, Nick Illingsworth finds the continual mithering about the weight of history not only a comparatively recent refrain, but a theory that doesn't hold water. 'I didn't really come across it, even at school,' he says. 'It was only when we went down to the Second Division in 1974 that it started, and even then it seemed to be more of a one-way thing – a kind of siege mentality. After years of that, Saints fans started to hate Pompey back.

'The navy divide and the working-class fighting myth seems to be a popular way of looking at it, but I don't really buy into that. Take some of the violent cities in England – Manchester or Birmingham. No one's gone to war *en masse* from there, apart from on each other. I think the analogy can be used in part, but I don't think it's the root cause. Pompey fans, or at least the more violent element, would like to glorify it, but that's a theory I've only heard in the last year or so.'

He continues: 'In general Saints fans don't hate Pompey as much as Pompey hate Saints. You could walk down the street in Southampton with a Pompey shirt on and no one would take any notice. But just try wearing a Saints shirt in Portsmouth! You get the feeling Pompey consider themselves to be the club with the history – "We've won the title, you haven't, you're nothing". Saints fans would say, "Fair enough, but we've been above you for forty years and you're showing us no respect", and so it's gradually built up. And the fact that it's two disparate cities living so close together lends it that edge. Other derbies, people live in the same houses, work in the same places and have an empathy. With this, it's like Newcastle and Sunderland. Even if it was tiddlywinks, everyone would go that extra yard to have a go. There's not a lot of friendliness.'

To the uninitiated, it must be a baffling state of affairs. We're not talking about the Old Firm, after all, with its centuries of sectarian baggage. These are supposedly southern softies: the seaside, candy floss, kiss-me-quick hats, scenic walks on the South Downs, *Howard's Way*, gin and tonics on the catamaran, and New Forest ponies. But on Sunday 21 March, the festering bitterness will reach boiling point in Portsmouth when Southampton pitch up for the first league meeting at Fratton Park since 1987–88, Pompey's last top-flight campaign. Until this season, it was the club's solitary spell in the big time since 1959.

You can take your piffling thirty years of hurt, it's now forty-one since Pompey last finished above Saints and time, far from being a healer, has created a festering sore. As Steve Woodhead observes, 'When I think of that club, I see a bunch of people who enjoy the status that should be ours and take it for granted.'

While once-proud Pompey, First Division champions in 1949 and 1950, slowly sank down the divisions – fans clinging to sepia-tinged photos of Dickinson, Harris, Reid, and Scoular – finally reaching the basement at the fag end of the 1970s, Saints were disappearing in the opposite direction, nudging their way into Division One for the first time in 1966. A decade later, under Lawrie McMenemy, they lifted the FA Cup as a Second Division outfit (though any Pompey fan will gleefully point out that their Wembley hero, Bobby Stokes, was a son of Portsmouth).

Promotion to Division One swiftly followed, as did the sensational signing of Kevin Keegan, whose bubble perm was the last thing anyone in a hastily-convened media scrum expected to see when McMenemy called a surprise press conference in July 1980. 'I want you to meet somebody who will play a big part in Southampton's future,' he told the astonished gathering. He was right.

The signing of Keegan – the deal had secretly been done months earlier – showed the depth of McMenemy's ambition. His twelve-year tenure revolutionised the Saints, and he remains fiercely proud of his record against Pompey. 'We played them five times and won every one – four league games and an FA Cup match,' he recalls. 'Unless you reside in, or have attended games in, this area, it's difficult for people to understand that the rivalry's just as great down here as in Scotland or the north east, Manchester, Liverpool, and London. Unfortunately, whether Pompey want to admit it or not, Southampton have been in a higher division more often. We were promoted in 1978–79, have been there ever since, and had a very good run in the days when there were a lot of big clubs in contention for honours. That period was a purple patch in the club's history, and I think it really hurt them down the road.

'Always in my team talk before a derby game I said: "You've got to remember that tomorrow morning, the two groups of supporters work together in the docks, factories, and offices. You want your fans to be waiting outside for the doors to open, their heads held high, not hanging low."'

The FA Cup game to which McMenemy refers, a fourth-round tie at Fratton Park in January 1984, was perhaps Portsmouth's blackest day off the pitch. The first meeting since a last-gasp Mick Channon goal had condemned Pompey to Division Three eight years earlier and sparked running battles in the surrounding streets, it was, in the words of Pompey goalkeeping stalwart Alan Knight, 'a real blood-and-thunder affair'. In front of 36,000, the game was won by the visitors with a goal from Steve Moran in stoppage-time added for a head wound to Saints full-back Mark Dennis courtesy of a coin thrown from the terraces. Dennis, a gifted player with a firecracker temperament of his own that had earmarked him as one of the 1980s bad boys, said at the time he could fully understand the sentiment.

Nick Illingsworth recalls a recent chat with Dennis. 'What he remembered most was getting back to the dressing room and seeing Lawrie McMenemy covered in spit. He said that day was the most hate-filled atmosphere he'd ever come across.'

Moran, a Saints fan raised in nearby Warsash, hasn't forgotten it either. 'When we drove up to Fratton, it was like passing through a war zone. There was a chilling atmosphere, some real menace in the air. We were all pretty anxious about getting home, especially after Steve Williams was threatened in the players' lounge, but they waited and slipped us out under cover of darkness. I can't tell you what a relief it was to get out of the place.' Moran was later thumped in a disco by a (soon to be ex-) Pompey apprentice.

'It was extraordinary,' says McMenemy. 'I remember picking up £5.50 in change and 2lbs of bananas, because we had Danny Wallace playing.' Others recall a deluge of flying chocolate bars, given out as a promotion before the game, raining down on the away support. Eighteen fans were hospitalised in what the *Portsmouth News* dubbed the 'Battle of Fratton', with fifty-nine arrests and damages totalling £8,000.

Trouble flared again in January 1988 at The Dell, before, during, and after a 2–0 success for Pompey, their sole victory in the fixture since 1963. Of the 116 arrests, 113 were Pompey fans, many members of the club's notorious hooligan gang, the 6.57 Crew.

The first thing Portsmouth chairman Milan Mandaric reached for when promotion was sealed last season was not a bottle of champers, but a banner which read: 'Step aside Saints, Pompey are in the Premiership'. But so far, things have not quite gone according to plan. In their first season in the Premiership, Portsmouth have discovered a very different Southampton Football Club.

With prudent husbandry, Saints have stealthily slipped their feet under the top flight table. Compared to the revolving door that doubled as the Portsmouth manager's office until Harry Redknapp's settling influence, the Saints job has been less a hot seat, more a tepid one. Between 1955 and 1991, the club had just three managers. Glenn Hoddle originally joined the club after leaving the England post, and European football – albeit briefly – returned to Hampshire for the first time since Lawrie McMenemy's heyday on the back of last season's FA Cup final appearance.

Steady progress is, says Nick Illingsworth, 'the only way to move forward long term. Some sides have spent millions and seen it wasted. We kept a tight grip on the purse strings and are reaping the rewards. Reaching the cup final was a natural progression. That and European qualification are reasonable targets for a team of Saints' standing.

'In the mid-1990s, there was a feeling among Pompey fans that getting back to the top was a matter of when, not if, and when they got there they would automatically be a top-four club. Their attitude was, "All you lot do is survive. When we get there we'll be a much bigger and better side. We won't just survive, we'll challenge for Europe." But in the past ten years, football has changed beyond recognition. It's now virtually impossible for anyone to break into the top five, but we're just outside that bracket, with a new ground, and sixth place is a reasonable target each year. Until Pompey came to St Mary's, I don't think their fans had much idea of the amount of work that's gone into Saints. Maybe their eyes opened a little bit.'

On 2 December 2003, Pompey arrived at St Mary's for a Carling Cup clash, the clubs' first meeting since a 1996 FA Cup third-round tie in which Saints' Matt Le Tissier ran the show in a 3–0 win. The evening was supposed to begin with a minute's silence for Ted Bates, Southampton player, manager, chairman, and president over a sixty-six-year period who had died just days before, but the 'silence' had to be aborted after twenty-five seconds of catcalls from the visiting fans. Trouble that night was minimal, but the fact that all police leave in Hampshire was cancelled, with 300 officers present – it's usually fifteen – tells its own story.

As Pompey fans were bussed in like POWs from the nearby park-and-ride, the air was thick with tension. 'It was my first derby,' says Portsmouth fan Claire Gurney. 'I travelled down on the train, but got a lift home. Having made the walk from the station, I really didn't fancy doing it again – as much because of my worry about how our fans would react after losing.'

The league meeting on 21 December was little better. PC Gary Morgan of Hampshire Police's Football Intelligence Unit reported the 'nastiest scenes I've witnessed in ten years of policing Pompey games'. Small wonder then that even the reserve league fixture prior to these two encounters was made an all-ticket affair.

If familiarity breeds contempt you shudder to think, for this has to be English football's least-played derby. To date there have been only twenty-seven league meetings, Southampton winning thirteen to Portsmouth's eight. When Saints stride onto the Fratton Park turf, looking to complete a league double over Harry Redknapp's relegation-haunted charges, it's fair to say few will have experienced the powder keg they will find there.

Fratton Park, a boil on the beautifully-branded face of the Premiership, is not a place for the faint-hearted at the best of times. Facilities – the club plans to revolve the pitch ninety degrees by 2005 for a £35 million development – are best described as idiosyncratic. Until the arrival of Mandaric, toilet paper was something of a luxury.

Now a non-smoking stadium, the concourse underneath the North Terrace, thick with the fug of fags, is so Dickensian – appropriate, considering he was born less than a mile away – you half expect to see Bill Sykes chatting with Fagin while his urchins fleece an unsuspecting old crone.

Yet the switch in the clubs' fortunes, far from cowing Pompey fans, seems to have made them more grimly determined to hold onto a history they feel establishes them as the region's top dog. 'It's like the Dalai Lama,' says season-ticket holder Dave Cauvin. 'We believe we'll be restored to our rightful position eventually.' Quizzed on the 2–0 and 3–0 defeats at St Mary's, he shrugs and smiles. 'We just might have a slightly longer wait than we expected.' It's a touchingly unswerving loyalty, akin to watching a drunk clutch a bottle with just a dribble inside as if his life depended on it. Some are so keen to 'stand up if you hate the Scum', it'd be a surprise to find a sofa in their lounge.

Talk in the pub after Pompey's defeat at Chelsea three days after Christmas wasn't about the game, or Abramovich's millions. It was all about Wayne Bridge. Having been 'scummed' incessantly for an hour, the Southampton-born ex-Saint celebrated his goal by cavorting along the touchline in front of the visiting fans, face contorted with glee. Bridge was soon shopping for a new mobile phone. His number, apparently passed on by an old mate, had become rather busy.

If this Premiership adventure lasts just a season, it won't make any odds to Pompey season-ticket holder Mike Hall. 'Southampton shouldn't even be bothered about us, but they are. Their problem is not really the fans, it's what everyone else in the country thinks about the two clubs – that Pompey is the proper club, the bigger club, the working-class club with the passionate fans and the singing. We're seen as a sleeping giant, they're a club that got lucky.

'They really want to beat us. They've got an inferiority complex, which I love to poke. They go out of their way to try and rub it in, while we're like the knight in *Monty Python and the Holy Grail* who fights on while his limbs are chopped off. They can beat us as many times as they like, they're not a bigger club and never will be. They've taken a tiny club and made a success of it. What they've had in their favour is superb and stable management – we had forty years where if there was a decision that could be taken for the worse, we took it. We've been monumentally impotent and things had to get as bad as they got at Pompey before people came in who realised it would cost more than a fiver to turn things around. People who get involved with Southampton are businessmen, because we're a sleeping giant we attracted the vainglorious and self-aggrandising. Southampton could carry on as they are, but they'll never be any bigger – we're limitless,' he adds, citing the potential catchment area to the north and east of Portsmouth of anything between 750,000 and a million people.

Perhaps the last word should lie with the late Marty 'Docker' Hughes, a Pompey obsessive who stood for Parliament in the General Election of June 1987. Hughes, the mascot of Pompey's 6.57 Crew, polled 455 votes on a manifesto that, though mostly verging on the bizarre – the banning of 'Robsons' and 'Waddles' as acceptable hair-cuts – demanded that Portsmouth be removed from Hampshire. It was enough to split the vote in Portsmouth South, Liberal Mike Hancock losing his seat by 205 votes.

The M275, arcing out of the city past the ferry terminal and the tower blocks of Stamshaw and Buckland, fast-tracks you to the M27 and Southampton in just thirty minutes. For many inhabitants of this fiercely-proud island, it might as well be Mars. Crumbling Fratton Park, with its Archibald Leitch stand and mock-Tudor entrance will groan with the weight of history in a couple of weeks. 'It is a doubt to me if there is such another collection of demons upon the whole earth,' wrote General James Wolfe of Portsmouth in 1758, days before leaving to meet his death liberating Canada from the French.

For anyone wearing red and white, it will seem precious little has changed when that whistle blows on 21 March.

'Getting on with the Neighbours?'

Millwall v West Ham, March 2004

It is billed as the ultimate hate match, but is the eternal feud between Millwall and West Ham really just a chirpy Cockney squabble?

> *'DON'T do it, chums! DON'T throw soil, cinders, clinkers, stones, bricks, bottles, cups, fireworks or other kinds of explosives, apples, oranges, etc. on the playing pitch during or after the match. DON'T barrack, utter filthy abuse, or molest in any way the players of the visiting team.'*
>
> **Millwall warning notice 1949–50**

'Oh, Wisey! Woah ah ah oh! Oh, Wisey! Woah ah ah oh! He's only five-foot-four! He'll break your fackin' jaw!' Flooding out of the New Den into glorious afternoon sunshine, you've never seen so many cheerful, rosy-cheeked and twinkly-eyed south Londoners. 'From henceforth, Mother's Day shall be known as Scummer's Day,' chortles a wit. Millwall have just beaten West Ham and dozens of delirious dirty (and not so dirty) denizens are on their mobile dogs, imparting this information to a woman apparently called Anne.

'Four-one! ANNE it could have been seven! ANNE we missed two penalties! ANNE their keeper got fackin' sent off!'

I'm trying to fit in. By not looking like a soft, middle-class, Northern homosexual who likes opera, real ale, and kittens. I've done me homework. I've got a copy of the Millwall fanzine *The Lion Roars* in me sky rocket. Inside is a savage attack on an *Evening Standard* article entitled '50 Things Every Londoner Should Do This Year'. Number 17 is 'Go for pie and mash'. To which a disgusted reader replies: 'Do not do this as a novelty, do this as part of everyday life.'

> ## EIGHT GREAT HATE DATES
>
> ## 1903
> ### West Ham 1 Millwall 7
>
> ---
>
> After reaching the FA Cup semi-final for the first (but not the last) time, Millwall also reach the semi-final of the Professional Charity cup. Where they thrash the Hammers 7–1.

So there I am. Trying to blend in. Trying to look like the sort of tasty geezer who has lavverly-jabberly pie & mash (& 'licker') *on a routine basis*. And who hates West Ham, not because they're Cockneys but – get this – *because they're not Cockney enough*. Which they achieve by, er, being too Cockney (choke on THAT, surrealism fans).

Of course nobody in football really needs a reason to hate the scum from up the road. But Millwall make a pretty decent fist of it. *The Lion Roars* fanzine hates West Ham 'because they won the World Cup and are the "Academy of Football" and are loveable, cheeky barrow boys and that lovely Alf Garnett, wasn't he funny? Grrrrr!'

From the Millwall perspective, says Garry Robson, author of *No One Likes Us We Don't Care – The Myth And Reality Of Millwall Fandom*, the rivalry with West Ham 'is played out entirely in terms of toughness, virility, and cultural authenticity within *Londonness*.'

John, a Millwall fan quoted by Garry Robson, states this in plainer language: 'They're all fakers over there – the "East End", all that "loveable Cockney" bollocks. And this thing with the Krays, and it's gone on and on and on and on. Like they're all loveable Cockney rogues. They all love the Queen Mum and it was bombed during the war. With us it's, like, they're all thieves and gangsters over there, but with them it's, oh they might be thieves, but they've all got hearts of gold and they all have nice street parties and they're not really bad lads. Like they keep saying about the Krays – you could always leave your door open. It's all bollocks.'

West Ham, on the other hand, would 'rarver fack a bucket/wiv a big hole innit/than be a Millwall fan/for just one minute'. And tend to look down on 'Scumwall' as 'pikeys'. 'They really are scum,' explains Hammers fan Pete. 'I mean, I was on the train once and there was this Millwall fan. He was asleep, he was about 60, really revolting looking. And he had "I Love Sex" tattooed on his hand. That says it all, really.'

So you get the picture. This is Ronnie Kray vs Charlie Richardson. Martin Kemp vs Luke Goss. Dirty Den vs Del Boy. Jim Davidson vs Hale and Pace. Iron Maiden's Bruce Dickinson vs Nick Heyward from Haircut 100. This is an argument with no real rhyme, reason, or rationale. Two predominantly white tribes – both increasingly drawn from far-flung suburbs in Essex or Kent – at loggerheads over which best represents an ever-more multicultural East London. Total bollocks, really, when you think about it. So it's a good job nobody really does.

'Where were you at Upton Park?' sing the 2,000-odd visiting West Ham fans, all apparently pointing at me. I blush. Because this is actually my second attempt to see a West Ham vs Millwall game this season. A furious West Ham press officer refused me access to the first.

'Why do you want to see the game?'

'I'm doing an article on the rivalry …'

'There IS no rivalry! There is NO rivalry between West Ham and Millwall! It's just a game! OK!? It's JUST a game!'

'Yes, but …'

'I said – "*IT'S JUST A GAME!*"' (end of conversation).

OK, OK – so it's just a game. So why am I feeling just a little bit nervous? Well I've done me research, see. And most fans, academics, journalists, and media pundits agree – visiting Millwall is like walking naked into a pit full of grizzly bears. With a sign saying 'grizzly bears are puffs' around your neck. While on really bad acid.

Arsenal's *Gooner* fanzine babbles about the 'Dickensian surroundings with water drip-

---

EIGHT GREAT HATE DATES

1904
West Ham 3 Millwall 0

Ten thousand see the first ever game at Upton Park. Local lad Billy Bridgeman scores West Ham's first goal at their new home.

---

ping from the dank viaduct' and claims that leaving the ground is 'like being on manoeuvres in some enemy infested outpost in Vietnam'.

And here's Billy, a West Ham fan, recalling his first trip to Millwall: 'We all got there early, and we was singing and shouting and that, having a great time. Millwall was really quiet. We was well taking the piss. Then all of a sudden this noise started, like moaning, they was all sorta *moaning*. I thought, what the fuck's going on here? It was so fucking loud, and they was all doing it, and it went *on* and *on* and *on* … West Ham just shut up.'

John King, in his seminal hoolie novel, *The Football Factory*, gibbered that Millwall has a history of 'a hundred years of kicking the fuck out of anybody who strays too far down the Old Kent Road'.

Which shows how much Mr King knows: 100 years? Try 400. In the 17th century panicking Puritan pamphleteers condemned the area as a bolthole for every species of 'dissolute, loose and insolent' wide-boy, ruffian, 'evill dispozed person' and 'sturdy beggar' on the planet. South London, wrote bible-basher Donald Lupton in 1632, is 'better termed a foul den then a faire garden' (and the name kind of stuck). In 1837 Charles Dickens set Fagin's den on Jacob's Island in Bermondsey: 'the very repulsive lineament of poverty, every loathsome indication of filth, rot and garbage.' And in 1996 the US State Department 'red-flagged' the area as a 'no-go' zone for American tourists, claiming that it was as dangerous as Guatemala (which, at the time, was overrun by right-wing death squads).

This, as former Millwall player Eamon Dunphy so eloquently put it, is quite simply 'the wrong part of London'. And – if the press are to be believed – Millwall FC are the living embodiment of unredeemed sporting evil. 'The New Den, like the old Den, remains unparalleled, a uniquely poisonous, malevolent, ugly, depressing venue,' hyperventilated Keith Pike of *The Times*. 'To watch Millwall is to journey into a valley of hatred,' blathered Ken Gorman of the *Daily Star* as he stared fearfully at 'a sea of scowling vengeful faces bounded by beer-fuelled loathing for any outsider. To talk of hatred in people's eyes,' ranted Ken, his nostrils dilated in animal terror, 'is not to exaggerate the most evil stench of wretchedness I have ever encountered.'

So that's why I'm doing my breathing exercises and fingering my energy crystal and trying really hard not to shit myself as I walk from the tube station, past the yuppie-flat building sites (with all the bricks and scaffolding poles conveniently shrink-wrapped and stacked for easy access), down past the railway lines and under the dank, dripping, graffiti-covered Victorian brick arches. Past evil-looking crows that go 'Caw!' And the glue-head wobbly scrawled sign that reads 'west ham will not make the den!'

OK, you want menace? I'll give you f***ing menace. This morning, before setting off, I tuned into Talk Sport Radio. Tony Cascarino and Andy

---

EIGHT GREAT HATE DATES

1957
Millwall 1 West Ham 3

Millwall make it to the final of the London FA Challenge Cup for the first time since 1938. And lose 3–1 to West Ham.

Townsend were discussing the Hammers/Millwall derby and engaging in a strange hyperbolic willy-waggling that made the game sound like a showdown between Freddy Krueger and the KKK. 'West Ham–Millwall? I wouldn't take my daughter to it!' said Cascarino. 'Ooh no! I wouldn't take my wife to it!' one-upped Townsend. And the two of them then segued seamlessly into a discussion about Republic of Ireland games in Belfast during the height of the Troubles – and al-Qaeda,

---

EIGHT GREAT HATE DATES

1972
Millwall 3 West Ham 5

It's the season that Millwall legend Harry Cripps plays his 300th game for the club. At his testimonial, West Ham win with Geoff Hurst scoring a hat-trick. The party is further spoiled by Millwall and West Ham fans battering the crap out of each other.

---

armoured cars, and guards with guns. And I'm stood there, electric toothbrush in my gob, absolutely f***ing terrified. Thanks, lads.

The press build-up to this game has bordered on the hysterical. *The Observer* refer to Millwall as 'the Mike Tyson of football'. In *The Guardian* Zoe Williams is told not to go by her brother because 'the one thing they hate more than each other are journalists'. A gentleman called Forest Gate Phil tells a lads' mag, 'I fully expect there to be murder'. The *London Evening Standard* claims that it was 'a blessing for football' that the two clubs have met so infrequently. And former West Ham hooligan Cass Pennant is quoted as saying that 'the atmosphere of hatred in unreal'.

Millwall and West Ham 'are like two brothers,' says Cass. 'But only one of them can be king. They have the same blood but would kill each other to take the throne.'

Cass, of course, is the author of the definitive history of West Ham hooliganism, *Congratulations – You Have Just Met The ICF*. The chapter on Millwall/West Ham games does not make for pleasant reading. It involves boots, fists, knives, machetes, and – in one horrible instance – giant British Rail track spanners. And this history is well known by the Burberry baseball-hatted adolescent twat-psychopaths who keep the flame of hooliganism alive on the Internet. And some of them are positively *drooling* over West Ham's visit to the New Den.

So it's no wonder then that, according to the tabloids, this game is going to be like the opening scenes of *Dawn of the Dead*, with grown men tearing each other apart with their bare teeth. They should make a film about it. In fact they are doing. It's called *Hooligan*. With Elijah 'Lord Of The Rings' Wood in the lead role as an American student who is 'seduced by the world of football hooliganism' at a Millwall/West Ham derby. Seriously. It's kinda *Fight Club* with hobbits and Stanley knives. And it's going to make *The Texas Chainsaw Massacre* look like *Finding Nemo*. Apparently. I mean, what the f*** am I doing here?

But, to be honest, the sun is shining on the railway sidings and the spring flowers are poking their dainty heads through the cracks in the

---

EIGHT GREAT HATE DATES

1993
West Ham 2 Millwall 2

In an echo of the current season, Millwall are jostling for automatic promotion to the top division. On an atrocious pitch, Jamie Moralee puts Millwall ahead after forty-five seconds. Kevin Lee gets a goal back for the Hammers in the 13th minute. And thirty seconds later – while Millwall are still arguing among themselves – Trevor Morley puts the home side ahead. Millwall manager Mick McCarthy goes for broke and sends on strikers John Kerr and Tommy Gaynor – but it's Lions defender Keith 'Rhino' Stevens who heads the equaliser.

quaint Victorian arches. And if this bit of South London is Dickensian then it's most definitely the 'Consider Yourself One Of Us' scene out of *Oliver*. (Rather than that bit where Bill Sykes smashes Nancy's skull in with his stick.) Besides which – these mums and dads and kids and that? I reckon I could have the f***ing lot of them.

Twenty minutes before kick-off and the West Ham fans start singing Bubbles. And the Millwall fans respond with their trademark howl. But it's all a bit ritualistic. A bit too intimidation-by-numbers. (He said, smugly, knowing full well there are over 1,000 police at this game.)

Meanwhile – as is traditional – the stands nearest the visiting fans are full of mime

EIGHT GREAT HATE DATES

2003
Millwall Supporters Club 3 West Ham Supporters Club 1

On a rock-hard Hackney Marshes pitch the youthful West Ham side are no match for the more experienced Lions. The West Ham team are also severely hampered by the fact they field five players called Dan. But, as the Hammers' manager comments after the game: 'Who'd have thought West Ham and Millwall could contest a game without a single foul or free-kick?!'

artists. One young man is particularly effective. He could probably earn a living doing this in Covent Garden. The American tourists would love his act – especially the bit where he combs a huge imaginary quiff, pretends to be a tea-pot and then uses his arms to suggest that West Ham are 'all marf' (by imitating the jaw movements of a large prehistoric fish).

The game itself is farcical. Especially if you're a West Ham fan. Millwall miss a penalty. West Ham score an own goal. With an hour gone the score is 3–1. West Ham's keeper is sent off. Millwall are awarded another penalty (which they also miss). And that's when some of the West Ham fans decide to 'attack' the Millwall fans. Sort of. Or maybe invade the pitch. Maybe.

What happens is that a couple of hundred West Ham fans are, er, 'held back' by a very, very thin blue line. Consisting of five coppers. 'Enraged' and 'frustrated', the West Ham fans jump up and down for a bit and demolish a 'Kick Racism out of Football' banner. More coppers turn up. Some on horses. And about ten minutes later some policemen in riot gear amble over. It's all a bit 'hold me back!' Utterly ritualistic and without any real menace. But it'll allow a few arseholes some bragging rights on the hoolie websites tomorrow. *'We'd've took Millwall if it hadn't been for those five coppers asking us politely to sit back down'* etc. And that's the main thing.

So where did it all start then, this jellied eel-fuelled blood feud? This inter-Cockney palaver? This interminable geezer vs geezer bitterness? West Ham Pete thinks he knows.

'There was a big strike at the ironworks about 1912 and the Millwall lot were the ones who

---

EIGHT GREAT HATE DATES

2003
West Ham 1 Millwall 1

More than 700 of the Met's finest police guard 31,626 fans in what is claimed to be the biggest police operation ever at a UK sporting event. Recently relegated West Ham are brought down to earth with a bump as they draw 1–1 with Millwall in the first East London derby for ten years. The game sees four bookings but fails to live up to the media hype, on or off the field. Hammers caretaker-manager Trevor Brooking ruefully admits: 'We've got to expect to do better if we are going to get out of this league.'

crossed the picket line. So basically they're the scab team.'

But this, alas, turns out to be an urban legend: at best, total bollocks at worst and – at a pinch – a garbled re-telling of the Portsmouth/Southampton story.

'Look, if this rivalry went that far back,' says Phil, a West Ham fan, 'then, when the Den was bombed during the Second World War, why did West Ham offer to ground-share? There's always rivalry between South-East London and the East End, yeah? That's obvious – coz we never had rats in the East End until they built the Rotherhithe tunnel.' 'It's all bollocks' agrees LSD, a Millwall fan. 'I mean where was Millwall's ground in 1912?' 'In the East End, on a fackin' mud chute in the middle of the Thames,' chimes in West Ham Ian, unhelpfully,

We're in a pub in London's neutral West End. West Ham fans Ian, Phil, and Pete are trying to shout down Millwall fans LSD and Jane. Some of the fans present might be described as former hooligans. Nobody is using his or her real name.

An outsider witnessing this maelstrom of shouting, swearing and extremely aggressive table-banging, fist-waving, and finger-pointing would probably find it hard to believe that all the people here are friends. And that (Millwall) Jane and (West Ham) Pete are girlfriend and boyfriend. The Dickensian ambience is heightened still further by the fact that a certain extremely drunk 1970s punk rock star is also sat at the table. He will take no part in the conversation, however, as he is

---

EIGHT GREAT HATE DATES

2004
Millwall 4 West Ham 1

Five goals, three penalties (two missed), a red card, a spectacular Christian Dailly own goal – and 1,000 coppers. This is a game that will be remembered for a long time, if only for the headline 'CHRISTIAN THROWN TO THE LIONS'.

far too busy engaging in the latter stages of foreplay with an extremely drunk young lady.

Is it not true that this rivalry is really overblown and that a lot of Millwall fans and West Ham fans are actually friends?

*Ian: No!

+LSD: No!

*Pete: Oh come on! You know it's fucking true!

*Ian: Thing is, West Ham don't consider Millwall to be any sort of challenge. Tottenham are our main rivals.

+LSD: Yeah, right. And then Arsenal and Real Madrid. But not necessarily in that order.

*Ian: HA HA HA! Thing is, south London are obsessed with east London. 'Cos they're rubbish!

*Phil: It's because no one sells pegs round our way and they see us as a potential market.

Do Millwall have a problem with the way that West Ham are always banging on about how they won the World Cup in 1966?

*Ian: No, it's just the fact we wear shoes!

+LSD: Yeah, normally white ones to match your socks.

*Ian: Oh hark at Captain Reebok! It's all down to the Jubilee Line extension. South London's always been gutted because they can't get anywhere and now they're getting ideas. Oh, which way to the Bernabeu?

*Phil: It used to be that people would go to West Ham one Saturday and go to Millwall the next.

+LSD: That's quite true. In the '40s and '50s. The antagonism started in '73 when a fan went under a train at New Cross.

But which is the real London? The East End or South East London?

+LSD: They both are. Yes, definitely. Without a doubt.

*Ian: But you lot ain't Cockneys.

*Phil: Well, neither are you!

*Ian: And neither are you, you Barking c***!

*Pete: Ian! Aye! Steady!

*Ian: No, whatever happens, we'll bash the journalist c***!

Is it not true that both teams increasingly draw the bulk of their support from the suburbs, which makes all the argy-bargy about 'Londonness' somewhat redundant?

+LSD. No!

*Ian: No!

*Pete: Whoah, hang on!

*Ian: Well not with Millwall, anyway, maybe West Ham.

*Pete: With West Ham it's definitely true.

*Phil: East London's changing all the time. The area around Upton Park is far more Asian and a lot of the West Ham support have moved out to Essex.

+LSD: Look, what I'm *trying* to say is that the two areas of London with strongest identity of where people come from are east and south London, yeah? Which basically came from the Romans up to the modern day.

*Phil: What the fuck are you talking about?

*Ian: In the City of London, the rogues were taken to the east gate and thrown out. Which created the East End. Then they went across the river on their little round boats. So it's the same people somewhere down the line. Like Chelsea supporters and Arsenal supporters can come from anywhere. Chelsea don't even know if they're in south London or west London!

If you walked into a pub of east London football fans, is there any way you'd be able to tell them apart?

*Phil: If they was trying to sell you heather and pegs ...

+LSD: There is a way – you won't like it. Black geezers.

*Phil: You see, you got no style, you got no soul ...

+LSD: Millwall supporters see it as a bit like the attitude there used to be in the East End. It's still very strong in Bermondsey. They see it – wrongly or rightly – as the last white, working class bastion of inner London.

*Ian: It's a fackin' island!

+LSD: And it's going to change. And I'm not saying it's right. I'm just saying that's the way it is. And south Bermondsey, round where the football ground is, it's not a good place to walk around if you're black. There are black supporters of Millwall, I know some. But they're very, very few. The black community don't want to associate themselves with Millwall and the white community who go to Millwall don't want to associate themselves with black people. West Ham is totally different.

*Ian: Can't we just all get together and kick fuck out of the journalist?

*Phil: There's always been a progression of races coming through east London but we've welcomed everyone. And there's black and white – and everyone'd turn up and give Millwall a slap!

+Jane: With Millwall it's passed on. If your dad supported them, you do. It is quite exclusive – it's kept in the family almost. Whereas West Ham is anyone – it's like Man United.

+LSD: If you like, Millwall are a dinosaur.

What happens if Millwall go up and West Ham don't? How are you going to deal with not having that chip on your shoulder any more?

+LSD: I ain't got a chip on me shoulder!

+Jane: It's pride.

+LSD: I'm *prahd* of supporting a little club in south east London that's got no money. Whose back's against the wall – and the rest of the football league hates ya! We sing about it every week! We're *prahd* of it!

+Jane: I don't think much of West Ham, but then, as a Millwall fan, you don't think much of anyone. I mean, my dad really admired

West Ham for the whole Bobby Moore generation and could see the strengths of the team and stuff – but as a Millwall supporter you are Millwall, and that's it.

So does your dad know that you're going out with a West Ham fan?

+Jane: It's not going down well, let's put it that way. What you say about a lot of our supporters being in Kent, that's really true. I mean all the kids in Bromley support Millwall because of the bad boy reputation.

+LSD: I mean, you can't blame them. You can't hold your head up high and say you support Crystal Palace or Charlton, can ya?

*Phil: Yeah, but without being too damning, what's your average gate this season? Ten thousand?

+Jane: That doesn't come into it.

+Phil: But it does. West Ham have been relegated and they get 32,000. I mean, come on!

+Jane: That's not what it's about. We're happy without the popularity.

+LSD: Without a shadow of a doubt, Millwall are the only club in the world where the fans are more famous than the club. The celebrities are on the stand; they're not on the pitch.

*Phil: Millwall have always had something against us. They've always wanted to be better than us.

*Ian: They've always hated us more than we've hated them.

Is that true?

+LSD: No.

*Ian: Fack off! We don't give a fack about you!

*Phil: Remember when we played them in 1978–79 and Brooking scored twice and we put them right in their place and we beat them 4–0? When we used to play them, we just thought – mugs! But now they've gone above us in the league and they've got a game in hand, they're in the Cup final – you've nearly got to doff your cap.

+LSD: I hate Charlton more than I hate West Ham.

*Phil: Look, people support teams for all sorts of reasons – because they saw them when they was a kid on a little black telly – blah blah blah. Whereas Millwall fans are just born there – bang – and that's it. And the Millwall people I've met and work with, they're as genuine as I am. So let them enjoy their day. They had us over, I had untold e-mails about it. You've just got to say – well done and good luck to them. That's the way I look at it.

And all is peace and harmony. But just then the 1970s punk rock star notices that someone has just nicked his pint. A right old hoo-hah ensues. The 1970s punk rock star is screaming in rage and fury. A fight almost starts.

And the West Ham and Millwall fans smile at one another and shake their heads. Some things just aren't worth fighting about...

More Than a Game
Cliftonville v Linfield, January 2004

When predominantly Protestant Linfield clash with overwhelmingly Catholic Cliftonville, the football often takes second billing to the religious divide – though gradual progress is being made to eradicate sectarianism in the sport.

The convoy of escorted buses carrying 800 Linfield fans is due at any minute. No other supporters of Northern Ireland's biggest and most successful club will be coming to today's big game. Strict security restrictions mean that any fan who wants a ticket had to meet at a leisure centre car park an hour ago, from where a fleet of buses has carried them through the divided communities of North Belfast. Many Linfield fans used to making their own way to matches resent the restrictions. Others accept that this is no ordinary away game. It is not so long ago – just six years – that it was not deemed safe for Linfield fans to make this journey at all. For their destination is Solitude, the home of arch-rivals Cliftonville.

Known by various monikers including 'the murder mile' and 'the killing fields', more lives were lost in the area around Solitude during the Troubles than in any other part of Northern Ireland. This neighbourhood of North Belfast is a patchwork of working-class communities living cheek by jowl, but divided by religion. It may not have the iconic status of West Belfast's Shankill or Falls Roads, but there are political murals, flags and painted kerbstones aplenty. Not two miles from Solitude is Holy Cross, the primary school which achieved infamy as a sectarian flashpoint two summers ago.

Outside Solitude the police presence is organised but low-profile. Armoured Land Rovers discreetly block passageways in the tight streets around the ground to secure an area for Linfield fans to pass through. Meanwhile officials of Cliftonville, Ireland's oldest football club, scurry about making sure everything is in order for their guests' arrival. And everything is well, mostly. The man in the burger van seems anxious when told that he'll be serving the Linfield fans. And the hundred or so alcohol-fuelled lads in baseball caps waiting behind Irish Tricolours, Basque and Palestinian flags in the squat, decrepit, main stand are clearly not there to exchange cordialities with the visiting support.

The increased hubbub on the police radios indicates activity and almost at once the first Linfield fans appear at the top of the street. Flanked by their own stewards, they move steadily towards the away turnstiles. The whole operation is watched by observers from Belfast city council and fifteen minutes later the travelling fans are inside the ground, some busying themselves by putting up an assortment of red, white and blue flags adorned with the words 'Londonderry' or 'Shankill'. The turnstiles are closed and the police stay outside the ground.

Such is the conflict between Linfield, with a reputation for being a predominantly Protestant (or unionist or loyalist) club, and Cliftonville, a predominantly Catholic (or republican or nationalist) one – the only such club in the top division since Belfast Celtic folded and Derry City started playing games south of the border – that for twenty-eight long years at the height of the Troubles, no games between the sides were permitted at Solitude.

East Belfast's Glentoran – whose fans have taunted Linfield with chants of 'Gerry Adams's your MP' because Linfield's Windsor Park ground is close to the Sinn Fein territory of West Belfast – may be a truer rival when judged by success and support, but Linfield's clashes with Cliftonville have always had religious connotations and been viewed as a microcosm of sectarian strife in the province. And that was too big a chance for the security forces to take.

'The location of Solitude represented too much of a risk, not so much to the players, but to the security forces who would have been vulnerable to attack,' says Padraig Coyle, author of the acclaimed *Paradise lost and found, the story of Belfast Celtic.*

'During the Troubles, the police argument would have been that that they were too tied up to police a Cliftonville v Linfield match in what is a largely nationalist North Belfast,' adds the BBC's Ireland correspondent Mark Simpson.

So instead, every time the two sides met, the game took place at Windsor Park, also the venue for Northern Ireland's internationals. 'The police are not as acceptable in nationalist areas of Northern Ireland as they are in unionist areas and Windsor Park is in a unionist area,' explains Simpson.

Though neither set of fans was happy about the arrangement, from 1970 to 1998, there was nothing they could do. Adjacent to a motorway, which aided pre- and post-match segregation, Windsor Park was considered safer. But it was not always safe enough.

'We played there three days after an IRA bomb which killed two soldiers in November 1991,' recalls Steven McKillop, treasurer of Cliftonville. 'We were standing behind the goal and the UDA [the Ulster Defence Association, an outlawed loyalist group] threw a hand grenade over the wall towards us.'

Life was seldom straightforward for Cliftonville fans, wherever they went. 'Because we were the only club with a big perceived Catholic support, people would turn up wearing Rangers shirts at grounds just to wind us up,' McKillop recalls. 'We were given a police escort to most games and had our coaches stoned at almost every ground. There used to be a competition in our fanzine called "The Golden Brick" – it was awarded to the supporters whose bus had their windows put through the most times during a season. We can laugh about it now but at the time it was serious.'

And divisions were easily magnified. 'Cliftonville were known as "Sporting Sinn Fein" by some Linfield fans who barely differentiated between them and Gerry Adams,' explains a Linfield fan in a pub in Belfast's fast-gentrifying city centre. 'Maybe people liked to believe that. Football fans are about exaggerations and the more nationalist Cliftonville fans were portrayed, the more nationalist they became, bringing Irish flags and singing IRA songs.'

Linfield were the perceived antithesis. 'Recently Linfield have made big strides by selecting players solely on ability rather than their political background, but it wasn't always like that,' says Padraig Coyle. 'In the 1980s, Linfield played their European matches at Wrexham because of crowd trouble. I was told of a Linfield supporter who travelled to a game and waited outside the ground to listen to the team being announced. When he heard a Catholic was playing he decided against going in.'

It wasn't always thus. In fact, the enmity between Linfield and Cliftonville was late to develop. Until the 1970s Cliftonville were an amateur club founded in what was originally a Protestant area before population shifts around Solitude changed the religious make-up. Up to then, religious bigotry had been far more common at games between Linfield and the long-defunct Belfast Celtic.

'Belfast Celtic's ground held 60,000,' says Coyle. 'And they attracted 30–40,000. They had a Protestant manager who had a non-sectarian policy and he signed the best players. But at Windsor Park on Boxing Day 1948, the Celtic centre-forward was attacked at the end of the game by Linfield fans. It had been a heated game and they tried to kill him. That summer the Belfast Celtic directors decided they'd had enough of playing in the Irish league and the club was wound up. Their fans' allegiances gradually transferred to the other Celtic in Glasgow, or to Cliftonville.'

And so, in the 1970s and '80s Cliftonville–Linfield games became yet another expression of the troubled times, the ranks of the true fans swelled by interlopers from both sides intent on indulging in anti-social behaviour and naked sectarianism. The police presence was high, the atmosphere vicious.

'Cliftonville–Linfield did become a match involving both communities,' concedes Malcolm Brodie, Northern Ireland's most renowned sportswriter.

'In the past, football has always been a victim of the social element of Northern Ireland,' adds Gerard Lawlor, a committee member at Cliftonville. 'Somebody from the New Lodge [an almost entirely Catholic district of North Belfast], for instance, may have come to Solitude because it was the nearest they came to seeing a Protestant. And they came to sing sectarian songs.'

These days, says Lawlor, that would not be tolerated. 'We can't stop 100 lads singing, but people have been evicted. It's a difficult problem, but all the clubs are working together to eradicate it. We really are.'

In fact, it was the two sets of fans working in tandem that eventually brought Linfield back to Solitude. 'To be fair, Linfield and their supporters wanted to come and in 1994 we began to campaign,' says Steven McKillop. 'We won the league in April 1998, the Good Friday peace agreement was signed in August 1998 and three months later Linfield came back for the first time.'

'It was fantastic,' says Padraig Coyle of that first game back. 'It was symbolic in that it marked another step on the road to trying to get back to normal. It was another barrier removed.'

'It was no coincidence that we had the peace process and Linfield being able to go to Cliftonville,' agrees Mark Simpson. 'Things have moved along an awful lot in Northern Ireland. The political climate is a lot better.'

Behind the scenes, people worked tirelessly to ensure the day passed off peacefully. Police liaised with both clubs and their supporters, one of whom was Billy Hutchinson, the Loyalist councillor and member of the Mid-Shankill Linfield Supporters Club. 'They spoke to me and to Gerry Kelly, a Sinn Fein representative who is perhaps notorious for getting done for blowing up the Old Bailey in London,' says Hutchinson. 'Gerry Kelly and I would often work together. He spoke to his community and made sure that the Linfield buses wouldn't get attacked and it passed off OK.'

The situation improved further a couple of years later when a group of Cliftonville fans approached some Linfield supporters about going to the match in unison to make a cross-community gesture. 'We walked to the ground together,' recalls Hutchinson, 'but because we were not members of Linfield we couldn't get tickets for the game. We went along anyway but Linfield's health and safety person wouldn't let us in the ground because we didn't have tickets. We paid to go in the Cliftonville end but it turned quite nasty around me, got a little bit sectarian, and we had to be moved.'

There's no quick fix, but even two steps forward, one step back represents progress. So improved is the climate that when Linfield announced that they were no longer willing to arrange buses for their fans to travel to Solitude, there was a surprise offer of assistance: from Cliftonville. The club secured sponsorship for the transport from the 174 Trust, a non-denominational Christian organisation that facilitates essential community projects in North Belfast. Admittedly, financially-challenged Cliftonville wanted the ticket revenue from the Linfield fans, but the positive intentions were clear.

Sadly, Cliftonville are not alone in Northern Ireland in seeking every penny they can get. Football is struggling in the province, the state of the grounds an accurate barometer of the current condition of the game, with the crumbling Solitude typical of many. Although there are plans for a new stand to match the one that houses the visiting Linfield fans, two sides of the ground are condemned and Cliftonville would be lucky to be accepted into the Conference in England. It's hardly their fault. Northern Ireland was not a beneficiary of public money to improve stadiums after the Taylor Report, and it shows.

'Football here is in a dire situation,' says Malcolm Brodie. 'Many clubs are facing bankruptcy, mainly because there are diminishing gates and people have more diverse interests. Wall-to-wall football on television from England, Scotland, Europe and South America doesn't help either. 'There aren't enough players of a sufficient standard to go round the 16 teams in the Premier League,' he continues. 'Irish league football is currently semi-professional, but with the money coming in, an amateur or non-contract set-up would be more realistic. Clubs simply can't pay out more than they are getting in and what you are left with is a product that isn't marketable to sponsors.'

'Business doesn't want to be associated with football,' agrees Billy Hutchinson. 'Perhaps people who don't go to the game only associate football with sectarianism. There are still elements, but it really isn't the problem it used to be. Well over half of the players are Catholics. There are still some Linfield fans who don't want anything to do with Catholics but it's a minority and it's quite clear among the fans that the Catholics in the team don't take any stick.

'Sometimes the politics can have an adverse affect on the game though,' he concedes. 'Coca-Cola used to sponsor youth development of the Northern Ireland team, but because Northern Ireland play at Windsor Park, the Irish lobby in America thought that they were sponsoring Linfield and put pressure on Coca-Cola who threatened to withdraw their sponsorship.'

There's also the problem of rival leagues with far more glitz and glamour. 'There's generally a swing towards Manchester United, Arsenal, Celtic and Rangers,' says Malcolm Brodie. 'Those are the shirts you see worn by the young kids on the streets in Belfast now. It saddens me because you used to see people walking around in Distillery or Linfield shirts, but that's life.' (Ironically, the English teams attract support in equal measures from all sides of society and some of their supporters clubs were cited as examples of successful cross-community initiatives by the then Northern Ireland Secretary, Mo Mowlam.)

'There's probably 20,000 travelling to England and Scotland each week to watch Celtic, Rangers, Man United or Liverpool. That's another drain of potential match-going fans,' says Padraig Coyle.

But Cliftonville's David Begley doesn't agree. 'People complain about the fans who travel to England or Scotland to watch matches, but exactly the same thing happens in the Republic and yet the Eircom league is going really well. The difference is that that league is run in a more professional manner.'

'There's a lot of in-fighting between the Irish League and the Irish FA,' admits Coyle. 'But people don't want to go to games when the facilities are so dire and the arrival of the Belfast Giants ice hockey team has also been a blow to football. The new Odyssey arena holds 7,000 people and crowds average about 4,500 – more than any football club. And there's rugby too, with Ulster doing well. Sometimes rugby has a higher crowd than the aggregate crowd for all the Irish League premier games. Ice hockey came in with a non-sectarian agenda and said: "We represent everybody. We are not nationalist or unionist. We represent ice hockey." If you wear a football shirt, you're asked to leave the arena and people have started bringing their families to this safe environment. With certain football clubs parents don't feel the same way. Some clubs are making a big effort, but it's going to be tough.'

It gets worse. RTE, the Irish broadcaster, have signed a deal for live Premiership television with Sky starting from next season. Viewers in Northern Ireland can pick up the RTE signal and will be able to watch Premiership matches live at 3 p.m. on Saturday. Yet more competition.

Political fighting, lack of funds, decaying stadiums, and competition from England, Scotland and other sports: it's fair to say things don't look rosy. But to paint an entirely grim picture would be an injustice to the efforts of those who are so passionate about football in

Northern Ireland. For two hours before the Linfield game, I am given open access to anyone and everyone at Cliftonville Football Club. It is a joy to witness so many genuine football people showing their passion for the game with a positive attitude.

The Cliftonville manager Marty Tabb appears. He hasn't come to offer his views. 'No, I've just sneaked up here for a fag so my wife doesn't see me,' he says with a smirk. He inhales deeply. 'But I'll tell you one thing. All the clubs deserve credit just for surviving the Troubles.' And with that he's gone.

Cliftonville and Linfield, like many other clubs in Northern Ireland, have been proactive in reaching out to the locality in recent years. 'We started our cross-community initiatives about five years ago,' says Cliftonville's Gerard Lawlor. 'We realised that we were perceived by the community to be a Catholic nationalist club and nothing could be further from the truth. But the thing is, we, as a club, had done nothing to change that. So we started going into schools and coaching children, giving kids from both sides of the community tickets to games. For so long this football club was a building at the end of the street which remained closed except on a Saturday afternoon. Now we have youth groups, education schemes and we're seeing real progress. We're getting a lot more young people at the game, Protestants and Catholics, and that wouldn't have happened before. We try to educate the kids that we are here for football, that we are here for enjoyment and that politics has nothing to do with it. We're getting there, slowly but surely.'

It's ninety minutes to kick-off and Lawlor is summing up his thoughts on the edge of Solitude's six-yard box. Behind him, two young lads from Cliftonville's youthful supporter group, the Red Renegades, are fixing their red-and-white flags to 'the cage', an unused covered terrace with a fence so high it touches the roof of the stand. None of the banners convey a hint of sectarianism. Asked why they don't follow football in Scotland or England like many of their mates, one replies: 'I want to support my local team. And I have no interest in

Scottish football because of the bigotry there.' The £3 admission fee would hardly discourage them from coming here either.

'The truth is, we actually did better when we had to play our home games against Linfield at Windsor Park,' says Cliftonville chairman Hugh McCartan with a mischievous smile. And true to form Linfield win the game 4–1 in front of a crowd of barely 3,000. McCartan and his fellow board members, some of whom once ran Cliftonville's fanzine, are limited to seeing snatches of action, so engrossed are they in their duties. One board member checks that the dressing rooms are OK, another that the tea will be ready for half-time. Their love for the club seems unconditional.

'We're like Barcelona in that we are owned by our members, every one has a vote,' says one board member. It's unlikely, though, that a director of Barcelona is found working the turnstiles at the Nou Camp half an hour before the game.

There is sectarian chanting inside the ground from a minority of fans on both sides, and a few kids aim their invective towards the Linfield players as they hurry towards the tunnel at the end of the game, but that aside, the edge is more about football, like cross-city rivalries the world over. As the game draws to a close, the Linfield fans tease, 'Go home, you might as well go home.' Given that the Cliftonville fans are held behind after the game while the visiting fans are escorted back to their buses, it's not like they have a choice. They have to stay and suffer.

Thirty minutes after the final whistle and Solitude befits its name. The only activity is in the dressing rooms and the boardroom, where suited officials stand and sip tea at either side of a huge oak table.

The chairman of Cliftonville steps forward to thank his equivalents from Linfield for being exemplary guests. He wishes them well in the league (which they go on to win). It's absorbing to see the focus and intensity on the faces of all in the room. It feels like a significant moment in history. A Linfield official steps forward and reciprocates the gesture. It's appreciated. The mood is positive.

'Things have started to change, but the changes are not happening quickly enough and money urgently needs to be spent improving the facilities at grounds,' says Billy Hutchinson. 'But I'm in favour of the peace process and I'm optimistic about the future of football in Northern Ireland. We need to start developing communities, and if a football club is not part of the community then it's not worth being there.'

The Clasico
Argentina v Brazil, June 2005

Between them, they've won seven World Cups and produced the two greatest players of all time, but Argentina and Brazil are neighbours from totally different planets. And they don't half bear a grudge …

The Argentinian view

A chilly mass of polar air advances through the misty streets of Núñez, the neighbourhood where River Plate's Estadio Monumental stands. It's 2 a.m. on one of the worst Buenos Aires nights of the year. A persistent drizzle soaks a group of 800 people sat clustered around the stadium as a howling wind whips in to compound their misery.

Some sit on improvised chairs made from boxes, others search for shelter under plastic bags and blankets. Broken beer bottles and cheap wine boxes are scattered around them. It's a sordid scene, but though the social situation in Argentina is parlous, it's not so severe as to see homeless camp sites springing up in one of the most exclusive areas of the capital. No, these people are here for a reason, the most compounding reason of all: football, Argentina vs Brazil, the ultimate derby.

In eight hours, 15,000 *populares* (standing tickets) will go on sale. And no matter how wet or sick they become through waiting, real fans will do anything to get their hands on one. It is, after all, the biggest home game of the last decade, and it kicks off in forty-eight hours. 'Even if it means camping on the wet pavement and being fired from work, I don't care, all I want is to be there,' says 29-year-old Alfredo. 'Nothing's more enjoyable than witnessing how our boys smash some Brazilian arses.'

There's a common opinion in Argentina, reinforced by the last decade of Brazilian domination. Brazil are the best, but when they visit Argentina, their players panic and lose. Yet if Argentina lose when they travel north, it's because the Brazilians are technically superior, not because our boys can't stand the pressure.

As time passes, the waiting crowd balloons. By 4 a.m. there are 2,000 fans. Three hours later it's 7,000. At 10 a.m., 20,000 fans are singing songs against the despised *los brasucas* as a three-mile queue snakes across two of the five lanes of the Highway Lugones.

'It's amazing what people will do to get a ticket,' gasps Hernan Crespo. 'It gives us extra motivation. We have to beat Brazil because it's Brazil, because it's our derby, because we would reach the World Cup, but, especially, for every hour these people spent in that bad weather. Some were camping for up to two days.'

Though the Argentina–Brazil rivalry is old, it hasn't always been so fierce. 'In our time, our derby was undoubtedly against Uruguay. Brazil was not a real opposition to us,' says Francisco Varallo, the 93-year-old who played in the World Cup final of 1930.

The emergence of Pele in the '50s and the launch of the Copa Libertadores in the '60s were instrumental in heating up the new rivalry. In the years since, Argentina–Brazil has seen everything from hooliganism and attacks on the police to pitch battles and arrested players. This derby has had it all.

This time around though, from an Argentine perspective at least, the *clasico* holds extra importance for a variety of reasons, least of which, bizarrely, is that three points for either side will secure automatic qualification for the 2006 World Cup.

This game is the first *clasico* since last year's Copa America final, one of the lowest points in Argentina's football history when, having trailed all match, Brazil's second-string team equalised at the death and stole the trophy on penalties. It's also the first derby since Sao Paulo striker Grafite accused Quilmes defender Leandro Desabato of racial abuse in a Copa Libertadores match, prompting an incident that cost the Argentinian two days in jail and caused a massive scandal in both countries. Diego Maradona warned that such situations should be handled carefully, 'otherwise every time the Brazilians come to Buenos Aires, someone will find an excuse to nick a couple of them'.

In addition, this is the first meeting between the sides since the so-called 'water jug scandal' came to light. Two former players, Maradona and Jose Basualdo have now admitted that during the World Cup derby in 1990, Argentina's physio carried two bottles of water. One was fine; the other was fixed with sedatives, a 'gift' to any Brazilian who asked for a drink (a claim denied by the physio, Galindez, and the Argentinian manager Carlos Bilardo).

With tension rising in the build-up, Brazil coach Carlos Alberto Parreira tries to act the peacemaker, reasoning that as both teams have all but qualified, the game's 'like a deluxe friendly'. For Argentinians, though, it isn't. And when the Brazilians land on Argentinian soil, the atmosphere is as tense as hell.

The rumour that Brazil have brought their own food and water to avoid 'surprises' adds fuel to the flames, and is duly exploited by newspapers *Olé* and *Crónica*. Deriding the visitors, *Olé* even publish a full-page stained-glass window with a Brazilian kneeling as an Argentinian offers him a water jug. Local TV show *CQC* goes further, invading the Brazilian hotel to offer a water jug with 'the purest Argentinian water'. If it is designed to put the past behind them (and it almost certainly isn't), Cafu is having none of it. 'If it were sealed, I wouldn't mind,' he smiles, 'but this one isn't.'

It proves to be a wise decision, especially as rumours spread that three Argentinian players have spat in the water beforehand. Poor Parreira proves less canny, agreeing to sip the water in front of the cameras. Despite the *CQC* host later explaining that two water jugs had been used and that the Brazil coach had not swigged saliva, many wonder otherwise.

Practical jokes aside, the Brazilian squad enjoy a trouble-free atmosphere at their HQ. While the Argentina players are locked away in their hotel across the city, the Brazilians talk to the press for hours, always smiling, always patient.

The Brazilian approach continues to confuse Argentinians – how can they be so happy? An Argentine who played for many years in Brazil once offered his own take on it: 'A person is walking in the middle of the desert. Suddenly, he hears music. If it's a Brazilian, the first thing he'll do is dance to the rhythm of the song. If it's an Argentinian, he'll ask himself where the music is coming, why it's coming and whether it's a good or a bad sign. And he'll keep asking until the song is over, without enjoying it at all. It's how we are, but that personality helps when we've got to grit our teeth in tough games.'

He's right. You won't see an Argentinian smiling like Ronaldinho, nor will you find them saying they have fun when they play. But while the approach to the game may differ, defeat tastes exactly the same.

Diego Maradona knows the importance of winning the *clasico*. Having starred against Brazil at Italia 90 (the second most

FIVE CLASSIC CLASICOS

1990 World Cup
Argentina 1 Brazil 0

The most exciting and dramatic match ever played between the two saw Brazil outclass Argentina throughout, squandering countless chances and striking both posts. Inevitably, one spark of Maradona invention won it, the half-fit genius setting off on a run which took him past three Brazilians before setting up Claudio Caniggia to round Taffarel and score the only goal. Brazil were sent home as Argentina somehow stumbled into the final.

fondly-remembered game in Argentina, after England 1986), he can't resist visiting the Argentina team in the build up to the game.

'First he spoke to us as a group, reminding us what it means to wear the Argentinian shirt against Brazil and recalled some stories of derby games,' says captain Juan Pablo Sorin. 'Then he started calling us one by one to talk in private. We were like nervous students waiting for the professor to call for us. When he left, my heart was beating so fast. I wanted to play the Brazilians that very minute. It was 4 a.m. and I couldn't sleep for the Diego effect. I knocked on Kily Gonzalez's room and he was feeling the same. We soon realised we were all awake.'

Finally, the big day arrives. Just as for a Boca vs River derby, 1,350 police are deployed, their main objective being to protect the 4,500 Brazilians among the 63,000 crowd. As kick-off approaches, the Brazil fans keep warm by dancing. Each of them seems to sport a Brazil shirt – No.7, No.9, No.10, No.11 – not a single soul favours a defensive number. Scary...

It's an explosive start: Javier Saviola nutmegs Roque Junior in the first minute – a statement of intent from the hosts that sets the tone for the first forty-five minutes. Argentina's high tempo and precise passing begins to pay off, the Brazilians outplayed as never before. By half-time, the hosts are three *golazos* to the good. Not just goals, great goals. The Brazilians look puzzled and nervous, their tempers fraying. Ronaldinho squares up with Sorin, Kaka with Kily Gonzalez and Roque Junior with Fabricio Coloccini. 'The score today could be greater than the 6–1 of 1940', predicts one commentator at half-time. But the rout never materialises, Brazil scoring the only goal of the second half without ever suggesting they might repeat their Copa America miracle.

As the game plays out, ecstatic Argentina fans take to winding up their rivals, first with cries of 'Ole', then by breaking into song: 'Keep the dance, to the beat of the drum, tonight we're fucking the poofs of Brazil' and 'Look, look, look, take a photo, they go back to Brazil with their arses fucked.'

Clearly, if tango sensually suggests more than it shows, football is as sexual as a porn film in Argentina. No wonder that in the build up to a previous derby, Argentinian condom company Tulipán came up with a witty ad of a horizontal penis-shaped 'A' aiming at a vertical bottom-shaped 'B'.

In Argentina, football jargon is packed with explicit terms and sexual references. Rarely will a fan say their team 'beat' their opponents when they have the chance of using dozens of sexual slang terms. After Argentina's imposing performance, Hernan Crespo, who is getting married the next day, is asked by one journalist if he enjoyed his 'stag night party with a handful of Brazilians', while Sorin claims that 'beating Brazil was like a very nice screw'.

As in the most tempestuous of relationships, the more the two hate one another, the far greater their passion...

The Brazilian view

Middle fingers wave furiously in the direction of the yellow shirts occupying one corner of the Monumental stadium, rage glows in the eyes of the home

---

FIVE CLASSIC CLASICOS

2004 Copa America final
Brazil 2 Argentina 2 (Brazil win 4–2 on penalties)

After eleven years without a title, Argentina were clear favourites, mainly because Brazil had sent their second string. When substitute César Delgado made it 2–1 to the gauchos with four minutes to go, the game seemed to be following the script. But there was one final twist, as Adriano grabbed a 93rd-minute equaliser. After a fracas in midfield, Brazil emerged victorious on penalties. The defeated Argentinians hid their medals beneath their jerseys in understandable dismay.

fans, expletives fill the night sky. Argentina have beaten Brazil 3–1 in Buenos Aires and pandemonium is breaking out. For Argentina fans, this is the moment they've been craving, a wild, victorious celebration after too many years in the shadow of their closest and fiercest rivals.

Though their team has been thoroughly vanquished on the night, Brazil's fans understand the outpouring of emotion and bitterness directed at them. After all, before tonight's game, images of Brazil's reserve team beating a full-strength Argentina in the final of the 2004 Copa America were still fresh in everybody's minds. So too was Brazil's own 3–1 victory in their home World Cup qualifier in June last year, not to mention the *Seleção*'s triumphant World Cup campaign of 2002 as Argentina's favourites fell at the first hurdle.

Victory in Buenos Aires seems to have washed away all the recent failures, however. Argentina's newspapers gush about their team's global supremacy, the sleeping flame burns again on the road to Germany 2006. Forget Ronaldo, Henry or Shevchenko, Chelsea flop Hernan Crespo, two-goal hero against Brazil, is the most lethal striker on the planet. Ronaldinho's World Player of the Year award should be handed over to Juan Roman Riquelme immediately. Oh, and Maradona was way better than Pele!

But as Buenos Aires and beyond erupts in celebration, Brazil merely shrugs. 'Argentina celebrated as if they had won a title,' sneers Brazilian newspaper *Diario de S. Paulo* patronisingly. Victory may have booked Argentina's place in Germany next year and left Brazil's own qualification unresolved, but the champions' presence at the 2006 World Cup is not in doubt: one more game – at home to Chile – should be enough. Which leaves Brazil nursing nothing more than dented pride, and with both teams taking part in the Confederations Cup in just a few days' time, there may even be an opportunity to deal with that one...

It's worth remembering that the Confederations Cup is a tournament designed for the continental champions, the world champions and the World Cup hosts. Argentina's last international trophy was won twelve years ago, the 1993 Copa America, but because Brazil lifted both the 2002 World Cup and the 2004 Copa America, Argentina, South America's runners-up, have been invited to make up the numbers.

Not that entering via the back door stops Argentina's players from travelling to Germany with a new swagger. The *Albiceleste* fans, too, are rubbing their hands at the prospect of another easy victory, another chance to prove the balance of power has finally shifted.

So, with a sense of inevitability, Brazil and Argentina progress to the final on 29 June. Exactly twenty-one days have passed since Uruguayan referee Gustavo Mendez blew the final whistle in the Buenos Aires qualifier, three weeks in which the Argentinians have been able to brag about their superior football, their superior players, their superior coach. We Brazilians sincerely hope that they made the most of it, because as the final kicks off, we know football's rightful order will soon be restored.

Statistics say that in games between the two countries, Brazil and Argentina boast thirty-three wins each, with twenty-two draws. Well matched, it seems, until you

FIVE CLASSIC CLASICOS

1957 South American tournament
Argentina 3 Brazil 0

The forerunner to the Copa America saw one of Argentina's greatest ever teams, Los Carasucias, thrash the same Brazil that would win the World Cup a year later. Inspired by Humberto Maschio, Enrique Omar Sivori and Antonio Angelillo, Argentina's romp in the penultimate game of the tournament secured both the title and the tag of favourites for the 1958 World Cup. A year on, in what Argentinians would refer to as 'the disaster of Sweden', Brazil emerged victorious.

consider that since Argentina's last silverware, Brazil has amassed two World Cups and three Copa Americas, not to mention picking up six FIFA World Player awards through Romario, Ronaldo, Rivaldo and Ronaldinho. Argentina's A team? Nada.

Three times in a decade, Brazil have eliminated their southern neighbours from the Copa America, most famously – and most infuriatingly for the Argentinians – in 1995 when, leading 2–1, Argentina conceded a late equaliser after Brazilian striker Tulio touched the ball with his hand before scoring. So a Brazilian Hand of God took the game to the penalties, where the *Canarinho* won 4–2. Argentinian complaints about the foul play (yes, the irony) prompted a melee on the pitch.

'I don't know what goes on in the heads of the Argentinians,' sighed Brazil right-back Jorginho afterwards. 'They think they're more manly than all others. But only *they* think that. They don't understand that it's not a war, it's a game of football.'

He may be right, but Brazil–Argentina has frequently come close to full-scale war, none more so than in the so-called Battle of Rosario in the 1978 World Cup. In one of the most brutal encounters between the two teams, Argentina's Ricky Villa and Brazilian Batista seemed hellbent on kicking anything that moved. The game ended 0–0, ensuring that Argentina would have to better Brazil's final group result to progress. With the *Seleção* beating Poland 3–1, Argentina went into their game with Peru knowing that only a four-goal victory would see them through. They scored six, with the finger of suspicion pointing at Peru's Argentinian-born goalkeeper Quiroga.

Though tensions have cooled since 1978, hostility is never far from the surface when Argentina play Brazil. 'Don't doubt that we are going to win,' declares Argentina forward Luciano Galetti ahead of the final. 'We are better than them.'

Frankfurt in June has never been so hot. On the eve of the match, the two squads meet briefly at one of the exits of the Waldstadion, as Argentina leave their final practice session just as Brazil arrive for theirs. With the 3–1 win fresh in their minds, the Argentinians provoke their rivals. 'They tried to make fun of us,' spits Brazil striker Adriano. 'You can't do that, you can't disrespect our shirt and go unpunished.' As tensions fray, *Diario de S. Paulo* adds to the hype: 'Let's see who'll have the last laugh.'

Despite fielding a team blessed with exceptional attackers – Ronaldinho, Kaka, Robinho, and Adriano – Brazil are ready for a physical battle. 'If a defender tries to hit us, we'll fight back,' vows pint-sized Robinho. 'They're dirty, we've seen it in past games,' echoes left-back Zé Roberto, 'but we'll stand tall against them.'

In the Argentina changing room, coach Jose Pekerman engages in a little psychological warfare, refusing to reveal his line-up until minutes before kick-off. 'Not even the players will know,' he declares. Nevertheless, Argentina will be ready. 'We have to be,' insists forward Luciano Figueroa. 'We must give it everything.'

Fifteen minutes in, however, Brazil are 2–0 up courtesy of sublime strikes from player of the tournament Adriano, and Kaka. Two more in the second half, from Adriano and Ronaldinho, settle the score, rendering Pablo Aimar's header a mere consolation, and inviting the *Seleção* to start their Samba Show. The Brazilians dance joyously

FIVE CLASSIC CLASICOS

1964 Nations Cup
Brazil 0 Argentina 3

Prior to winning the World Cup in 1986, this victory secured Argentina's most important title ever: not only had they beaten the world's best (Portugal, England and Brazil) without conceding a single goal, they had also taken the trophy on enemy soil. In the final at Sao Paulo's packed Pacaembu, Roberto Telch scored twice, Amadeo Carrizo saved Gerson's penalty and a nervous Pele broke Messiano's nose with his elbow, though the ref saw nothing.

FIVE CLASSIC CLASICOS

1982 World Cup
Argentina 1 Brazil 3

In an attacking masterclass, the Brazil of Zico, Socrates and Falcao swept the world champions aside, scoring three and missing a host of other chances. Argentina's only goal came in the final minute, by which point a bearded Maradona had seen red for kicking out at his tormentor Batista. Brazil advanced to the quarter-finals, where eventual champions Italy knocked them out in the match of the tournament.

---

around their powerless rivals until the final whistle, at which point the real carnival begins. *Pandeiros*, *tambores* and *tamborins* are brought onto the pitch and the players celebrate in style, with Ronaldinho the master of percussion.

'Party!' screams sports paper *Lance* the following day. 'Beating Argentina was the cherry on the *Seleção*'s cake', gushes *Folha de S. Paulo*. 'So sweet!' cries *Diario de S. Paulo*, adding: 'This result crowns the incontestable Brazilian dominance of the football world.' For Brazil fan Denis Moreira, who watched the game in a sports bar in Sao Paulo, the meaning is more simple: 'Suck it, Argentina!' he chuckles.

Back in Buenos Aires, the party has stopped. In the build-up, sports paper *Olé* predicted another easy win, including one cover of Pele as a voodoo doll. But the day after their 4–1 surrender, the tabloid runs a blank cover with a post-it note which reads: 'Error. For technical reasons, we can't print this cover. Sorry, see you tomorrow.'

It's an understandable response from an Argentinian. Theirs is a nation of dreamers. They dream of being the greatest team on the planet with the greatest players and the greatest coach, but they're deluded.

There's a constellation embroidered above Brazil's crest – five World Cups, won thanks to a dynasty of players including Pele,

Garrincha, Didi, Amarildo, Rivellino, Carlos Alberto, Romario, Rivaldo, and Ronaldo. Argentina has only two – one won in questionable circumstances in 1978, the other thanks, in part, to the Hand of Maradona in 1986. Their chances of adding a third in Germany next year are remote, especially if Brazil are in attendance.

The Rivalry That Time Forgot

Southend v Colchester, September 2005

Fifteen years have passed since the last league derby in Essex. White stilettos are in the loft, XR3s have seen their last fluffy white dice. But the football hatred hasn't ever gone away ...

As his car grinds to a halt an inch from the bumper in front, Steev Tovey is greeted by the sight of a snotty youth flicking the V's his way. He's been sitting bumper to bumper for more miles than he'd care to remember, heading for a place he'd rather forget. On the horizon sits Southend-on-Sea, home of 'the enemy'. Given the choice, Tovey would steer clear of the place, but today his team Colchester United are in town for the first Essex league derby in fifteen years.

The fact he's moving at snail's pace doesn't help raise his spirits, and neither does the fact that to avoid trouble between the two sets of fans, the Football League suits have brought forward the kick-off to a midday slot. To make matters worse, he and the other U's fans caught up on the A127 know that unless they take something from a game they very rarely win, the return trip will be ten times more painful. 'I didn't want them to get promoted, I've always dreaded the thought of getting them in cup games, and I'm not looking forward to this,' he sighs. 'Just as long as we don't lose ... I don't want that feeling in the pit of my stomach again.'

Tovey fronts a heavy metal band. Right now, two hours before kick-off, he feels sorely tempted to head bang his skull into the steering wheel.

Welcome to Essex and the derby that time forgot. Never a fixture to catch the eye outside of the county at the best of times, the lack of regular meetings between the Shrimpers and the U's is reflected in the attitude of many younger fans. To them, this is just another game. For more seasoned campaigners, though, it's far more than a half-forgotten football match. This is a battle for the soul of the county.

Essex has had a bad press since the last league game. One of England's largest, oldest, and most diverse counties, its million-plus inhabitants found themselves the butt of the nation's jokes in the 1990s. The boys and girls of Essex were portrayed as pasty teens doing unpleasant things in the back of pimped Ford Escorts, fluffy dice banging on the windshield.

They were chavs, a full decade before they existed, with Southend-on-Sea as the epicentre. 'There is some truth in that stereotype,' sighs Jamie Forsyth, editor of Southend fanzine *All At Sea*. 'I grew up with the XR3 and white stiletto stuff. You just get used to it.'

Colchester, on the other hand, is in the rural middle-class north of the county, so close to the border with Suffolk that many outsiders don't realise it's in Essex at all. If they were a smidgeon further north, and a bit higher in the league, their derby

HEROES AND VILLAINS

Southend United
Roy Hollis

Colchester United only entered the league in 1950, and Hollis seemed intent on sending them straight back again. The Shrimpers' record scorer was the scourge of the U's defence as Southend dominated that first decade of derbies, chalking up a 6–3, two 4–0s, and a 4–1 FA Cup mauling. Colchester's self-esteem never quite recovered.

would be against Ipswich. Not that they're ashamed of their Essex roots, they just blame their southern rivals for sullying the good name of the county. 'We're actually very vocal about being from Essex,' says Steev Tovey, 'and we'd rather see ourselves as being representative of the county. It's quite quiet and relaxed in Colchester. When you go to Southend it's the opposite. It all just seems a lot … dirtier.'

'But Colchester is a footballing backwater,' retorts Forsyth. 'They have a different accent to us, being forty miles apart, and they're more East Anglian than Essex, really. They're carrot-crunching inbreds, farmers married to their sisters and all that.'

In fact, Colchester is the oldest recorded town in the country, built around a centuries-old army garrison, but increasingly a commuter suburb these days. The football team has been happily treading water in League One for seven years now and are generally seen as a decent footballing side, but something of a soft touch. 'We don't have the history of mixing it,' says Tovey. 'If it becomes a battle, we lose,' he sighs, which is somewhat ironic given the town's status.

Southend's history is more chequered. The decadent old seaside town became a popular migration spot for those escaping downtrodden East London in the 1940s and '50s. As the East End has regenerated recently, however, Southend seems increasingly out on a limb. House prices are low for a seaside town so near the capital, and there aren't too many takers. 'Southend is mostly made up of old Londoners,'

HEROES AND VILLAINS

Southend United
Glenn Pennyfather

Loathed at Layer Road, Penny-father was Southend's 1980s hit-man, a tough-tackling mid-fielder in the Graeme Souness mould – in more ways than one. 'He was a fan of the elbows and high-tackling midfield approach,' says U's fan Steev Tovey, 'plus he had this awful poodle perm thing going on …'

agrees 62-year old Shrimper, Geoff Mills. 'But I don't think anyone wants to move out here any more, apart from maybe asylum seekers ...'

While Southend's population was swelling postwar, so its football club's ambition became bigger and brasher. By the 1990s, they considered themselves far superior to their neighbours. 'They were the more "professional" team in certain respects,' says Richard Wilkins, who played for Colchester in the last league meeting between the clubs at Easter 1990. 'They were a very physical team, always well-organised, quite intimidating

> ## HEROES AND VILLAINS
>
> ### Southend United
> ### Peter Daley
>
> ---
>
> A reserve centre-half whose only notable contribution came with the crucial second goal in the 1990 game at Layer Road. 'He was supposed to be the new Ron Yeats, but was more like Eddie Yeats, the Coronation Street bin-man,' recalls old colleague David Crown. 'He got so excited when he scored that day that he dived into the crowd and head-butted one of our supporters.'

at times. I'll always remember one of their boys taking a piece out of me in that game.'

That now-legendary match was perhaps the quintessential Essex derby, as promotion-chasing Southend invaded Colchester's Layer Road, and overpowered their hosts in a 2–0 win. It proved a pivotal moment in both sides' recent histories. 'It was a big game for both teams, very tense,' recalls David Crown, Southend's star striker at the time. 'To be fair, they were struggling then, while we had a very strong, well-organised side, under David Webb. Even so, I didn't think the club would go on to achieve what it did.'

Having gained promotion from the old Fourth Division that season, a contract dispute saw Crown leave Roots Hall in the summer of 1990. He missed out on the club's most successful spell, with David

Webb guiding them up into the old Second Division and to within touching distance of the Premiership's inaugural year in 1992, before quitting following a row.

Enter Barry Fry, who unleashed Stan Collymore on the world before leaving for Birmingham City. His replacement, Ronnie Whelan, was soon replaced by Alvin Martin, but both discovered that for an over-achieving outfit, the only way was down. 'Whelan wasted all the Collymore money,' says Jamie Forsyth ruefully, 'and Alvin Martin couldn't organise a piss-up in a brewery.'

After flirting with the Conference, Southend then managed to alienate their remaining fans by appointing an ex-Colchester manager, Steve Wignall. 'It was a strange decision,' admits David Crown. 'He was just too synonymous with Colchester.'

When the axe eventually fell on Wignall in November 2003, a pre-dogging Collymore was interviewed for the vacancy, but the club opted instead for ex-Shrimper Steve Tilson, who steadied the ship before winning promotion to League One last season. 'The ambition is to get into the Championship,' says Forsyth. 'We're now expecting to beat teams like Colchester. We're a bigger club than them by some distance.'

For the U's, meanwhile, that 1990 defeat was another nail in the coffin as they slipped out of the League and into the Conference at the season's end. It proved to be a blessing in disguise though, and in 1992 they gained promotion on goal difference and won the FA Trophy. Promoted again in 1998, beating Torquay in the Division Three play-offs, the U's swapped places with their plummeting rivals. 'When you think they're both classed as lower division clubs, it's astonishing that they haven't played for fifteen years,' says David Crown. 'There's this whole generation that have missed it.'

As they languished in the Conference, Colchester developed a new rivalry, this time with Wycombe Wanderers. 'We hate Wycombe because of what Martin O'Neill, then their manager, said about us during our FA Trophy win,' says Steev Tovey, the resentment still simmering nicely. Spurned, Southend turned their targets on League Two rivals Leyton Orient, their nearest London neighbours. 'Sadly, we had too much in common with them,' says Forsyth. 'Both sets of fans would be singing "You all support West Ham" at each other.'

There is in that a grain of truth, with Southend enjoying a love-hate relationship with the Hammers. For a time, West Ham fans were welcome guests at Roots Hall, boosting attendances when their own team were playing away. The relationship soured when the Hammers began to muscle in on Southend's territory. 'They opened a shop in the town,' says Forsyth. 'But it got vandalised and closed down pretty quickly.'

With fifteen years apart and their bile directed elsewhere, it seemed the Essex rivalry had been all but forgotten. Hatred dies hard, round here, however. If the fans had merely taken their eyes off one another, the players were utterly clueless until their clubs arranged a couple of pre-season friendlies. Ill-advised friendlies, as it turned out. 'That was when I realised the Southend thing existed, when there was trouble in a friendly,' says current Colchester captain Karl Duguid.

Last year, the two sides met in the LDV Vans Trophy. 'The LDV games really showed what

HEROES AND VILLAINS

Colchester United
Roy McDonough

A rumbustious striker-cum-defender who helped relegate Colchester to the Conference in his previous life at Southend, McDonough returned to Layer Road and became a managerial legend. Typically brave, the mullet-and-moustachioed manager succeeded because (a) he won more than his fair share of matches, taking the U's to their 1992 non-league and cup double, and (b) he'd always lived in Colchester anyway. The club was in his blood.

HEROES AND VILLAINS

Colchester United
Steve Wignall

The George Graham of the Essex derby, his switch proved far less successful. Wignall played almost 300 games for the U's before he too became a hero in the hotseat, leading them to their current League One status. His subsequent spell at Roots Hall proved disastrous, however. Never a Southend man, he lasted six months. 'I did not see the passion in his eyes,' explained the chairman.

these games were all about. There was so much tension around them.'

Under new boss Phil Parkinson, Colchester were enjoying a great spell, heading for their highest ever league finish in League One, and looking forward to a well-deserved day out in Cardiff. Barring their way, in the LDV area final, were their struggling League Two neighbours. The U's had one eye on the final. 'We thought we'd win it comfortably,' says Duguid. 'But there was so much expectation and it got very nervy.'

Southend appear immune to nerves in this fixture though, and returned home from Layer Road with a 3–1 win. Stung into action, Colchester levelled the tie at Roots Hall before being undone in one of the Essex derby's most contentious incidents. With a Colchester defender lying injured in the box, and playing him onside, rather than kicking the ball into touch, Southend striker Drewe Broughton helped himself to what turned out to be the winner. 'That incident made us hate Southend again,' says Tovey. 'It went nuts after that.'

Thankfully, the local constabulary were already out in force that night. They'd been caught cold at the first friendly in 2001, as groups of rival 'fans' left Roots Hall early for a pre-arranged battle. According to Tovey, the Colchester firm had been formed just for the occasion. 'They weren't people you ever saw at home games,' he says. 'It all kicked off near the train station, so the police just shepherded them inside, locked the gates, and let them go at it – they filmed it and then nicked them all afterwards. 'It's nothing new,' he adds. 'When I was a kid, my family wouldn't let me go to the Southend games, because there were always brawls on the terraces.'

'The violence was directed more against the police than the Colchester fans,' recalls Southend supporter Dave Collins. 'The first time I saw trouble at Roots Hall was in 1971. It was quite a nasty, niggly sort of game, and it sparked reactions in the crowd. The police dogs were brought in to calm things down.'

The return fixture was equally eventful, with the police intervening to quell an 'incident' among the away supporters. 'It was just a rendition of "Knees Up Mother Brown", a popular East-End ditty,' recalls Collins. 'Only we'd jump up and down while we were singing it, four or five hundred of us in this wooden stand, and the stand was moving and dust coming out of the rafters. So the coppers intervened – "The next one who starts that is out." It was all good-humoured, with a certain amount of aggressive passion behind it, but then a load of our fans tried to smash the train up on the way home, pulled the seats up, tried to smash the windows. I stopped going soon after that … until now, that is.'

Two hours before kick-off, and there's a hefty police presence around Roots Hall. A booze ban is in place until 4 p.m., and the locals are restless, aggrieved, and thirsty. 'I've had kids in all day moaning why aren't we selling booze,' complains the owner of a corner shop near the ground, her stash covered by a thin green canvas. With little sign of trouble so far, the policy appears to be paying off – though it obviously helps that many of the Colchester fans are stuck in traffic on the A127.

Inside the only open pub in town, the Southend Supporters' Club bar, the locals are showing few signs of pre-match nerves. 'I think the whole rivalry is more from their side than ours, because we've beaten them every time I can remember us playing them,' one fan says. Clearly in no great rush to soak up the pre-match atmosphere, he orders himself another pint despite there being only ten minutes until kick-off. 'Canvey's the real rivalry,' pipes up his young companion, 'because it's a crap place that nobody likes.'

By the time the 1,000-strong visitors finally arrive at the ground, they appear, for the most part, sober and subdued. They've clearly arrived expecting the worst.

The hosts' cause hasn't been helped by the suspension of prolific striker Freddy Eastwood, who despite having never played against Colchester is already a hate figure for the visiting fans. To them, Basildon-born Eastwood embodies the 'other' side of Essex, and they later join in a charming song that suggests he was born and raised on a caravan site.

Colchester themselves are missing captain Duguid – himself a hate figure for Southend fans – and he's clearly itching to put right the injustice of that LDV defeat. 'It's more a fan's thing really, but I was desperate to play today. There was bad feeling after those games and it'll be a massive boost if we beat them.'

As the game finally kicks off, you sense a draw would probably do for Duguid and his supporters. Southend's Shaun Goater has his own agenda, though, and after a strangely sedate first three minutes, he races onto a long ball and smashes his new side ahead in front of the Colchester end. The visiting fans look like they'd rather be back in traffic.

As the 'One team in Essex' taunt rings out, Colchester's fans spark into life, quickly followed by their players. In the 18th minute, right-back Sam Stockley deservedly rifles home past keeper Daryl Flahavan, then runs the length of the pitch to celebrate with visiting fans. For the next ten minutes Colchester are by far the better side and revenge appears to be on the cards until, in the 30th minute, they self-destruct.

In a moment of madness, Colchester winger Mark Yeates sends an aimless punt across the centre circle, inviting Mitchell Cole to race away and score. Having wrestled the advantage back, Southend finish it late on, when Goater runs onto another long ball and lobs home. With that, the Southend fans celebrate as if they've 'relegated the rurals' again.

With the game all played out and thankfully fracas-free, a Southend fan, old enough to remember those 1970s clashes sullies the result by spitting at Stockley as he retrieves the ball. Having ordered the offender out before blowing for time, referee Rob Styles describes the incident as a 'storm in a teacup'. Steev Tovey sees it differently, however. 'They didn't actually throw him out like they should have done,' he says, 'they just stood chatting to him for five minutes, then at the final whis-

HEROES AND VILLAINS

Colchester United
Greg Halford

A prominent derby figure – if for all the wrong reasons. The versatile England Under-20 international was said to be attracting Premiership interest, but flopped in the edgy denouement of the LDV area final. He took things a stage further in the long-awaited league game, rashly scything down various Shrimpers, which endeared him to the Colchester fans. 'It was more laughter than hatred though,' says Southend fan, Jamie Forsyth. 'He would have looked more at home in a circus.'

tle they walked him right in front of the Colchester fans – it was almost like they paraded him – and he pulled a moony on us. We couldn't believe it.'

Half an hour later, and the Colchester fans are back in their cars and coaches, 'Easy' chants still ringing in their ears as they contemplate a miserable drive home. Back at the ground, meanwhile, local hacks converge on Southend's Steve Tilson, who's playing down the win. 'It's no different from any other game,' he claims, but Colchester's Phil Parkinson, standing lonely to his right, would surely disagree. As his young daughter hugs him for several minutes, it's hard to know who needs it most.

The return fixture and a chance for revenge is on 4 March next year. You get the impression, however, that if Colchester didn't see their neighbours again for another fifteen years, it wouldn't be a day too soon.

Battle of the Bosphorus
Fenerbahce v Galatasaray, December 2005

The Istanbul derby: so violent the authorities tried to ban it, so bitter the whole world is watching, so important the fans of two teams will do anything. Welcome to hell indeed...

'You are all sons of whores,' come the chants of Galatasaray fans, as they tear up their seats and hurl chunks of red and yellow plastic onto the pitch of their team's crumbling Ali Sami Yen stadium.

By Istanbul derby standards, the 351st clash between 'Cim Bom' and their arch-rivals Fenerbahce has been a fairly quiet affair. The target of the home fans' vitriol is not, though, their enemies from across the Bosphorus, who have just sneaked a 1–0 win, but their own club's management and directors. It is probably just as well that Galatasaray's prim and polite chairman Ozhan Canaydin has boycotted the match in protest at Fenerbahce fans being allowed to attend.

In all some 1,000 away supporters, crammed into one small corner of the stadium, have managed to make it into the ground, and their mood is, by contrast, ecstatic.

Victory has set a Fenerbahce club record of twelve league wins on the trot and carried the champions six points clear at the top and well on track for a historic third straight title. To add considerable insult to

Galatasaray's latest injury, the small blue and yellow wedge of Fener fans, though outnumbered thirty to one, have severely embarrassed the massed red and yellow ranks of the Cim Bom.

'Ali Sami Yen's gone silent, they're all listening to us,' sang the jubilant away contingent in the second half, and they had a point. During the first half, the drums, whistles and songs of the Galatasaray fans drowned out whatever noise the small cluster of 'Yellow Canaries' dared to make. But by the 80th minute, after yet another failed attempt by faded national icon, Hakan Sukur – these days known even to Galatasaray fans as Donkey Hakan – the home support is utterly subdued.

'We won the football match, but we also won the fans' "game" decisively,' beams Cuneyt Aytac of Fener supporters group Antu after the match. 'We are very happy with this result.'

Indisputably the biggest event in the Turkish football calendar, the showdown between the Yellow Canaries and Cim Bom is a game with a global dimension too. Supporters munching on their doners and meatballs outside the Ali Sami Yen have travelled from across Turkey; some have even ventured from across Europe, with fans from Germany and Holland swelling the numbers. And with a sizeable football-mad Turkish diaspora scattered across the planet, the games also draw a crowd in smoke-filled cafés from Hackney to Moscow.

'Forget Glasgow. Forget Barcelona. This is the biggest derby in the world,' boasts Galatasaray supporter Gökhan ahead of the latest set-to. The 20-year-old has made the 870-mile journey from Gaziantep near the Syrian border – a twenty-six-hour schlep on the train. 'I've been coming since I was 12. I don't smoke or drink, I just save all my money for this,' he adds, munching on pine nuts, the nibble of choice for the Turkish football fan.

Two hours later, it seems an awful long way to come for what has been, by common local consensus, one of the flattest derby encounters in years. His team look a pale shadow of the flagship Turkish side that used to humble European giants on a routine basis and that defeated Arsenal to win the UEFA Cup in 2000.

But even in defeat, Gökhan can draw comfort from slagging the opposition. 'Fenerbahce are the worst team in the world,' he mutters. 'The foulest, the lowest, the most dishonourable. They're nothing and their fans are even less. We don't hate them because they're big and rich, it's more than that. Galatasaray are an ethical team, honourable. But Fenerbahce are all about money and buying success.'

A Cim Bom banner inside the ground reinforces the view that these days Galatasaray find themselves clutching at reasons to be cheerful: 'Success comes and goes,' it tells the players, 'but your nobility is enough for us.'

Istanbul derbies don't fit neatly into any of the classic paradigms for local rivalries. There is no ethnic split between the clubs and no religious divide, though historically, at least, social class played a part in forging the identity of each.

In the 1970s, Kurthan Fisek, a leading Turkish academic (and Fenerbahce fan) summarised the differences between Istanbul's three leading clubs thus: Galatasaray, he said, were the club of the Europeanised aristocracy, Fenerbahce the club of the bourgeoisie, while the city's third club, Besiktas, were supposed to be the team of the working classes.

Fisek's definition holds some water but, according to local sportswriter and radio broadcaster, Bagis Erten, the modern reality is more fluid. There are unsurprisingly, plenty of posh Besiktas fans and no small number of poor Galatasaray supporters.

'Other major derbies may have ethnic or religious differences or class at their roots, but in Turkey, things are different,' says Erten. 'Here, choice of club is like a kind of democratic citizenship. Anyone can become a supporter of any club. Each of the three big clubs has to compete for every new-born child.'

Besiktas, Istanbul's oldest club, having been founded in 1903, represent a third way of sorts. They don't inspire the same intense hatred among either of their neighbours, and any success is tolerated by both. The perception of Besiktas as the team of the working classes is bolstered by the fact that in recent decades the club has drawn much of its core support from the traders, porters and labourers who work in the maze of shopping lanes around the old fish market in the Besiktas district, on the European side of the Bosphorus. They have also tended to attract the sympathies of Istanbul's beleaguered minority groups, the Greeks, the Armenians and the Jews.

Galatasaray's roots, meanwhile, lie at the opposite end of the social spectrum. The club was founded by old boys from Istanbul's equivalent of Eton. The Galatasaray High School in the heart of the European part of Istanbul is a 400-year-old institution built to provide a French-language education for the elites of the Ottoman Empire, and it was there, in 1907, that Ali Sami Yen convinced a group of his friends that they should start a football team, presenting them with a ball repaired with leather cut from his own shoes. 'Our aim,' he wrote, 'was to play in an organised way like the English do, to have a set of colours and a name and to beat non-Turkish teams.' Two years later, in the first ever Istanbul derby, they defeated Fenerbahce 2–0 with one of the goals scored by an English ex-pat by the name of Horace Armitage.

Armitage was the first of fifty-four players to play for both clubs. Changes of allegiance being relatively commonplace, they don't tend to generate too much heat. The recent case of Israel international midfielder, Haim Revivo is a notable exception. A Fener fans' favourite, Revivo walked out on them suddenly in January 2003, claiming ill-treatment and, not short of offers from around Europe, appeared to cock a snook at his old employers by signing a two-year deal across the Straits. He probably thought better of his decision when, during a stint laid-up in hospital, he looked out of his window to see the building besieged by angry Fenerbahce fans brandishing banners bearing the legend 'Traitor'. A few months later he was heading back to Israel.

Today, all three big Istanbul clubs are a fusion of a wide variety of commercial and sporting interests. The leading Turkish clubs are rarely, in fact, just football clubs, but go under the broader sobriquet of sports clubs. Besiktas is nominally a gymnastics club. Galatasaray has its own basketball team, an athletics squad, a rowing team, and even a team of equestrians. And it has even gone back to its educational roots by establishing its very own eponymous university.

With commercial growth, the fanbase of all the clubs has expanded, and now embraces supporters from across Turkey, with all of the country's ethnic minorities well represented. The Kurdish rebel leader Abdullah Ocalan – as far from the image of a French-speaking aristo as you could hope to find – may have spent the 1980s and 1990s waging a violent separatist campaign against the Turkish state, but he still found time to follow the fortunes of his favourite team.

Clues to Galatasaray's Frenchified past are still occasionally evident, though. On the night I visit the Ali Sami Yen, a banner pays homage to the 'Le Lion de Bosphore'. And though the bilingual, privately educated elites that once formed Galatasaray's fanbase are now a small minority, they still dominate the boardroom, something which continues to irk the club's rank and file support.

'Galatasaray comes from a private school but most fans are not,' says Mehmet Aktop of ultrAslan (ultraLion), the club's biggest supporters group. 'And that creates problems. The management has always distanced itself from the fans. They treat us like stepchildren.'

Fenerbahce, on the other hand, have, under current chairman Aziz Yildirim, managed to put decades of internal fighting behind them. More than any other Turkish club they have cracked the merchandising game, selling branded paraphernalia by the bagful at their Fenerium stores. Yildirim has also invested in the ground, making Sukru Saracoglu stadium, on the Asian side of the Bosphorus, by far the best purpose-built football venue in Turkey.

In this sense, Fenerbahce – a club built on the new money of an economically thriving Anatolia – is a microcosm for the rapidly modernising Asian Turkey: ambitious, hardworking, financially astute. The club's identity with the Asian hinterland goes all the way back to Fenerbahce's most famous fan: Mustafa Kemal Ataturk, the hard-drinking general and statesman who is regarded as the founder of the modern Turkey in 1923, and who is supposed to have blessed Fenerbahce with a wish for their 'eternal success'.

Laying claim to the support of such a talismanic national icon is controversial, but most now accept that Ataturk did have a special affection for Fenerbahce, and the story of the great man's visit to the ground by the shores of the Marmara Sea in 1918 is enshrined in the club's official history.

The club and its fans are fiercely proud of their support for the war Ataturk fought against invading Greeks to establish the Republic of Turkey on the wreckage of the Ottoman Empire. Club folklore tells of midnight intrigue when Fenerbahce took advantage of its waterfront location to help smuggle arms and support from then-occupied Istanbul to Ataturk's army in central Turkey.

'This is the reason the older generations love Fenerbahce,' explains Antu's Aytac. 'The club played an important role in Turkey's war of independence,' he says, 'and we are very proud of that.'

Though falling some way short of matching Ataturk's iconic status, the players from both clubs are fully aware that the Istanbul derby is their main opportunity to earn their stripes, a chance to write themselves into the history books. Take the example of Tuncay Sanli, whose goal opened the floodgates in Fenerbahce's now legendary 6–0 win over Galatasaray in November 2002. He says it was the game that set him up for the rest of his career. 'That was my most important match ever. It was my first Galatasaray match and I scored. There have been other important derbies for me but doing well in the first one is very, very special as a Fenerbahce player.'

That pasting added further heat to what was already a particularly spiky encounter. There had been more trouble than usual before the game, the kick-off being delayed by thick clouds of smoke from scores of flares, and visiting fans had to be frogmarched out of Sukru Saracoglu stadium by the police for their own safety.

These days restrictions on away supporters mean that sort of situation is avoided, but Sanli mourns the old days when the grounds were split 50–50 between the two sides. 'Nobody wants trouble, but in the past the atmosphere was better and of course we need our fans, we want to hear them.'

The 6–0 win probably ranks at the top of Fenerbahce's many recent derby victories. Close behind is another 1–0 smash and grab at the Ali Sami Yen, back in 2000. Galatasaray, then boasting Georghe Hagi in his pomp, were reigning supreme at home and in Europe, beating all-comers on their way to their UEFA Cup triumph. Predicting a basket-ball score for the match, the Galatasaray officials had enraged rival fans by requesting an enlarged scoreboard for Fener's visit.

But it didn't go to script. The only goal of the night was scored by the visitors' Ghanaian Samuel Johnson, and the victory inspired a Fenerbahce corruption of a Galatasaray song that Yellow Canaries fans love to this day:

'Galatasaray say they're conquerors of Europe.
They say all their fans are gay.
They say they are a star in people's hearts and moon upon their
   souls.
But we fucked their mothers nicely, Galatasaray.'

Nothing is so guaranteed to enrage a Turk as an insult directed at his mother. But the Galatasaray fans return the insult with interest, with a reference to one of Fenerbahce's frequent European debacles.

'You went to Europe
And disgraced us.
The gay canary,
How Barcelona fucked your mother!'

Given Fenerbahce's Champions League mauling at home to AC Milan several days before they face Galatasaray in the first derby of the 2005–06 season, the jibe can be easily tweaked to suit the circumstances and remains a particularly effective response. Local kingpins they may be right now, but their aspirations to join the European elite look as unattainable as ever – a fact that their own head coach Christoph Daum admitted recently. 'There's a big difference between the Champions League and the Turkish Supercell League,' said the German. 'Let's be realistic about Turkish football's place in the international scheme of things. Before we run around saying how great we are we need to develop young players more effectively and we need to stop throwing things at buses and players.'

All in all, the last couple of years have been a rapid comedown for Turkish football, following the delirium of Galatasaray's UEFA triumph in 2000, and a third-place finish for the national team in the last World Cup. The fact that their clubs have reverted to whipping boys in Europe, has been compounded by the national team's failure to make it to Euro 2004 or Germany 2006.

That stark reality makes the battle for local bragging rights all the more important. Fenerbahce head the overall tally with 130 wins to 113. And these days, Galatasaray have to delve some way back in time for derby victories to cherish. One that stands out is their Turkish Cup victory in 1996, the infamous match in which head coach Graeme Souness earned a place in the derby pantheon with an act of adrenaline-fuelled bravado – he planted a massive Galatasaray flag in the centre of the turf at Fener's Sukru Saracoglu stadium. It ensured him hero status with the Cim Bom faithful; but he almost sparked a riot in the process.

Dean Saunders, who spent a season with Galatasaray in the mid-'90s, and whose goal it was that gave Galatasaray a 1–0 first-leg lead recalls the encounters vividly. 'I'd scored from the spot in the first game; I'd probably have been hung if I'd missed. And then we went to

Fenerbahce for the second leg. It was hostile, very hostile, but great fun to play in.'

With the aggregate scores tied after normal time, Saunders was on target once more in the 115th minute, clinching a 2–1 aggregate win for the visitors. 'The next thing I remember is Graeme rushing past me with the flag,' Saunders says. 'I hear they're still selling T-shirts with that picture on it.'

The win was a triumph for the small group of Galatasaray fans who'd braved the trip over the water. 'All night we'd felt under pressure. We were outnumbered and it felt like we were Millwall fans away at Chelsea,' remembers Aktop. 'Then we won and Souness came up to us and took one of our flags and planted it. It was the most natural and spontaneous thing.'

Such scenes are a far cry from the prevailing mood of the Galatasaray faithful for much of tonight's derby.

Before the start of the current season, representatives of Istanbul's three big clubs met with the police and the city governor to discuss how to handle their matches. Their decision to ban away supporters from all of the city's derbies caused fury among fans, who blame hysterical media and club managers for exaggerating the level of violence at Turkish grounds.

In the aftermath of the violent scenes at the Turkey–Switzerland World Cup play-off last November, the authorities have been more determined than ever to use the Istanbul derbies to show the world, and FIFA in particular, that Turkey is capable of organising high-profile matches without trouble on or off the pitch.

Yet, predictably enough, the ban proved completely impossible to enforce. Earlier this season, ahead of their derby away to Besiktas, some 200 Fenerbahce fans disguised themselves in the black and white of the opposition to enter the stadium, before stripping off en masse to reveal their true colours. Surrounded by thousands of Besiktas fans, it was a risky move, but one that saw them score a major tribal triumph.

'The moment we started chanting, the two sides just separated naturally. The Besiktas fans gave us space. But then the police came in and kicked us out,' laughs Antu's Aytac. 'I don't understand why the police were so surprised. We'd already written and faxed them saying that we didn't accept this ban and that we were going to the match anyway. We even gave them our names and phone numbers. We're not going to stop supporting our team just because some jackass says we can't go.'

In the end, the 'jackasses' backed down in time for tonight's game, yet the arrival of the Fenerbahce team at Ali Sami Yen offers as clear an illustration as you could wish to see of the gulf between fan culture and the sterile FIFA fairplay paradigm that the Turkish authorities are keen to embrace. Outside the ground, a phalanx of police, in full body armour, muscle onlookers out of the way to form a corridor that will allow the Fener bus into the ground. Galatasaray fans who can get close enough, hurl plastic cups and obscenities at the curtained windows.

Once inside, however, the Fenerbahce team are greeted with a bouquet of flowers. As they step off their coach, Galatasaray club officials hand out chocolates and splash lemon-scented cologne on the visiting players. It is the kind of slick piece of PR posturing that infuriates and alienates many Galatasaray fans. 'Cologne and chocolate?' says an exasperated Aktop, shaking his head in disbelief. 'Sure, you shake their hands. You welcome them. That's normal. But cologne and chocolate? It's just embarrassing.'

Under the watchful gaze of the police, the Fenerbahce fans assemble near the ground, before squeezing through a single narrow stairway into their allotted space in the south stand where their presence is, in a manner of speaking, welcomed by the home fans. The fact is that no true football supporter wants the Istanbul derby to be stripped of its fan rivalry.

'Look at Italy. Look at Greece. Can you tell me a derby anywhere where things haven't been thrown? The idea that you can ban away fans is an idiocy. How can that be possible?' asks ultrAslan's Aktop. 'This is our reason for existence – it shouldn't threaten people.'

'They even want to stop us swearing,' fumes Antu's Aytac. 'It's unbelievable. That's part of the culture!'

Dean Saunders agrees that the passion of the Turkish support is something to be celebrated not sanitised. 'Football means an awful lot out there. Players like Tugay (Kerimoglu) and Emre Belozoglu are more famous than the president. And sometimes the fans may go a bit berserk but that's better than having no passion at all like some countries,' he says.

Tonight, fans and players alike seem to lack passion. The game's only goal arrives seconds before the half-time whistle. Brazilian Marcio Nobre leaps to get his boot onto a high ball and send it past Galatasaray's onrushing keeper Faryd Mondragon.

It's the one moment of drama in an otherwise uninspiring game, dominated by Fenerbahce's midfield enforcers Marco Aurelio and Stephen Appiah. Their pixie-like winger Tuncay Sanli shows the odd flash of inspiration down the flank, but for the most part there is little to coax a lonely Nicolas Anelka out of his default sulk mode.

The Galatasaray fans' protest after the final whistle notwithstanding, the match passes without any of the predicted trouble. 'Our fans were a little subdued,' admits Aktop. 'Partly because after the Switzerland game there was a wave of stress and, in my opinion, excessive self-criticism.'

But then contrary to the image sold by the local and international media, most Turkish supporters will tell you that football violence has been on the decline over the last decade. 'There used to be all kinds of fights with stones and bats,' remembers Antu's Aytac. 'Then in the early-1990s these fist and stone fights became more dangerous and knives started being used and people started being killed rather than beaten up. I remember a guy killed in Macka, and another in Taksim.'

By the mid-1990s the three groups had agreed a 'terrace peace' that laid down the basic 'rules' for ambushes and outlawing of knives.

'Though there were isolated incidences of beatings here and there, after that there were no more clashes of large fan groups,' continues Aytac. 'Things are much more "in order" compared to 1980s and 1990s.'

Galatasaray fan Mehmet Aktop agrees that fans now police themselves more effectively than the authorities and he blames the media, who continue to represent Turkish fans as unemployed louts, and the 'industrialisation' of Turkish football for blowing out of proportion fears of violence.

If the establishment's recent efforts to sanitise derby matches have done one thing, it is to strike a rare note of harmony among both sets of rival supporters. 'One reason tonight's derby was not one of the best,' muses Aktop, 'was because they are doing their best to kill off all the pleasure and the tension that surrounds the game'.

His voice tails off as he shakes his head in dismay, but the glint in Aktop's eye suggests neither Galatasaray nor Fenerbahce will back down without a fight. The next time the two sides meet, at the Sukru Saracoglu stadium on 23 April, expect normal service to be resumed.

Unholy War

Hapoel Tel Aviv v Maccabi Tel Aviv, December 2005

When Israel's biggest rivals clash you don't expect songs about Hitler, the Holocaust and suicide bombers. But at the Tel Aviv derby, decency goes flying out of the window …

I can feel the eyes of the soldier holding an M16 burning into the back of my head. It's his job to guard the heavily fortified American embassy in Tel Aviv, Israel. It's mine to write about the derby match between the city's biggest two football clubs, Maccabi and Hapoel. A game where the invective is so pernicious that songs are sung referencing the Holocaust, Nazis, and Hezbollah.

Just fifty metres away families are playing on a Mediterranean beachfront closer in appearance to Miami's South Beach, all conspicuous high-rise chain hotels and beautiful people. Even in early spring, people are swimming. This is not the Israel Natasha Kaplinsky talks about on the evening news.

Resting my rucksack at my feet, I hail a taxi and ask for the training ground of Hapoel Tel Aviv, where the club's Ultras will be watching their team's final training session before taking on Maccabi. 'I'm not taking you there,' says the agitated driver. 'Hapoel are shit. Get out if you want. I'm a fan of Beitar Jerusalem. You are my last job and then

I'm driving to see the best team in Israel. Why don't you come with me instead and see some real football?'

Jerusalem is an hour away. I think about it. 'How much?'

'200 shekels (£22) – and I'll get you back to Tel Aviv by 10 p.m.'

'Alright then, why not.'

'Now call those Ultras and tell them to fuck off! Isn't that how you say it in English? But first, pay me the money.'

We settle on 100 shekels, and ten minutes later we're heading out of Tel Aviv, Israel's biggest city, a modern sprawl with shimmering skyscrapers and busy intersections, following motorway signs for Jerusalem. The driver is hollering along to his favourite CD of Beitar songs. 'This one is about a great Beitar man who was killed by a suicide bomber,' he says, briefly lowering the volume. At the same time he pulls out a small monitor and inserts a DVD showing great Beitar moments.

We speed past United Nations trucks en-route to the West Bank, passing busloads of yellow-and-black-clad Beitar fans. The driver beeps as he passes each. 'Beitar,' he says, 'the best.' In the distance we can see the red lights of the border posts, the controversial West Bank barrier and, beyond, dimly lit Palestinian settlements.

I'm confused. One because he keeps saying the phrase, 'Chick, chat' and I've no idea what he means. But more pertinently, the driver looks like an Arab, and Beitar, whose fans have a reputation for being staunchly right wing, are the only Israeli team never to have fielded an Arab. Either I've got it wrong or I'm speeding to Jerusalem with a driver with a death wish.

'I'm Israeli,' he assures me, 'but some of my family came from India. Now tell me about Steven Gerrard. Will he come and play for Beitar? Our owner is Gaydamak and he can afford any player. He's got as much money as his friend Abramovich.'

Arkady Gaydamak is the Russian billionaire who holds four citizenships and has revolutionised Israeli football since taking over Beitar at the start of this season. He raised the club's budget from £3 million a season to a projected £18 million next season. He is also the subject of an international arrest warrant in France probing the illicit sale of Russian arms worth £450 million to Angola. His son Alexandre is now well known to Premiership fans, particularly those of Portsmouth.

His investment in Beitar has brought him popularity among the club's supporters. He strolls onto the pitch in Israel's best stadium before the game resplendent in his trademark pin-striped suit and yellow scarf. The owner then milks the applause after unveiling the club's latest signing, 31-year-old Jerome Leroy from Lens on a £880,000 a year contract. Previously the best-paid Israeli player was Avi Nimni on a reported £120,000.

Despite the huge disparity in resources, Beitar are unable to overcome lowly Netanya in a 1–1 draw. The superb atmosphere from the 14,000 crowd more than compensates for the deficiency in entertainment.

Afterwards, the taxi driver takes me back to Tel Aviv – after a one hour diversion to his ex-wife's house and fruitless sales pitches for a sightseeing trip back to Jerusalem, cocaine, and a 'beautiful' Russian hooker.

'The Tel Aviv derby is the craziest game in Israel,' he says, finally offering an opinion about something other than Beitar as we arrive outside the hotel by the American embassy. 'You'll enjoy it tomorrow.' The same guard with the M16 is still staring fixedly. He hasn't moved in six hours.

Such is the standard of Israeli domestic football, most fans follow a second team in Western Europe – the usual suspects of Barça, Manchester United, Liverpool, Juventus. Chelsea's popularity is increasing, especially after Jose Mourinho's visit last year and the links with Pini Zahavi, the Israeli über agent who is popular among his compatriots. What Israeli teams lack in quality, their fans proudly make up for in passion. No club has taken a bigger away following to Old Trafford in the Champions League than the 4,800 febrile fanatics of Maccabi Haifa in 2002. Hapoel Tel Aviv, meanwhile, took 10,000 to the San Siro for a UEFA Cup game in 2002.

Hapoel were founded in 1923 and have always associated them-selves with socialist ideology and the Histadrut, Israel's largest trade union association. They've won the league thirteen times and reached the quarter-finals of the UEFA Cup in 2001–02, knocking out Chelsea en route. Their chief slogan: 'The whole wide world hates Hapoel and only I love her!' isn't really true in Israel, let alone the rest of the planet. Neighbours Maccabi are loathed and loved in greater measure.

The older of the two, Maccabi Tel Aviv were formed in 1906 and have won a record eighteen league championships, not to mention gracing the Champions League last season. The club's fans are proud of their right-wing reputation and the fact that they attract heavy support from Tel Aviv's wealthy northern suburbs. To mark their centenary this season, they spent heavily to bring in several big names, including ex-West Ham and Manchester City star Eyal Berkovic. The Israeli press lavished their new signings with the tired 'galacticos' tag, and the fans responded by snapping up a national record 11,000 season tickets before the season had begun. While Maccabi can proudly boast of being the nation's best-supported club, Hapoel lag behind on gates of just 8,000, with Maccabi Haifa and Beitar a bigger pull.

It helps Maccabi Tel Aviv that they boast Avi Nimni, a goalscoring midfielder and Israeli national captain. So enamoured are the fans with him that when he was kicked out of the team by a foolishly brave coach and moved to Beitar Jerusalem in 2003, many boycotted matches and wore black until their hero returned two years later, via spells at Atletico Madrid and Derby County. Nimni has been the most powerful name in Israeli football for some time, a player who is considered bigger than his club and a man whom many have strong feelings about.

'I wrote a negative article about him and I was beaten up down an alleyway soon after,' says Maccabi fanatic and journalist Haim Shadmi. 'Two guys came behind me, threw my glasses away and attacked me really hard, kicking me and punching me all over my body. I believe it was my warning to watch out, because he is like the Jesus of modern Israel.'

Despite the incident, Shadmi remains a Maccabi fan and Nimni's popularity remains undiminished as he enters the twilight of his career. The fans love him because he has time for them. He's a regular guest at fans' Bar-Mitzvahs – he even attended one where a 13-year-old boy in the north of Israel said he'd kill himself if Nimni didn't show.

'Maccabi are seen to be rich, bourgeois, arrogant, and successful because usually we are,' says their former coach, Nir Klinger. 'We are educated people. We only care about Maccabi. Hapoel are obsessed by us, but we don't care about them. Winning is more important to us. Unlike Hapoel, we have no link to any political party and this is one reason why we have been so successful and they have not. Players concentrate only on winning every game, politics does not interfere.

'Maccabi players and fans think they are better than anyone,' says Shadmi. 'They are schooled in Maccabism – a passion and a will to win.' Sadly for the garrulous Shadmi, results of late contradict their assertions of supremacy.

To get a better understanding of the current rivalry, it helps to rewind a decade, to when Maccabi did the double with Nimni at his most potent. The manager then was Dror Kashtan, who received the sack for his efforts and now manages their great rivals.

He wasn't the only one to cross the divide, for when Maccabi won the league in 2002–03, their star was an Ethiopian Jew, Baruch Dego. Effectively a replacement for an out of favour Nimni, his own fans taunted him with racist abuse, blaming him for their hero's departure. Under a barrage, Dego's form dipped, he got injured and suffered from stress. Finally recovered, he joined Kashtan at Hapoel in 2005.

The indignity was tempered by Nimni's return, alongside Eyal Berkovic. The former Hammer is known in Israel as 'The Magician', but, as John Hartson can testify, Berkovic's personality can grate. Few doubt his ability as a player, but many question the high opinion he has of himself, and when he makes comments, as he did on TV when he said that he supported Switzerland in their game against Israel because he was not selected to start, their aversion is understandable.

In the week leading up to the derby, chaos reigned. Maccabi Tel Aviv coach Nir Klinger stepped down, while Berkovic was reported to have an illness which would leave him out of the Hapoel game. As the rumour mill cranked into gear, other sources suggested that he'd be dropped and that he was now contemplating retirement. The papers made hay.

I am sitting in a workers' café in central Tel Aviv, watching fans scoop hummus onto thick slabs of bread. It's the morning of the game, and the regulars are nursing Sunday morning hangovers from the city's electrifying nightlife, unconcerned that they're eating in one of the few cafés in the city without a security guard on the door to check would-be suicide bombers.

Tsadok is part of Ultras Hapoel, a supporters' group formed in 1999. A largely youthful collective who look more like a group of skateboarders than the Italian ultra groups they profess to admire, they bang giant drums at matches, sell merchandise, arrange travel to away games and make flags bearing legends such as: 'Born to be Red', 'Red or Dead' or 'Workers of the World Unite.'

But Tsadok is clearly on edge this morning. 'Hapoel fans are used to being disappointed,' he sighs. 'We are used to being losers and finishing in second place, but the derby is above everything and I can't face coming second today. It's much more than three points.'

He refuses to have anything yellow in his house on the grounds that they are Maccabi's colours, to the point that you sense he's annoyed that his urine is the wrong hue. He's wearing a red Ultras top, which he lifts to reveal a tattoo of a hammer and sickle, part of Hapoel's badge, on his heart. The club's founding slogan was suitably socialist: 'Sport for thousands, not for trophies'.

'You should have come last night,' he smiles. 'We had 500 fans for training and we set off smoke bombs and flares. The police won't let us take flares to the game. They visited our houses to look for them before the game. We've spent a month preparing our flags though. We wanted to show the players the importance of this game.'

Asked what grates most about their city rivals, Tsadok snaps straight back: 'They look down their noses at us. Some of our fans call them Nazis, but that is not right. I hate them but I would not call them Nazis, although the Nazis thought they were the superior race, just as Maccabi fans do, so …'

If Tsadok sounds wary of crossing the line in terms of taste and decency, he drops his guard when discussing the songs both sets of fans will sing. There's the one about a former Maccabi goalkeeper, for example, whose troubled wife threw their baby out of a second floor window. The baby survived, but the goalkeeper was reminded of the distress when Hapoel fans bought plastic dolls to subsequent games. The death of another player's brother is frequently raised too, and neutral fans are advised to leave their taste at the turnstiles.

'You can sing anything when you are in a war,' says Tsadok. 'It's much more to us than a silly game of football. I want my team to win, of course, but the result is not the most important thing. You need political and social connections to form your identity. I hate everything that Maccabi stand for.'

Inconceivable though it might seem, Maccabi and Hapoel share the 17,500-capacity Bloomfield stadium close to Tel Aviv's ancient Arab port of Jaffa. For today's encounter, Hapoel are deemed to be at home. With Maccabi having sold their 3,000 away ticket allocation with ease, their fans have tried to buy tickets in the home sections in the build up to the game. To prevent this, representatives of Ultras Hapoel stood outside the ticket office and asked every potential buyer questions to find out their allegiance. If they suspected they were Maccabi fans, they'd set them the ultimate test by asking them to spit on a picture of Avi Nimni.

Even now, with just half an hour to kick-off, it's clear that their vetting process hasn't been entirely successful, as dozens of Maccabi fans spill out of the Hapoel end and into their own sections. There are skirmishes as they head to the no-man's land which separates the supporters, but the police presence is vast and disorder is quickly quelled. If back up is needed, Tel Aviv's principal Police station is directly behind the stadium. As it stands, a forbidding MAGAV unit, usually responsible for the border patrols with Palestinian territories, has been brought in to keep the peace. They're imposing, battle-hardened figures, the antithesis to the beautiful 18-year-old gun-toting female Israeli Defence Force soldiers regularly sighted on the streets – a three-year national service spell is compulsory for every Israeli.

The club's two owners sit close to each other in the main stand. Close by are the obligatory platinum blondes, ex-players and several high profile political figures with their box-fresh scarves. An election is approaching, and the nation's politicians want to be seen to like football.

The entire ground is bouncing, both fans singing their songs in harmony to a constant drum beat. The air is hot and dry and filled with vitriol. The Maccabi fans might be outnumbered, but they match the Hapoel fans for noise in the first half. Both factions hold up cards to form giant mosaics. Maccabi's is all black, symbolising the dark mood at their club, but in a clever twist, they turn the cards over to reveal the yellow of sunrise. The message is clever: the darkest hour comes before the brightest dawn.

Hapoel fans behind one goal are singing: 'We wish you another Holocaust' to their more nationalist rivals. In the past, Maccabi fans have sunk to similar levels by responding: 'We hope you burn in Treblinka' (the WWII Polish death camp).

Today though, they prefer a simple cry of 'Communists … Get out of this country, you are not Jewish'.

Things are only just warming up. 'Gate 5 (the main Hapoel section) is like a Gaza refugee camp'; 'Hapoel are Hezbollah' (an extremist terrorist group whose main intention is the destruction of Israel.)

And so it continues, long after the referee has blown to kick off the game. It soon becomes clear that what we're watching is the antithesis of most derby games, a tepid encounter where what unfolds on the pitch is a mere side attraction to many in the stands who enjoy the spectacle more than the sport.

Soon enough the main action occurs *in* the stands, when Nimni's followers in the wrong end take exception to the home fans taunting their hero. Gesticulations abound and punches are thrown before some are escorted into the Maccabi section. They enjoy their walk past the Hapoel fans.

Although the quality of football today impresses few, Israeli football is clearly in the ascendancy and standards are improving as the relative success of their teams in European competition shows. Whether Israel should even be allowed to play in Europe given that geographically it's in Asia is an altogether different issue, and not one for debate as the game rumbles on.

Up in the stand, a man paces the steps nervously. He stands out, not just because he seems edgy, but because he's wearing a peace T-shirt bearing both the Palestinian and Israeli flags. That man is Ari Shamay, a lawyer, journalist, hardcore Hapoel fan, and confidant of the players. He's renowned for his left-wing views, yet he controversially represented Yigal Amir, an ultra right-wing activist who so strenuously opposed Prime Minister Yitzhak Rabin's signing of the Oslo peace accords that he assassinated him in 1995.

Politics are never far away from Israeli football, or Israeli life in general. In recent weeks, the game has been used to promote peace, with a joint Israeli–Palestinian team captained by Nimni playing Barcelona in the Camp Nou in a match organised by the Nobel peace prize winner Shimon Peres's Centre for Peace. Now, as the Arab Walid Badier gives Hapoel the lead after half-time, any last shred of goodwill goes up in smoke.

'He's a suicide bomber,' sing Maccabi.

'War, war, war,' holler back Hapoel, and they're even singing in the posh seats.

At the end, with Hapoel adding a second goal, their victorious players dance in front of their delirious fans for twenty minutes.

The win takes Hapoel up to second in the table, ten points behind Israel's pre-eminent football force, Maccabi Haifa. Managerless Maccabi Tel Aviv, meanwhile, slip to sixth in the twelve-team top flight. It's simply not good enough for Israel's previously most successful team. Not that they care too much about that on the red side of the fence.

'Beating Maccabi is the highlight of the season for us,' says Hapoel legend Yehoshua Fangehboim as fans hug and kiss around him. 'It was the same when I played. Everyone wanted to play against Maccabi and we were extra motivated because we knew what it meant to the fans. The media used to write only about the game for the seven days leading up to it. The pressure built up so much that we couldn't face defeat.'

The fans disperse from the stadium flanked by heavy security. As in Glasgow, rivals use separate roads to leave the area.

'It was very emotional for us to beat Maccabi,' manager Dror Kashtan tells me. 'It really is more than a game. The Tel Aviv derby may not have the crowds that you have in England, but the passion is the same, always very hot and always very red.'

As they leave the dressing room, leftie lawyer Ari Shamay hugs each of the Hapoel players. The respect appears to be mutual. 'I've supported Hapoel for 35 of my 41 years, I've travelled all over Europe and now I write about them in a newspaper,' he tells me, welling up with pride.

But what if Hapoel are playing badly and every fan can see it? What does he write then? 'Then I don't write it. I'd write only against the management or the owners, I criticise only them.'

Three weeks later, Hapoel are bought by Lev Leviev, another Israeli–Russian billionaire who happens to be friends with Roman Abramovich (Israel has approximately one million Jews of Russian descent in its six million population).

Sources suggest that Leviev has become fed up watching how famous and popular his ex-partner Gaydamak has become through owning a football club. 'It's all a game for them,' says Yaron Spira from *Globes*, Israel's business daily. 'Football is their toy. [People like Gaydamak] come to "donate" or to clear their name and reputation, but not for the business, never for business. The fans love it when a rich Russian takes over their team but it leaves fans of other clubs like Maccabi depressed and searching for their own billionaire.'

Mention Israel and the world thinks of the Jewish–Palestinian divide. People are conditioned by BBC and CNN images of bloodshed and bombs and the mere sight of a bus fills those first-time visitors still prepared to venture into the country with unease. Yet the everyday talk in café bars or on the beach isn't of politics, but of football. Domestic Israeli life contains great fissures which are dramatized graphically in the sporting arena, and where rivalries burn every bit as deeply as they do in Milan, Manchester or Madrid. As Dror Kashtan said, 'It's always very hot, and always very red'.

Pride of North London
Arsenal v Spurs, April 2006

Arsenal have been annoying Spurs for years: they've moved in on their turf, stolen their captain, imitated their style and even managed to get them relegated. Could the final Highbury clash redress the balance?

Every football club and its fans like to nurse a sense of injured inno-cence, a myth of victimhood which can be trotted out to justify any unsporting act on or off the pitch.

For Arsenal, it is Manchester United, the Northern bully using its institutional weight to crush its plucky Cockney rival. For Manchester United, the capital M Media is determined to stitch them up every chance it gets. For Liverpool, the whole known universe conspires to do down the red half of self-pity city. As for Tottenham Hotspur, it is Arsenal, the carpet-bag club which moved in on their manor, tried to siphon off their fans, stole their top-flight status, hijacked their keeper, lured away their captain and, perhaps most gallingly of all, pirated their style.

All paranoid nonsense, of course. Except for the first one. Spurs have a case. Where most local rivalries are about no more than that, locality, Spurs' disdain of Arsenal carries the extra charge of morality. Arsenal hate Spurs for the usual reason: because they're there. Spurs hate Arsenal precisely because they shouldn't be there in the first place.

On 22 April 2006, a capacity crowd witnessed the final encounter between Arsenal and Spurs at Highbury, whereupon the junior club decamped a few hundred yards back in the rough direction of where it was founded, in the bowels of the arms industry south of the River Thames in Woolwich. From *dar-as-sina ah*, meaning place of manufacture, the very word arsenal is derived from Arabic, so the move to the Emirates Stadium marks a return to the club's etymological roots too. (As a teenager living in London, Osama Bin Laden followed Arsenal. Fact.)

In between its flit from the death factory in 1913 and up-market move to a converted rubbish recycling plant handily situated for the King's Cross red light district, Arsenal have cultivated an air of Establishment pomp. Just as a fly-by-night finance house will adopt the trappings of pillared and pedimented permanence to camouflage the fact that it's no better than a clip-joint or casino, so Arsenal marbled its halls and filled its boardroom with blazered Old Etonians. 'Good old Arsenal!' its fans in flat caps would cheer during the club's era of dominance in the 1930s – aptly known as the Great Depression – but it was good and old in the same way as a Georgian-style executive development is good and old: a thin veneer of sprayed-on class that may fool snobs but not connoisseurs.

10 CLASSIC DERBIES

31 January 1934
Arsenal 1 Spurs 3

Arsenal bossed the '30s, Spurs enjoying just two top-flight seasons that decade, suffering an aggregate 11–1 hammering in the 1934–35 relegation season. Even so, though Arsenal ended 1933–34 as Champions, Spurs finished third, outclassing their neighbours before a 68,674 Highbury crowd.

For that amazingly successful transformation, Arsenal owe everything to a bent businessman and Tory MP called Sir Henry Norris. Norris was a self-made and very well-connected property developer who knew who to lean on, whose wheels to grease and where the bodies were buried. Already a director of Fulham FC, his ambition was to command a London super-club.

Woolwich Arsenal had a mud-heap pitch, a fan-base restricted to an inaccessible corner of Kent, and a load of debt. Like Chelsea nearly a century later with Abramovich, the Woolwich Arsenal board nearly bit his hand off when Norris made his approach. While retaining his directorship of Fulham, Norris became Woolwich Arsenal's chairman and tried to merge the two clubs to play at Craven Cottage, crucially north of the river. The League weren't having it, nor his follow-up plan for each club to maintain separate identities while playing at the Cottage.

Plan C was to relocate Arsenal to Highbury, just far enough south of Tottenham and Leyton Orient to have a chance of attracting the masses of potential fans in the inner suburbs just north and east of the City of London. The underground railway station at Gillespie Road – renamed Arsenal in 1932 – would deliver the punters direct to the turnstiles, guaranteeing gates that would justify Norris's £125,000 investment – £50m today – in the hitherto dead-end club.

Plan C provoked outrage from all quarters: fans of Woolwich Arsenal, Spurs, Orient and even Chelsea united in condemning a scheme that would abandon

---

10 CLASSIC DERBIES

6 October 1962
Spurs 4 Arsenal 4

In the space of five years the North London rivals fought out three 4–4 draws: the second was a Geoff Strong-inspired Gunners fightback against Spurs' three-goal lead. 'Unbelievable!' gasped *The Sunday Times*.

one set of supporters and undermine the other three. The *Tottenham Herald* caricatured Norris as a spike-collared Hound of the Baskervilles prowling round the Spurs roost, and mounted a campaign to keep the 'interlopers' out. 'They have no right to be here!' the local paper thundered, a sentiment echoed by Spurs fans ever since.

Norris, a ruthless political operator as well as malignantly visionary strategist, was not going to be over-ruled by the FA a third time. He packed their inquiry with allies and got

---

10 CLASSIC DERBIES

15 October 1963
Arsenal 4 Spurs 4

Again Spurs let it slip against a battling Arsenal before a 67,857 crowd. Of the Spurs scorers, Jimmy Greaves, Bobby Smith and Dave Mackay were artists at the top of their game, as were Arsenal's George Eastham and Joe Baker, while Strong again grabbed the last-gasp equaliser. A classic.

---

the vote. Next, he squared Highbury residents fearful of a riff-raff invasion every other Saturday, and, thanks to a personal testimonial by his old pal the Archbishop of Canterbury, reassured the Catholic Church that the six acres of land belonging to St John's College of Divinity he proposed buying as site for the club would observe the Sabbath and be free of intoxicating liquor. Arsenal played their first competitive game at Highbury, against Leicester Fosse in the Football League Second Division, on 6 September 1913.

What of Spurs? Originally a cricket club, Hotspur FC was named after the rebel son of the Earl of Northumberland, whose family had owned Northumberland Park and other land around Tottenham. Sir Henry Percy, nicknamed Harry Hotspur, was immortalised by Shakespeare as the chivalrous anti-hero of Henry IV Part One (his catch-phrase: 'By heaven, methinks it were an easy leap/To pluck bright honour from the pale-faced moon'). The aristocratic cavalry to

10 CLASSIC DERBIES

3 May 1971
Spurs 0 Arsenal 1

A decade after Spurs became the first 20th century side to do the Double, Arsenal repeated the feat, edging the Championship by a point in the last game of the season – a Ray Kennedy header settling the game in the 86th minute. A quarter of a million fans jammed the Lane for hours before the game, with only a fifth gaining admission.

Arsenal's roundhead artillery, the gulf in class between the two clubs goes right back to their roots.

The first London team to win the FA Cup – as Southern League amateurs, to boot – Spurs joined the booming Football League in 1908 and were promoted to the First Division in 1909. From that peak they slid until bottoming the table at the end of the 1914–15 season, when the Great War intervened. Ending, meanwhile, the last pre-War season fifth in the Second Division, upon the return of peace Woolwich Arsenal did not expect to resume League football in the First Division. And yet they did – at Tottenham's expense.

Now there is a theory that Tottenham had repeatedly been frustrated over the years in its dealings with the Southern League, London FA and Football League because it had already acquired a Jewish support which was not smiled on by the football establishment in those days of widespread and open prejudice. Moreover, so the conspiracy theory goes, the FA waved through Norris's plans to build Highbury at the other end of the Seven Sisters Road from Spurs for the same reason that the Catholic church granted the land – to undermine London's top club on the grounds that it was too Jewish. Nothing can be proved.

What is certain is that Norris persuaded the 1919 FA League Management Committee that the fairest way to expand the First Division by two clubs was for the bottom club (Spurs) to be relegated and the next-to-bottom (Chelsea) to be reprieved on the grounds that its position was entirely due to a result that the High Court ruled had been fixed. Manchester United's 2–0 victory over Liverpool had saved the Red Devils' top-flight status at Chelsea's expense; that result reversed now doomed United and saved the Pensioners. Three clubs from the Second Division would make up the twenty-two – the top two at the end of the 1914–15 season ... plus Arsenal, the fifth.

The official reason the committee gave was to reward Arsenal's 'long service to League football', despite the fact that Wolves, who'd finished a place above Arsenal in 1915, had actually been in the League longer. The idea that visiting First Division directors might have voted for Arsenal because they looked forward to weekends away in the capital with somewhat more relish than trips to Wolverhampton or third-lying Barnsley is, of course, absurd. As is the suggestion that the Committee President, 'Honest' John McKenna of Liverpool, in championing Arsenal's cause was repaying Norris for his support in white-washing his own club's murky role in the 1915 match-fixing scandal. Or indeed that he received a cut-price house in Wimbledon through Norris's estate agency ...

When the news of their unwelcome new neighbour's bizarre promotion at Tottenham's expense reached While Hart Lane, the club parrot, which had been presented by the captain of the ship on which Spurs voyaged home after their 1908 tour of Argentina, fell ill and expired. Hence the football cliché 'sick as a parrot'. Arsenal have that on their consciences too.

Since then the fortunes of the clubs have see-sawed, seldom in equilibrium. Arsenal have never left the top flight; Spurs have oscillated. Tottenham's glory years in the '60s coincided with Arsenal's spell in the wilderness that touched bottom on 5 May 1966 when just 4,554 turned up at Highbury to watch them lose 3–0 to Leeds. Tottenham have never fallen quite that low.

For the fans, the animosity really started upon Tottenham's return to the First Division after their 1919 relegation: on 23 September 1922,

10 CLASSIC DERBIES

23 December 1978
Spurs 0 Arsenal 5

Back in the top flight after a season in Division Two, Spurs had signed Argentine World Cup-winners Ossie Ardiles and Ricky Villa but it was Arsenal's Liam Brady who bossed the midfield, with Alan Sunderland netting a hat-trick.

trouble spilled out from the pitch onto the terraces at White Hart Lane when Spurs lost to two Arsenal goals scored by, wait for it, Reg Boreham. 'Spurs … the finer artists … extreme daintiness,' *The Sportsman*'s match report puffed its pipe appreciatively; 'but Tottenham lost because they had nearly all the bad luck going in an amazingly strenuous contest … yet one could not help feeling impressed by the sledgehammer opposition of the Arsenal.'

Never mind that Spurs did 'em 2–0 at Highbury the following Saturday: that first outcome has been all too typical of the fifty-six defeats Tottenham has conceded to Arsenal in the league, compared to forty-five victories and thirty-six draws – artistry bludgeoned by industry, playing the game with a more noble but less effective philosophy than winning at all costs.

Nor has Spurs been lucky in its off-pitch dealings with Arsenal. Very few players have crossed the divide, but two stand out for the damage done to the morale of Spurs fans at vulnerable moments in the club's fortunes: Pat Jennings and Sol Campbell.

It seems bizarre to think that Jennings remains a White Hart Lane hero, given that the Northern Ireland goalkeeper deliberately signed for Arsenal to embarrass Spurs directors, not one of whom thanked him for thirteen years' illustrious service when he was released for just £45,000 at the end of Tottenham's 1976–77 relegation season. Spurs fans may not have liked the direction Jennings chose to be pushed, but pushed he was, and it was four years before Spurs had a keeper fit to fill Pat's outsized gloves.

Being pushed was forgivable. Being pulled wasn't. The last time Sol Campbell played for Spurs, it was as captain in April 2001 against Arsenal in an FA Cup semi-final at Old Trafford, injuring his ankle in a heroic effort that kept the margin of Spurs' defeat down to 2–1. The next time he played at White Hart Lane, in November, it was in an Arsenal shirt. He had gone on a free that July after Arsene Wenger had publicly stated in April he would like to sign him. The Arsenal manager achieved his ambition in the teeth not only of Spurs offering Campbell 80 grand a week to stay but also a reported five-year contract offered by Barcelona.

Never in living memory was the derby so bitterly contested by Spurs fans as upon Campbell's return; the phrase 'cauldron of hate' was coined for such atmospheres. Nor has the venom and vitriol directed towards Campbell by Spurs fans much abated, though the tone has softened since the initial purging hatred of the banners, boos and Judas chants. Today you'll occasionally hear sung from the cheaper seats knockabout ditties about his rumoured private life that, with some clearly vile exceptions, are homocomic rather than homophobic: the idea of this rock-jawed juggernaut in a romantic clinch with Michael Barrymore (to the tune of Verdi's 'La Donna E Mobile') makes him a figure of fun who can be laughed off rather than an object of hate who can't. Whether such mockery is less acceptable in a football ground than it is in the BBC's comedy hit *Little Britain* is a topic for a heated debate on another occasion. Spurs officially are

---

10 CLASSIC DERBIES

4 April 1983
Spurs 5 Arsenal 0

Five years later, revenge against the odds as an injury-hit Spurs without Glenn Hoddle, Steve Perryman, Ardiles and Villa hammered an unusually demoralised Arsenal.

taking no chances: 'strong action will be taken against those guilty …
of harassment whether it concerns race, religion or sexual orientation,' threatens the matchday programme.

But, after four years, the fans seem to have got to Campbell. His
performance at White Hart Lane in October 2005 was a model of
panicky ineptitude which set the standard for the rest of the
season. When Arsenal fans, as they now do, grumble that Spurs are
welcome to have Campbell back, Tottenham fans can at last feel
satisfied that rough justice has been done: disloyalty is rewarded
with disloyalty.

(Not that the bitterness penetrated the boardroom. Where relations between the two sets of directors in the past had been coldly
formal, today Arsenal vice-chairman David Dein's son Darren is married to former Spurs vice-chairman David Buchler's daughter, having previously dated Alan Sugar's daughter. As an insider explained, belonging to the Premiership is too much of a good thing to let the small matter of time-hallowed mutual dislike get in the way.)

Campbell's decline for Arsenal coincides with Ledley King's assured establishment as Tottenham's defensive rock, captain and frequent England choice. The Spurs end of the see-saw seems to be swinging back up. Even St Totteringham's Day – the date on which it is

---

10 CLASSIC DERBIES

4 March 1987
Spurs 1 Arsenal 2

The two legs of this League Cup
semi-final had ended 2–2 on
aggregate after another Arsenal
fight-back (losing 0–1 at home,
winning 2–1 away). In the replay,
Clive Allen put Spurs ahead, but
sub Ian Allinson scored an
equaliser that made him a Highbury mini-legend and David
Rocastle grabbed a late winner.
George Graham's side went on
to lift the first of several trophies
under his stewardship.

mathematically impossible for Spurs to catch up Arsenal in the league; 'it seems to come round earlier each year!' gloat the Gooners – might not be celebrated this season.

With Chelsea's lock on the Championship probably secure for years to come, Arsenal's rivalry with Manchester United now seems no more than a sideshow, so the North London derby looks set to resume its traditional status as the most keenly awaited fixture of the season by both sides.

'It's About the Suffering'
The fans on Arsenal v Spurs

Danny Kelly, Spurs
'Being born and brought up near Highbury, I should be an Arsenal fan, and I used to get taken there and to White Hart Lane – my family are mostly Arsenal, and my girlfriend now is a season ticket holder. But even then I saw one lot was the Foreign Office in red shirts while the other were the true spirit of rock'n'roll – the white shirts represent purity to me. At school in Islington I was in a minority but it wasn't such a huge issue then – you didn't define yourself so much by who you were against. For me the crisis came in 1971 when Arsenal won the Double and held the victory parade in Islington. My family trooped off with cardboard trophies, leaving me behind to hear the roaring from the High Street. That was the moment I realised that life was not necessarily going to be fair.'

Lloyd Bradley, Arsenal
'In the '60s I went to school between the two grounds. Arsenal were the underdogs then. Most of the First XI supported Spurs, while more black kids, including me, played for the Arsenal playground team. My mates and I would go to Arsenal one Saturday and Spurs the next – and we'd support Spurs against any Northern side. All real football

fans are the same: it's about suffering, so you don't get on someone more than gentle geeing up. You couldn't fight with kids then sit together in class on Monday. Spurs fans would talk about how we hadn't any class, so in recent years we've loved taking the piss because we were more successful and playing good football. That's what perturbs me about this season – Spurs aren't the idiot cousin down the road you can patronise anymore.'

Jim O'Neill, Spurs

'The rivalry is more intense now than in the '60s and '70s. When Pat Jennings left Spurs for Arsenal, he got applauded when he came back to the Lane, while Sol Campbell needs an armed guard. Back then, people would alternate, Tottenham one week, Arsenal the next. When Arsenal won the Double in '71, I spotted a bloke on telly that my brother stood with in the Shelf (at White Hart Lane) supporting Arsenal at Wembley! Couldn't happen now, and not just because of the cost and having to book ahead. No one lives near the grounds anymore, they live out in Harlow, Stevenage, the suburbs. Also, the need to win at all costs and at all levels – managers, players and fans – is more intense. I love watching Arsenal lose now almost as much as watching Tottenham win.'

Paul Elliott, Arsenal

'I've always had loads of Tottenham friends, and I love the banter but hate the dread. On derby days at Spurs, I hate walking past the Corner Pin

---

10 CLASSIC DERBIES

14 April 1991
Arsenal 1 Spurs 3

The North London rivals split the top domestic silverware in 1991. And Spurs' route to FA Cup Final victory came via this even sweeter semi-final win at a packed Wembley, with Gazza's virtuoso free-kick goal from thirty-five yards out opening proceedings.

pub and hearing they want to kick the shit out of me. The 3–1 Wembley FA Cup semi-final in 1991 was the only good game of football I've seen between the two sides, though losing it really hurt because everyone saw it on the telly. When my mates say they hate Chelsea or Man U, I have to remind them who the real enemy are.'

Simon Kanter, Spurs

'Arsenal have always been the enemy and always will be, whatever Chelsea's aspirations.

---

10 CLASSIC DERBIES

17 November 2001
Spurs 1 Arsenal 1

Sol Campbell returned to a cauldron of hate at White Hart Lane after his defection to Arsenal that summer, Judas balloons, chants and boos greeting his every touch. For once, Spurs grabbed the last-gasp equaliser, and honour was satisfied.

Arsenal were the dour and unattractive alternative to Spurs' glory glory side. In 1971 they ground their way to the Double, unlike Spurs' 1961 free-flowing Double side. Until the Wenger era that remained so. It's been hard to stomach watching Wenger's Arsenal playing Spurs-style football, especially while we've been so woeful in that respect.'

Nick Hornby, Arsenal

'In *Fever Pitch* I wrote that Spurs fans had a smug air of ersatz sophistication. That Arsenal under Wenger have played the space-age version of the football Spurs aspired to must have been extremely galling. The derby stopped being a big game, just sound and fury. Then they turned a bit nasty, like in 1999. When Sol said he was leaving Spurs for Arsenal for football reasons, everybody knew what he was talking about and that ratcheted up an already bitter situation. Yet Spurs could absolutely have done what Arsenal did – they could have had Bergkamp, Petit and even Wenger. Now, this season, with Carrick, Robinson and Defoe, it's beginning to look the other way.

10 CLASSIC DERBIES

13 November 2004
Spurs 4 Arsenal 5

Martin Jol's reign as Tottenham coach started with a home defeat that Spurs fans half-celebrated as Arsenal's so-called Invincibles conceded four in a thriller suggesting the quality gap of the previous eight years was closing at last.

The last few weeks I've remembered what it feels like to be a football fan. For ten years it's been like going to the cinema or a rock concert – you're entertained, but at a distance. If Arsenal beat the likes of Sunderland by less than four goals, it felt poor value for money. Abramovich has brought back the importance of the derby. The Premiership doesn't matter because you can't win the fucking thing anymore.'

Spite, Suits & Binmen
The players reveal their derby motivations

Arthur Milton (Arsenal 1945–55)
'We were winning 1–0. I pulled the ball back and Jimmy Logie popped it into the net. Jimmy came rushing over and gave me a hug. I said: "What are you doing giving me a hug?" "Well," he says, "my tailor said he'd give me a new suit if we beat Tottenham".'

Malcolm Macdonald (Arsenal 1976–79)
'Spurs players were always arrogant and that helped in the North London derby: "OK, lads, let's go and do the arrogant bastards!" Their arrogance gave the edge to the opposition, never themselves, and they never saw that.'

Kenny Sansom (Arsenal 1980–88)

'I used to dread losing, especially when a big England game followed soon afterwards because I shared a room with Glenn Hoddle and he wouldn't miss a chance to wind me up.'

Gary Mabbutt (Spurs 1982–98)

'If we got beaten, our binmen would wear their Arsenal scarves just to rub it in.'

Niall Quinn (Arsenal 1983–1990)

'Pat Rice was our youth coach and he drummed into us that Tottenham were the enemy from day one. All the caricatures were used – flash, fancy dans – and after a month that's what I believed.'

Steve Williams (Arsenal 1984–88)

'I used to lick my lips and look forward to it. Everyone says every game's the same. Not for me. I want to beat Tottenham and I want to beat them often.'

Teddy Sheringham (Spurs 1992–97, 2001–03)

'I hate Arsenal. With a passion.'

On the Frontline
Wrexham v Chester City, March 2006

It's pride of North Wales against their posh neighbours from across the border. But tough times for both and eleven years without a derby game have done nothing to stop the hatred.

Wrexham's Frontline hooligan firm have given me the nod to travel with them on the train to Chester, home of their most hated rivals. We've brought a photographer along, although it's been made abundantly clear by our hosts that if things 'go off', then the camera will have to do the same. On arrival in Chester, we'll spend time observing a major police operation – one that has prevented officers from fifty miles away taking leave – to keep the rival fans apart.

We'll also meet supporters from both sides of the divide, and while no Chester or Wrexham fan pretends this is the biggest derby in football, they do believe the clash is genuinely more than a game. It's a unique encounter, one that's as much about class and nationality as football. Given that Wrexham have historically tended to play in a higher division, border skirmishes between the teams from middle-class Chester of England and working-class Wrexham of Wales are not played out with the regularity of other derbies. So as the two clubs prepared to meet in the league for the first time in over a decade, the words 'eagerly' and 'awaited' began cropping up in local newspapers as frequently as police warnings that any hooliganism would not be tolerated.

It's 8.57 a.m. on Wednesday, 28 December 2005, a normal working day, when we walk into the cavernous Wetherspoons pub in Wrexham town centre. Inside, around 100 lads aged between 16 and 50 are already drinking. Most would happily classify themselves as members of the Frontline, a long-established group of wily casuals whose website opens to the Stereophonics song, 'As Long As We Beat The English'. One of Wrexham's nicknames is the Red Dragons, yet the only evidence of red in this boozer is the discreet Prada Sport labels worn by many. A Wrexham fan wearing a replica shirt here would look as incongruous as Father Christmas riding a cow in the Grand National.

The intention is to get the 11 o'clock train ten miles to Chester. The monied post-Christmas shoppers who flood the city will be in for an unpleasant surprise if they see Wrexham's marauding mob. The police, who wait by the train station to escort the Frontline and prevent such an occurrence, are fully aware of the potential for disorder and have made the game a midday kick-off to reduce the probability of trouble. It hasn't gone down well with fans who've had to take the day off work.

English and Welsh police are co-operating closely, with intelligence officers monitoring the Frontline's movements. At the moment, these consist of frequent visits to the bar. The leaders in the Frontline are doubtful that they'll get a chance to attack Chester's '125' firm, but they live in hope.

A gaunt and dishevelled figure enters the pub. He doesn't look like he'll make it to the bar, let alone Chester. He begins scrounging for money. The lads don't give him any but they tolerate him, some shaking his hand. 'Twenty years ago he was one of the top lads in Wrexham,' explains one hooligan. 'He always had the best trainers, girls, everything. He's a smackhead now. Shame.'

The drug addict won't be going to Chester, but the violence addicts will, a band of brothers frisky with anticipation as they prepare to cross the border into enemy territory. Several have just come out of prison or finished banning orders for smashing up a pub opposite Chester station in 2004. One has the incriminating CCTV footage that was used in evidence against the perpetrators on his mobile phone. It lasts for five minutes, as twenty or thirty deranged Frontline persistently attack the Deva Mail and Sports Club with bottles, poles, and any other objects they can muster. 'Cost me my flat and missus that,' says Chas, one of the main Wrexham heads. 'If I hadn't been nicked I would have probably left all this behind. But I'm back here now, aren't I?'

Chester and Wrexham haven't met in the league for eleven years and it's the blues of Chester who remember the 1995 Valentine's Day meeting more fondly than Wrexham's reds. Reduced to nine men, Chester came back from 2–1 down to draw 2–2 at the Racecourse Ground.

'I've never played in a game that had as much incident as that one – two sent off, a missed penalty and four goals,' says Gary Bennett, who turned out for both teams during a distinguished lower league career. 'Everyone in the Wrexham dressing room was gutted afterwards; we couldn't believe how nine men had got a draw against us. The Chester fans were singing, "You couldn't beat nine men,"' adds Bennett, still revered as 'Psycho' by Wrexham fans.

'Every player who took part in that game is held in such a high regard by City fans,' says Chester fan Jim Green, 'If Andy Milner ever falls on hard times I know 100 people who would give up their beds for him.'

Bennett has been on the winning side for Chester in the same fixture, too, in a 1987 third-round FA Cup. 'It was snowing and Wrexham led 1–0 at the break – but I managed to get two second-half goals,' he says. 'Wrexham fans always remind me of that one. I also played in a Freight Rover Cup game where fans were ripping up seats and throwing them. You have to expect the unexpected when Chester and Wrexham meet.'

What you can always expect is mutual disdain. One Chester website has a section called: 'They've scored against the Wrexham', which boasts: 'In a perfectly ordered society, streets would be named after them. When it comes down to heroes they're right up there with Spartacus, Hercules, Theseus and, yes, even Biggles. By scoring for Chester against our arch-rivals, the Goats, they have genius shining from every orifice.' Goats is a favoured Chester moniker for Wrexham, along with 'Wrectum' and 'Sheepshaggers'. Wrexham use many colourful profanities to describe Chester, the least offensive being 'Jester Pity'.

Back at the pub, bad news filters through: the game's been called off. Chester's pitch, which straddles the English and Welsh border, is frozen. The reaction is surprisingly measured, probably because the news is not entirely unexpected. 'Means the re-arranged game will be at night now,' offers one. 'That means a better atmosphere,' interjects another.

The Frontline considers going to Chester regardless, but the arrival of two police intelligence officers in Wetherspoons makes them reconsider. 'Boys,' says an officer in a firm, businesslike tone. 'We're passing on a message from our Chester counterparts that resources will now be focused in the Wrexham area for the rest of the day.'

Nobody replies, but the few nods indicate that they've got the message and the Frontline contemplates the long day ahead. They've got plenty of time – it's not even 10 a.m.

Wrexham's population of 43,000 makes it one of the smallest places to have a Football League club. Only the towns of relative newcomers Yeovil, Rushden, and Boston have fewer inhabitants. Wrexham grew because of industry, including brickworks, steelworks, and a brewery making Wrexham lager. Coal was also mined in surrounding villages, including Gresford, famous for its colliery disaster of 1934. Yet mention Gresford to the Frontline and they talk about a riot that erupted during a 1990s Sunday League game between a Chester and a Wrexham-based team after hooligans from both sides came to watch.

The 1970s offered mixed fortunes for Wrexham. The side played in the European Cup Winners' Cup four times and reached the sixth round of the FA Cup twice, but the decline of Wrexham's traditional industries had a devastating effect. 'I can remember my dad losing his job and we wanted to leave Wrexham to get a job elsewhere,' remembers one fan, 'but everyone else wanted to do the same and house prices dropped so we couldn't. Everyone in my school seemed to be on free meals. But dad still found money to take us to the match.'

Wrexham's economic situation has improved in the last two decades, but it remains the antithesis of well-heeled Chester. Many Wrexham lads are happy that it stays like that and are proud of the hard-bitten reputation of their town.

Chester never relied on traditional industries like Wrexham, instead hosting a large white-collar workforce involved in financial services. Chester's riverside setting, cathedral, Roman walls, and historic racecourse have long been a tourist magnet. The clock on the town hall only has three faces, with the Wales facing side remaining blank because, according to the architects, 'Chester won't give Wales the time of day.' An archaic law states any Cestrian (a resident of Chester) may shoot a Welshman with a longbow if he loiters within the walls after sunset – although this law no longer offers legal protection against prosecution for murder. 'I'd like to see them try it,' says one Wrexham lad.

'Wrexham boys see themselves and the town as downtrodden by the well-to-do of Chester,' says Chester fan Jim Green, 'but parts of Chester like Blacon or the Lache are as bad as Queens Park in Wrexham.' Queens Park (remained Caia Park in an attempt to improve its image) is a troubled Wrexham estate of 14,000 which was plagued by riots between asylum seekers, residents, and police in 2003. Some members of the Frontline were involved.

With a population of 90,000, Chester is over twice the size of its rival, yet their support is around half of Wrexham's, partly because Wrexham attracts fans from all over North Wales. 'The people of Chester don't deserve a Football League club,' says Wrexham supporter Paul Baker. 'Chester's too posh for football. They're into rowing, lawn tennis, golf and all that.'

Baker – who is unlikely to be ever employed by the Chester tourist board – continues: 'The Cestrians are stuck up their own arses. Wrexham lads look out of place there. We wear sensible clothes; they wear pink shirts and have gel in their hair. We go out on the steam (beer), throw it down us and have a laugh. They just want to have a drink or two and chat up the ladies. That's why a lot of Wrexham girls go out in Chester – they like to be treated well and know we're a bunch of piss-cans.'

One irony is that the Frontline fuel Chester's prosperous economy by purchasing their designer threads in the city's superior shops. 'Most Wrexham lads buy their clothes in Chester as there's more choice,' says Wrexham fan Irish. 'But even as a teenager the Chester lads would stop you and ask where you are from. You had to have your wits about you.'

It's not just Wrexham fans who question Chester's support. When Chester were in turmoil under Terry Smith, the controversial American owner who briefly installed himself as team manager, Mark Lawrenson opined: 'The trouble is that Chester is not a footballing city.'

'There was an outcry over Lawrenson's comments but ultimately, as much as it pains me, he was right,' says Jim Green. 'We've a population of nearly 100,000 within the city yet cannot pull in 3,000 for a league game on a Saturday. I think the council and the city in general lack the passion of our counterparts in Wrexham – something I'm pretty envious of. Wrexham could, and previously have, pull in over 10,000 every week if they were doing well – something Chester will never do.'

Other Chester fans view it differently. 'Try telling people that Chester's not a football city when witnessing the passion at a Wrexham derby match or the tears that were shed when we were relegated to the Conference,' says Sue Choularton of the Chester Exiles, a long-standing supporters' group with 100 members around the world. 'Lawrenson's comments actually helped because they galvanised the Chester supporters' groups into action and ultimately led to the downfall of Smith.'

Green reckons there are differences in the identity of the respective populations. 'North Walians see Wrexham as their identity – if you tell somebody you live in Coedpoeth, a village five miles away, then nobody knows where that is, but people have heard of Wrexham. Chester, meanwhile, is a small city, overshadowed by Liverpool and Manchester. Until *Hollyoaks*, not many people outside the North West knew where we were. We've basically got five suburbs and that's it – villages any more than five miles outside of the city prefer to have their own identity. It's much more in keeping with the Cheshire mindset to tell people you live in Tarporley or Little Budworth than Chester, despite their close proximity.'

Three months later, I'm back in Wrexham, this time for the visit of Chester. It's late March and the teams have still to meet this season. A line of police riot vans is parked outside Wrexham General Station, just 200 metres from the Racecourse Ground. The police have again set a noon kick-off, but with daffodils hinting of spring in a blustery North Wales, there's little chance of this game being called off.

Despite an abysmal run of form that has seen them plummet to 92nd in the Football League, Chester have sold 1,340 tickets and around 250 of them, among them known thugs, are due to arrive at the station half an hour before kick-off. They will be met by a unit of handy-looking police in body armour who look like they've spent more time filling in hooligans than forms behind a desk.

'Our job is to facilitate the safe passage of visiting supporters,' says one Robocop. 'I used to work in a large Midlands city where we had serious problems. Now I'm based in North Wales where we get little storms in teacups. But this lot need keeping apart.'

Aware that the police will prevent them getting anywhere near the visiting supporters, the Frontline remain in a town centre pub. Some of them have hung a flag from a bridge of the Chester/Wrexham bypass to greet the visiting fans. It reads: 'Welcome to Hell', or at least it does for a short while before police remove it. There are even dark murmurings of bricking the train before it arrives, a little ironic on a train line that was built partly to transport bricks.

The vast majority of the 7,240 crowd, easily Wrexham's biggest of the season in a functional stadium that holds 15,500, has no intention of causing problems. They hold the hooligans in contempt, pointing out that their cash-strapped clubs haven't got the money to fund huge police operations, evidence of which is everywhere. Above in a dark grey sky, the North Wales police helicopter hovers loudly while dog handlers prevent groups of Wrexham fans forming on the ground. All the time CCTV cameras record events.

Irish points to one whirring CCTV camera. 'I hate that,' he says. 'It stops us doing anything.' He also identifies various individuals as they make their way towards the Racecourse Ground. 'He's a big Man City fan,' he says after shaking hands with a handy-looking lad who clearly doesn't visit his dentist as often as he should. By that, it's assumed that he's Man City *and* Wrexham. 'I once bit his City tattoo and it bruised for months,' adds Irish, who goes away with Manchester United. 'A lot of the lads will watch Liverpool, Everton, United or City too.' The lower-league club benefit from these two-team fans, who can often watch Wrexham at 3 p.m. on a Saturday, and still fit in a trip to Old Trafford or Anfield for whenever TV dictates kick-off time in the Premiership.

Five minutes before the Chester train arrives, Irish is back on his mobile. 'The Frontline are coming up through the town now,' he says, visibly excited. Sure enough, police are soon holding all Wrexham fans behind a roadblock 100 metres from the station. They want the area cleared so that the English can pass.

'You move – especially you!' bellows a policeman in a half balaclava which masks most of his face. He's talking to Irish. The Chester fans spill off the train into the station car park where they're surrounded by police. 'Ing-er-land, Ing-er-land, Ing-er-land!' they sing, a mixture of Burberry clad lads and straight, scarf-wearing supporters. 'Sheepshaggers!' they shout in the direction of the Wrexham mob behind the police lines.

'North Wales,' respond the Wrexham fans. You hear Welsh spoken among some fans. 'We're proud to be Wrexham and we're proud to be Welsh,' says Chas. 'South Walians don't always have it. They call us English or even Scousers, but for us it's Wrexham first and Wales second.'

The police operation works impeccably, as the Chester fans are escorted down Mold Road into the away turnstiles. Five minutes later, the Wrexham fans are allowed to follow and they attempt to catch up, but like greyhounds chasing a rabbit, their target is always just out of reach.

Most of the Frontline stand in the section adjacent to the away end which is named after former chairman Pryce Griffiths, a local businessman who has kept Wrexham afloat for much of the last twenty-five years. Griffiths was a fan who helped build terracing before he became a director in 1977, then chairman between 1988–2002. Now a life president of the club, his popularity endures, although some Wrexham fans criticised him following the sale of his shares to Alex Hamilton, the despised former chairman.

Hamilton wanted to knock down Wrexham's Racecourse Ground, their home since 1872, and replace it with a shopping development. This was the venue for the first ever Wales international in 1877, and is the ground where Anderlecht, Manchester United, AS Roma, Porto, and Hadjuk Split turned up to play Cup Winners' Cup ties, even if they left as soon as they could afterwards. When protests put a stop to

Hamilton's plans, Wrexham slipped into administration and were hit with a ten-point deduction which saw them relegated to the league's basement division last season. Still, at least the relegation meant that Wrexham got to play Chester.

Like many rivals, both sides have more in common than they'd like to admit. Despite their proud histories, both have recently been threatened with extinction because of serious financial problems. 'Because both fans have suffered from dodgy chairmen, a lot of the hatred is now being replaced by closet respect,' says Chester fan Nigel Hutt. 'There are many on both sides who hope that both clubs survive their problems.' Jim Green agrees: 'I have the greatest sympathy for what Wrexham have gone through over the last eighteen months having been there myself. I truly hope that they get through it – so we can stuff them next season.'

The feeling, however, isn't always mutual. 'I'd rather Chester didn't exist at all,' says Wrexham fan Paul Baker. 'I despise the club and a city which is full of people who are full of themselves. At the very least, I want Chester to go down.'

In the weeks leading up to today's game, Chester, whose record transfer fee received is still the £300,000 that Liverpool paid for Ian Rush in 1980, have suffered an alarming slump, losing twelve games from fourteen and slipping from sixth to bottom of League Two – perilously close to the Conference league which they left as champions in 2004. You know a club is struggling when the players registered as numbers thirty-five and thirty-six are in the starting line-up.

Their current malaise is evident from their deflated, woeful performance in a first half dominated by Wrexham, who take a two-goal lead and see a penalty saved. The second Wrexham goal is greeted by a stirring chant, to the tune of 'Men of Harlech': 'Wrexham Lager, Wrexham Lager, feed me 'til I want no more, feed me 'till I want no more.' They even sing along in the posh seats.

'Wrighty, Wrighty what's the score?' they add, pointing in the direction of Chester manager Mark Wright. In his second spell as manager, the former Liverpool and England defender looks forlorn. 'Going down, going down, going down,' add the Wrexham fans, from behind advertising hoardings for roof trusses, printers, and plastics. 'Going bust,' retort the Chester fans in the Eric Roberts (Builders) stand, unfurling a 'Goatbusters' flag.

Chester's second-half performance is more spirited and they pull a goal back through Jake Edwards in the 89th minute. A chance of immortality on the banks of the River Dee beckons for Chester's Paul Ellender, but he squanders a last-minute chance from six yards out.

Wrexham fans applaud at the final whistle, waving flags of St David in the direction of the visitors. Yet the Chester fans congratulate their team, too – they've witnessed a spirit absent in recent months. The police helicopter reappears above. The Frontline leaves the ground and cram round the exit from the away end. Hoods go up and caps go down, but the police have got everything under control and start pushing them back. Even the shouts of 'stand!' from the frustrated hooligans are half-hearted.

As I wait for the Chester fans to be escorted past to the station, two lads clock my photographer. They're keen to talk, but don't want to give names. 'I'm 49,' says one. 'I did all the getting married, having kids, and foreign holidays, but I got bored. I missed this. You can't beat following Wrexham. We know Wrexham is a shit hole, but we're proud of what we've got, proud of the number of lads who follow the team for the size of the town. Chester is bigger and our support is twice theirs. They don't want a football team in Chester.'

The Chester fans are soon being herded past the Turf Hotel in the corner of the ground where we're standing. 'Sheepshagging bastards,' one shouts. A lone Wrexham lad lurches forward. 'Come on then,' he taunts. A policeman pulls him to one side for an explanation. 'Look, there's hundreds of them and about ten of you. My shield is not going to offer much protection is it?' The lad takes his point and walks away.

'The police have got it organised today,' notes the ageing hooligan. 'We'd absolutely slaughter them if we could get near, but I can remember Chester coming here and running us all over the place,' he says.

'No they didn't,' objects his mate. 'They've never run us.'

'They did.'

'Chester have never done Wrexham.'

'They have.'

This one, it seems, will run and run.

The Coldest Derby in the World
FC Zvezda v Metallurg-Kuzbass, May 2006

Welcome to Siberia, a frozen land where the football-mad locals glug vodka to stay alive and where neo-Nazis run wild in the stadia. I head east in a thick coat …

'Vodka,' replies Denis, raising a glass as I shiver in his shadow. I've just asked him how football fans in Siberia keep warm at games when the temperatures have been known to drop to −50°C. His tone is matter-of-fact, and it soon becomes clear that vodka is the answer to almost everything in this vast region of Russia.

'It can get extremely cold during games here,' chips in his friend and fellow Zvezda fan Anton, in the broken, heavily-accented English usually reserved for James Bond villains. 'But this is Siberia, our home, and we are accustomed. If it is −20, −30, −40, −50°C temperature, snowstorm and blizzard, we go to the match in any case.'

On the trail of the Coldest Game On Earth, I've travelled to watch FC Zvezda play FC Metallurg-Kuzbass in Irkutsk, Russia. It's a remote Siberian city nearer Beijing than Moscow and nine time zones from London. For seven months of the year, temperatures in the self-styled 'Capital of Siberia' are unimaginably cold. This winter has been particularly bleak, hitting as low as −45°C. And although Siberian football runs through the summer, being a football fan at either end of the season requires absolute commitment, a thick jacket and evidently a lot of vodka.

Ahead of the game, our hosts, Anton, 20, and Denis, 27, have taken us to a sports bar near Zvezda's Soviet-era stadium, the Palace of Labour. The beer tankards are full and Anton's confidence in his team is overflowing. 'Today we will win 3–0,' he predicts.

'We must fill our bellies before the game,' declares Denis, charging his glass. What follows is a non-optional Russian tradition of proposing a toast and necking a large vodka. With six of us round the table, the guest is invited to go first. 'To Zvezda winning,' I say, and then gulp. 'Fucking our enemies,' says Denis. Gulp. 'Scunthorpe United,' shouts Anton, remembering this writer's own allegiance. Gulp... Gulp... Gulp. Gulp. It is three hours until Zvezda kick off the first home game of the season, and spirits are sky high. Yet today's game almost never happened.

When Winston Churchill described Russia as 'a riddle wrapped in a mystery inside an enigma' he might have been talking about the football fixture list, best described as 'fluid'. The scheduled game on 24 April came and went without any football in Irkutsk. Enquiries about the first home game at the Zvezda administration office were met by the now familiar 'Russian shrug'. The team, unable to play in Irkutsk due to an ongoing dispute with the ground staff over the state of the pitch, were forced to play away from home. And it's easy to understand why. One week before the game there were still huge chunks of ice on the pitch. Two weeks before that the Palace of Labour was packed for an ice hockey match in temperatures of −15°C. The ground, it would be fair to say, is not at its best.

'It's never been this bad,' says Alex Alioshin, Zvezda's strait-laced press attaché. 'Ten years ago it would have been fine by the start of the season, now we just don't have the money to cope with the circumstances of Siberian football ... and neither do I.'

The effect of such extreme temperatures is just one of many problems, including cash crises, unfathomable distances and right-wing extremism that constantly beset teams, and fans, in Europe's farthest-flung league: Russian Second Division – Siberia East.

It's a seven-hour flight from Moscow to Irkutsk, across the Ural Mountains and far into Asia. As the plane lands at Irkutsk airport on a freezing morning, I look upon a Russia only a tiny percentage of its people have ever seen. Less than a third of Russia's population is sparsely spread out in an area that covers 70 per cent of the country. Siberia is as foreign to most dwellers of Moscow and St Petersburg as it is to us: one Spartak Moscow fan I meet, only half joking, refused to believe there was even football 'out there'. Its perception as a vast untamed frozen wilderness has changed little in the 300 years since the newly formed Russian state plundered it for fur. Today exploitation of gas and oil has replaced fur but roubles still struggle to filter down to most Siberians, many living in ugly Soviet monoliths that scar the landscape.

Football, as ever, provides an antidote. The sight of people kicking a ball around a park in temperatures of −30°C and deep snow is common, and goal posts spring up wherever there is a patch of relatively flat ground. And while winter is merely an annoyance to Siberian football fanatics, the arrival of the first game is perhaps more eagerly awaited than anywhere else on the planet. It is the symbolic end of winter.

'The beginning of the season was a sure sign of spring and renewal,' wrote former British Spartak player Jim Riordan in his book *Serious Fun*. 'The special harshness of the Russian winter made this pleasure more intense … the opening day of the season was always a joyous "holiday".'

The populace of Irkutsk, though, have to wait a couple more days to celebrate, for Zvezda are forced to play an away game in Nakhodka, 2,625 miles further along the Trans-Siberian Railway. Covering an expanse larger than the United States for away games is inescapable for the thirteen teams that constitute Siberia East. Next time you moan about travelling to Middlesbrough or Torquay for an away game, bear in mind that supporters of FC Irtysh-1946 Omsk would have a round-trip of more than 6,250 miles to see them play FC Okean Nakhodka. That's the equivalent of Liverpool playing a regular away game in Baghdad.

To make matters worse these games are crammed into the depressingly short Siberian summer that stretches from snow-covered May to a spit-freezing October. And with up to six games a month, this gruelling schedule is a drain on the players' energy and a massive burden on a club's finances.

While Chelsea benefit from the oligarch Roman Abramovich ploughing in millions made from exploitation of Siberia's great natural resources such as gas and oil, Russian teams are left struggling to pay players, fly teams across the country once a week and maintain the pitch (not that his roubles have managed to sort out the Stamford Bridge playing surface). But far from being vilified by the football fans I met, Abramovich is widely praised for the hundreds of millions of dollars he's ploughed into his home province of Chukotka.

As it is, promotion is seen as the way out of the football 'poverty trap' of the Russian Second Division, with a guaranteed bonus. Competition, however, is fierce. The Russian League is split into three divisions. The Premier League, with sixteen teams, is dominated by European Russian teams such as Spartak and Dynamo Moscow. The nationwide First Division has twenty-two teams, most based west of the Urals, a notable exception being Luch-Energia Vladivostok, a third of the way around the globe from St Petersburg. The eighty-one clubs in the Second Division are divided into five geographical zones: West, Centre, South, Ural-Povolzhye, and Siberia East. Only one club is promoted from each zone, and although Siberia East is by far the largest zone geographically, it boasts just thirteen clubs.

'I am 100 per cent sure that we will be promoted this season. And the season after we will be in the Premier League,' forecasts Anton, draining another vodka. Zvezda, he tells me, are a team with an attacking tradition and renowned for playing with flair. 'Our fans are also known for being very dedicated,' he says. 'We'll be singing and shouting very loudly, it's the first game so many people will come.'

At a training session at the Palace, I ask the coach Alexander Petrovich if he too expects to be promoted. 'Of course,' he laughs. And then his smile drops. 'We have to be promoted this season,' he says seriously.

The implication is obvious. Zvezda as a club are as precarious as the cars that drive across the melting ice on nearby Lake Baikal. Only two years ago local newspaper headlines were announcing 'Zvezda is over'. They struggled through the 2005 season and finished in a commendable fifth place, but their sponsor-free shirt was testament to the dire situation they and many Siberian clubs find themselves in. Only a last-ditch cash injection this winter from the football-loving provincial governor saved them.

It's unlikely that fans will recognise many faces at the game, however. 'In Siberia when players become good they go to play in Moscow or Europe,' says my translator and football fanatic Alexei Protassov. Over the winter Zvezda's star player, Maxim Zuzin, a personal friend of Ukraine President Viktor Yushchenko, signed for Dynamo Kiev. 'There is no incentive for good players to stay in Siberia,' continues Protassov. 'But to encourage home-grown talent, no foreigners are allowed to play in the second division.'

After days of waiting, posters begin to appear around the city announcing that Zvezda will play FC Metallurg-Kuzbass from Novokuznetsk on 4 May: a round trip of just 1,400 miles for the visitors.

By matchday the great thaw has begun in Irkutsk. Rain has fallen instead of snow for the first time in nine months; blackened ice and slush remain under the shadow of the famous wooden gingerbread houses that fight against gravity and Stalinist blocks. The ice on the pitch has been dumped in the street, and despite the bitter nights that keep parts of the city's mighty Angora River frozen, the day of the match is unseasonably warm at 5°C. The sun has brought out thousands of socialites celebrating the end of another hard winter. They hang around a giant Lenin statue (an omnipresent fixture in Russia) and under the towering floodlights of the stadium that dominate Irkutsk's skyline. The Palace of Labour is the first thing a traveller on the Trans-Siberian Railway – still an essential lifeline – sees as it trundles into the city.

Everyone seems to be drinking, but then it's always beer o'clock in Russia. Practically regarded as a soft drink, it's not rare to see besuited businessmen on their way to work knocking back the popular Baltika Three lager. Life expectancy for a man in Siberia is 59, and as a consequence of the alcoholism ravaging the country, the government banned booze from football games. Attendances – and therefore gate receipts – instantly plummeted.

Anton remembers nine years ago, when Zvezda were in the First Division, 20,000 fans filled the stadium. Last season barely a quarter of the seats were regularly taken and at the miserably cold final game less than 300 made the effort. 'Football games are not very well publicised in the media,' complains Denis. 'And now you can't drink at the game, it has got even worse.'

Today, with free entry for all, more than 7,000 fans go through the turnstiles, one of the highest attendances in eight years. The number of Metallurg-Kuzbass supporters, however, is nil – a far from unusual head-count for travelling fans. 'Fans just can't afford to pay for the flights,' Anton laments in the bar. 'The only team that bring fans to Irkutsk are fucking Barnaul.'

FC Dynamo Barnaul are the nearest Zvezda have to a local derby, being only 800 miles away, but the intense rivalry is based on a long-standing grudge dating back to a humiliating defeat in 1996 which knocked Zvezda out of the First Division. The following season Barnaul joined them in the lower rung, and consequent games were marred by violence. 'There were very many fights,' says Anton, 'but that's because everyone hates Barnaul.'

These days, the Palace of Labour can expect to host no more than twenty-five away fans from their sworn enemy; Anton believes most are too scared to visit. For all other visiting fans, however, he's always happy to extend the hand of friendship. 'If there are any away fans we will always be their friends, have a drink with them, they are comrades,' he says. 'Except Barnaul.'

As we leave the bar, Anton and Denis hand me a red and blue scarf embroidered with CSKA, a Moscow team. Like many Siberian teams there simply is not the cash to produce merchandise, so supporters buy products that are Zvezda's colours. When scarves and pendants do appear, they're manufactured by enterprising fans.

Outside in the still-chilly air, rare Russian smiles are out with the sun. Men, accompanied by a good number of women and children, expectantly pile through the grand gates. Above them is sculpted the communist hammer and sickle. Within the emblem is the Soviet 'Red Star' that gives Zvezda (literally 'Star') its name. Hawkers selling pistachio nuts and sunflower seeds are doing a brisk trade. A lone merchandise seller is not so successful with her fake Arsenal, Manchester United and CSKA scarves and pendants.

As one side of the stadium fills, it's reminiscent of old black and white photos of British matches in the 1920s and '30s: men are wearing black flat caps and black leather coats, common dress in Siberia. Many cragged faces, aged beyond their years, stare out at the empty terrace on the other side of the pitch. Most are chewing sunflower seeds and spitting out shells through gold teeth. Fans are much livelier under the scoreboard where I see Anton and Denis singing. I head over.

'Scunthorpe United! Scunthorpe United!' chant a sizeable chunk of the vocal Zvezda fraternity. When the song eventually subsides, a drunken fan makes a move towards me. Anton and Denis – who evidently told their friends who I support – yank him back. He punches their hands away, jumps across the tops of rotting wooden benches and arrives inches away from my face. Through his gold-toothed grin and with a whiff of vodka, he loudly exclaims in English, 'Scunthorpe United now favourite English team.'

It's an impressive gesture. Then he draws back and I notice a silver pendant bouncing around on his black T-shirt: it's a swastika. He's sporting black rolled-up Levi's held up with a bulldog belt buckle, steel toe-capped boots and a Lonsdale bomber jacket with tartan check lining. His head is shaven. Looking around there are perhaps fifteen other young fans sporting the same uniform.

'We are all white supremacists,' the skinhead continues in slurred broken English while bending down to reveal a swastika tattooed on his shin. 'But England has best skinheads, yes? Russia skinheads are number two. We buy all clothes that English skinheads wear.' Several more yobs crowd round firing questions at me about English football hooligans: 'Which team has the best skinheads?', 'What do they wear?', 'Do they carry knives?' I edge away as they perform the Nazi salute and bark 'Heil Hitler'. Anton comes over and apologises for their behaviour, evidently embarrassed. 'They are crazy,' he tells me. 'Every country has them but it is a big problem in Russia.'

The proliferation of skinheads in Russia is well-documented, but whereas the authorities in Moscow begin to copy the anti-hooligan laws of western European countries by banning the 'uniform', out in Siberia the police have no qualms with a man decorated with swastikas screaming 'Heil Hitler' in public.

A couple of weeks after returning to the UK, I meet football sociologist John Sugden, the author of *Scum Airways*. 'As people in these societies get a glimpse of affluent people around them through mass communication, their resentment fuels right-wing extremism,' he says. 'Football is a gathering place and it tends to have the good and bad, but in more volatile societies the bad becomes more manifest. In a lot of these societies they have very underdeveloped civic institutions; before the Communist Party was involved in every part of life, now there is a vacuum filled by gangsterism and extremism. [Russia president] Vladimir Putin could do worse than spend some time in Irkutsk's stadium; football becomes a good thermometer for society.'

I watch the rest of the match failing to avoid drunken Nazis. An early Metallurg goal quietens the crowd a little, but Zvezda equalise through an own goal in the second half. The well-oiled crowd go wild and the Zvezda hooligans burst into song once again: 'Hey Zvezda, let's score some goals/Three goals in the net of the pigs.'

The song is neither catchy nor prophetic. The match finishes 1–1, and as the fans trudge back to their warm homes, a chilly wind swirls around the stadium. It is definitely not the Coldest Game On Earth, but such is the uncertainty of Siberian football, two weeks later Zvezda and their fans shiver in horrendous conditions of –10°C and a blizzard. Anton excitedly e-mails me after the game: 'Zvezda was superb! 5–0! And very many chance for more goals! I very hope in this season we'll do First League, very very hope! We merit it. For real supporters weather – nothing! Football, only football.'

Love Island

B36 v HB, July 2006

When you're an archipelago in the remote North Atlantic, there's no escape from gloating rivals after a crushing defeat. Lucky, then, that everyone gets on so well.

'We have no choice but to get on,' says Faroe Islands international midfielder Mikkjal Thomassen. 'Faroese have to live together because people can't escape to another city – there aren't any.'

After three days in Tórshavn, the word's smallest capital city, home to just 16,000 weather-beaten souls, not one football fan has said a bad word about another team. The strongest insult, delivered from the stands as Jakob a Borg, the Faroes' best player, is about to take a free-kick against his former team, is that he's 'not a good guy'. So stunned is A Borg by this vitriol that he stops playing and turns to quiz the detractor.

Lazy commentators used to describe the Merseyside derby as friendly, yet in comparison, the Tórshavn derby between the Faroes two biggest clubs, HB and B36, is some kind of love-in. 'I'll tell you a little secret,' offers one inebriated B36 fan, 'sometimes we say that HB are snobs.' It's the strongest comment I hear in four days on the islands. If you're looking for spewing bile and seething passion, best avoid the friendly Faroes.

Since 1948, the Faroe Islands have been a self-governing region of Denmark, with their own parliament and flag, but until 1988, the islands barely registered on the radar of most football fans – nor, for that matter, anyone who wasn't a regular listener of Radio Four's shipping forecast. Yet recognition from FIFA that year and UEFA two years later (one of only four non-sovereign teams with UEFA membership, Scotland, Wales, and Northern Ireland being the others) changed Faroese football irrevocably. Since then, the exploits of the national team have given the island a disproportionately high profile in relation to its population.

It started like a dream, the Faroes stunning even themselves by winning their first competitive international, 1–0 against Austria in a European Championship qualifier in 1990. From there, the only way was down, yet despite Wales putting nine past them over two games in qualifiers for the 1994 World Cup, results have gradually improved with experience. They still tend to lose by the odd goal or three, but in recent years, they have clocked up a memorable 2–2 home draw with Scotland in 2002 and were only beaten 2–1 by Germany in Hanover in a qualifier for Euro 2004.

'Respect for Faroese football is getting bigger and bigger,' says Jakob i Storustovu, the island's only licensed football agent. 'It's coming. Teams now see a game against the Faroes as a real challenge. When we played the Czech Republic, they needed all three points to qualify for the World Cup. Towards the end, a Faroes player was lying on the pitch injured so another of our players put the ball out of play. Patrick Berger took the throw-in straight away when the player was still lying on the ground and they scored, winning the game 1–0. The referee didn't do anything about it.'

Yet the biggest change to Faroe Islands football has not been at international level, it has come from the knock-on effect of Faroese clubs qualifying for European competition, and earning far in excess of their rivals. 'We get 500,000 Danish Kroner (£46,000) just for playing one round of the UEFA Cup and you get around a million for each

The girl from Ipanema –
but there's seldom order
and progress when
Argentina meet Brazil.

Above They know each other as 'the chickens' and 'the shits'. River Plate fans warming up for their war showdown with rivals Boca Juniors.

Below The *Bonbonera* – or chocolate box – before Boca v River, with downtown Buenos Aires in the distance.

assions run high in South
merica, whether it's local
valries in the Copa
ibertadores or international
lashes between the mighty
razil and Argentina.

ight All-action Anderson and local hero
teven Gerrard during England's biggest
ame, Liverpool v Man United.

elow The curva hisses like a snake
efore the Milan derby in front of 80,000
t San Siro.

Above The Anfield Kop, Liverpool: not the best place to witness a last-minute Manchester United winner.

Right Forever friends: the Faroes' derby, with grass behind the pitch and plastic on it.

Just the two of us: Dinamo Zagreb fans vent their spiel against Hajduk Split.

Above Hoops and Irish tricolours. Celtic fans sing: 'You'll Never Walk Alone' during an Old Firm game.

Below Arsenal's continental stars celebrate in the north London derby against Tottenham Hotspur.

Above Loud and proud: Happoel's Ultras in Tel Aviv during the derby against Maccabi.

Right Kolkata sees crowds of up to 120,000 for East Bengal v Mohun Bagan.

Below Donkey Lashers, Michael Jackson and Tom Finney: Preston v Blackpool in the West Lancashire derby.

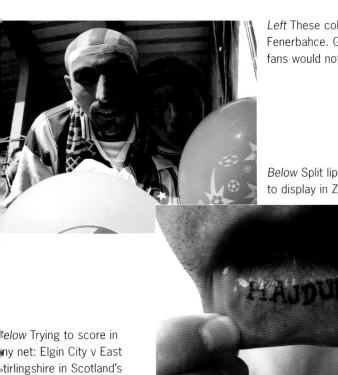

Left These colours don't run: Fenerbahce. Galatasaray fans would not approve.

Below Split lip: not advisable to display in Zagreb.

Below Trying to score in ny net: Elgin City v East tirlingshire in Scotland's ar north.

Above Tenerife's Brit friendly fans show their anti-Fascist colours.

Right Don't mention the whites: Barcelona and Madrid slug it out for supremacy.

Below The Essex Uniteds: Southend v Colchester at the cramped Roots Hall.

Champions League qualifier you progress through – that's just prize money,' says Steinfinnur Mittelstein, managing director of HB. 'It's huge money when you consider that we all work for free. We were close to playing Liverpool last season, but they drew TNS.'

Such riches have caused domestic problems. Players that had previously tied themselves to their local team out of loyalty found that they could supplement their incomes by earning a decent semi-professional wage at bigger clubs. They could further their careers by playing European football too, even if it usually meant a trip to Lithuania rather than Lisbon.

Not surprisingly, the smaller teams from villages in outlying islands – one club take a two-hour ferry journey to every away game – don't like the fact that their best players are snapped up by HB or B36, but the capital clubs have always been the best-supported and most successful.

Founded in 1904, HB – short for Havnar (the local word for 'Tórshavn') and Boltfelag (football) – are the older of the two. B36 arrived some thirty-one years later, formed by disenfranchised working-class supporters who disliked the perceived snobbishness of HB. They should be called B35 (after 1935, the year they were set up), but '6' is considered to be a more powerful number in the Faroes and, the fans say, B36 sounds better.

HB are the islands' most successful team with eighteen league titles – KI from Klaksvik, the second town of the Faroes with a population of 5,000, have seventeen – yet B36 are the reigning champions and, along with KI, were the first Faroese teams to play in Europe, in 1992–93.

The clubs usually get on, but the rivalry has its moments. In August 1991, B36 led the league by seven points before a game with HB. A couple of nights before the game, the HB players went out for a few beers. It was no surprise when B36 took the lead as expected, but it was when HB came back to win the game 8–2. After that, B36 imploded, picking up only one more point in their remaining games and losing the championship by one goal. If they had managed to keep the HB game to 7–2, they would have been champions. And that still smarts.

This season's derby coincides with World Cup quarter-final weekend. The shirts of the competing nations are on display in the window of Tórshavn's sport shop – no takers yet for the Ghana wristbands.

The league season used to run from April to September, but it was extended to ensure the players were fit for the crucial international games that are regularly played in March and April. The ten teams in the top division now play each other three times each in a twenty-seven-game league season (who gets the extra home game depends on the final table the previous season).

With the league out of synch with most of the rest of Europe, teams that qualify for the Champions League or the UEFA Cup can find themselves in the bizarre situation of being crowned champions in October yet not playing in European competition for another nine months. Changes may occur to bring the league into line with other countries, but winter football doesn't appeal to everyone.

Even today, in midsummer, drizzle drenches this isolated settlement from dawn until dusk – a long time given that the weak north Atlantic sun never truly sets.

It's always light in summertime Tórshavn; the sedate ambience is only disturbed by two summer cruise ships en-route to Iceland disgorging their elderly cargo into the narrow streets. The passengers conform to national stereotypes: the Americans are inquisitive and vigorously browse shops, the grinning Koreans take pictures, while a cluster of Spaniards stick closely together, looking puzzled and slightly anxious.

Such is the relaxed nature of these islands that the tourists are welcome to visit the prime minister's office, a tiny house with grass on the roof in traditional Faroese style (the sheep act as lawnmowers when the grass gets too long). Until recently, islanders could pop in and discuss issues with the PM. Now they have to go through the tiresome bureaucracy of making an appointment with his secretary. 'It's because some people were not always happy,' explains a local, vaguely.

Sidestepping the opportunity to meet the Faroese Tony Blair, a group of English tourists go in search of a bar to watch the Portugal–England game. Fifteen years ago they would have struggled – there were none, and limits were imposed on the imported alcohol from Denmark. Now, there are nightclubs which stay open until 5 a.m. and the Faroese brew their own beer, but most products are still imported. Cheap clothes and fleshpots can be found in Aberdeen, the nearest sizeable city, 200 miles to the south-east.

The Manhattan Bar is packed with a mixture of locals and tourists. Most of the locals are warming up for the derby tomorrow, but Oyvind Eysturoy is watching the England game. He's a fan of HB and Liverpool. 'Liverpool are the most popular foreign team here, the only one with a supporters' club,' he explains. 'It's partly because of their great teams in the '70s and '80s; and because of Danish players in the '80s like Jan Molby.'

Eysturoy's support for HB goes against a family tradition. 'All my family are B36 and my mum is on their board, but I'm HB, the rebel. B36 are our biggest rivals but there's never any violence between the fans. We are easy going people here.'

Jakob i Storustovu, the agent, is there too, reminiscing about how he became an agent by default after being a coach at B36. 'Clubs from Denmark and Norway started calling the players and making promises that they didn't keep,' he says. 'So players asked me to represent them. People thought I was crazy, that nobody would be interested in Faroese players. A couple of English clubs laughed and thought I was some kind of joker when I told them I was a Faroese agent, but one of them later called about a player.'

Storustovu now has twelve players abroad, most in Scandinavia, but others have been at Arsenal, Liverpool, and Manchester City, though none made the first team. He also attracts players to the Faroes from distant countries like Brazil, Nigeria, and the Ivory Coast. He sells the islands well. 'We have the things that a big city has yet we have nature too,' he says. 'Some people have never seen the ocean, but we live in the middle of it. I would like it to be a little bit warmer, but that has to be put into context – there is hardly any crime, children play in the streets and the economy is going up.'

Derby day dawns. With forty minutes to kick-off, the 5,000 capacity Gundadalur stadium is almost empty, but for the players warming up. One of the few watching is the injured Ingi Hojsted, a B36 player who joined Arsenal in 2002 as a trainee and later Birmingham City, where injuries limited him to forty-five minutes of reserve-team football.

Before long, the first of the 2,000 fans begin to arrive, taking a free match programme from a box by the turnstiles. Admission is about £7, while some fans are selling tickets for a sweepstake in which they have to predict the score. Where they go in the ground depends on who they support: HB and B36 share the council-owned stadium, but each club has its own stand which contains dressing rooms and fan facilities. Both stands are identical and are situated on the same side of the pitch, seating around 600. The majority view in the HB stand is that it's going to be tight – much like the league. The atmosphere is jovial, but there's no chanting.

The relative peace is broken by 'Football's Coming Home' bursting from the public address system as the teams take the field. As it's a B36 home game, both teams appear from the B36 stand – although the HB players changed in their own dressing room. A drummer begins playing in the HB stand, the common sense mentality evident in the harness he's strapped into – it would pass the strictest health and safety executive. A man with a formidable moustache says that his heart pumps for HB, then praises B36 for being 'a good club'. A minute's silence is held before kick-off in memory of those who have lost their lives in traffic accidents, before the players hold aloft a FIFA Fair Play flag.

The match is played at a fair old pace, the artificial surface sees to that. Before the first artificial pitch was laid in Gundadalur in 1986, teams had to play on sand, but these new surfaces have greatly assisted the development of Faroese football and it's now hoped that the fourth-generation of pitches will be accepted by UEFA and FIFA. It would help the national team. When they began taking part in international competitions in 1990, home games had to be played in Sweden because there were no grass pitches in the Faroes. With little flat land to build on, extreme measures were needed: in 1994, fifty tonnes of explosives were used to blow up a great mound of rock behind the village of Toftir (population 1,000) to make room for a pitch which would meet FIFA regulations.

The Toftir stadium held six times the village's population and visiting teams hated it. Arriving at the Faroes' tiny airport, the likes of Spain and Scotland were forced to drive for an hour around the islands' contours, through scattered settlements of simple housing, before boarding a ferry for a vomit-inducing forty-five-minute crossing. Although lashed by wind and waves, visitors can't fail to be impressed by the stunning scenery of jagged green peaks tumbling into the ocean – and the passion for football. Even the smallest villages have their own artificial football pitches.

By 1997, pressure had increased for Tórshavn to have a grass pitch capable of hosting international games. Plans were published showing grand designs for a new stadium adjacent to Gundadalur, but the end product was sadly different – think Milton Keynes national hockey stadium, only with three stands and without any shelter. If any national stadium should have a roof then it's in the Faroes, which averages fifteen wet days per month.

Fans prefer the adjacent Gundadalur. 'It's more enclosed and the atmosphere is better,' explains one. It's all relative, but with two open ends, one of which features a grassy knoll with wooden boxes for fans to perch on, it's hardly enclosed by British standards. A stream gushes behind one goal and sheep idly graze nearby.

The HB fans chant 'HB' and the B36 fans 'B36'. One lady at the front of the HB stand bangs a small drum and shouts encouragement. It's the mother of their number five. 'She's a very passionate lady,' someone explains. 'She even shouts at the referees if she disagrees with their decision, especially if they affect her son.'

She's quiet enough when B36 take the lead, though, more so when they score a second. In the neutral stand opposite a group of elderly men, supporters of both teams, sit together. One lives behind the ground and they all meet before each derby match for a beer. The B36 stand is understandably noisier, yet the fans are still nervous. 'HB are like the Germans, they always score,' explains one. But it's B36 who score next to make it 3–0. Then they get a fourth, a fifth, a sixth, all without reply.

'HB, HB,' chant the B36 fans in an ironic manner, while looking across to the HB stand. You sense they don't want to upset them too much, merely have a touch of fun at their expense. The HB fans are too busy trudging out of the ground to notice.

In the dressing room after the game, the B36 players celebrate by singing 'Football's Coming Home' in English. Most young Faroese speak English, as does their Nigerian striker Obele Okeke Onyebuchi. He started his career away from home in Poland, moving on to Serbia and Sweden. Then his agent arranged a move to the Faroes.

'Living here was very difficult at first,' he explains. 'People asked what the hell I was doing going to a place they had never heard of. You don't play on grass and you pick up injuries, but you get used to it and I'm happy to stay. It's very quiet here, but there's no corruption, the people are kind and trusting. People can leave their doors open and it's good if you want to have a family too – for education.'

Foreign players like Onyebuchi make around £2,000 a month, but can supplement their income by working, usually in fish factories. Fishing is king here: the fishing industry accounts for 97 per cent of the islands' exports while tourists tired of the island's natural beauty are encouraged to go on fishing trips – one company has even adapted Bill Shankly's most famous line in its promotional literature: 'Fishing isn't a matter of life or death … it's more important than that!'

In the bars of Tórshavn, the B36 fans are delighted with the 6–0 scoreline. One is sipping whisky and smiling. 'B36 means everything to me, but our rivalry is friendly,' he says. 'We shake hands after the game.' He's not a one-club man though. 'I'm a Tottenham fan too. It's because I have listened to the BBC for many years. I support Tottenham because of Jimmy Greaves. Tottenham played a UEFA Cup game in Iceland and I went to see them alone. People thought I was little crazy, but I have a great love for Tottenham Hotspur.' Unexpectedly, he bursts into song: 'Spurs are on their way to Wembley …' Another fan walks past, shouting that beating HB is better than sex.

Jakup Mork is a football writer for *Sosialurin*, the main Faroes newspaper with a circulation of between six and nine thousand copies. It has three football writers. With 5,000 registered players – over 10 per cent of the population – the people love their football, although the team names do take some deciphering, a bewildering array of acronyms: GI, NSI, KI, IF, VB/S, EB/S. It's not a good idea to read the league table after a few beers.

Mork played for B36 until he was 24. 'That helped when I started in sports journalism because I knew most of the players, but it also hindered because people thought I was biased towards B36.'

Another man approaches. 'Where are you from?' he asks.

'Manchester,' I reply.

'Manchester itself or Bolton, Bury, Macclesfield, Wigan, Stockport, Rochdale or Wigan?' he demands, listing every football league team in Greater Manchester.

Heri Simonsen is the stadium announcer, part-time comedian and font of Faroese knowledge. After an introduction to the Faroese Victoria Beckham – 'Yes, but I'm prettier,' jokes a player's wife who is indeed better looking – Simonsen offers me a lift back into town. Five Live is on his car radio. 'This is one reason why British football is so popular on the Faroe Islands,' he says. But it goes much further back than that, in part to the time when The *Arsenal Stadium Mystery* film was shown in the islands in 1940 – 'Many older men in their eighties still support Arsenal because of that,' explains Simonsen. But the real reason British football became popular, he says, was the war. 'On 9 April 1940, our motherland Denmark was occupied by the Nazis, but we were lucky because three days later the British rescued us from a hostile occupation.

'Faroese ships sailed to Grimsby, Hull, and Aberdeen to support the British fish market throughout the war, losing 250 sailors to mine attacks – about one per cent of the population. On 25 April 1940, sixteen days after the occupation of Denmark and thirteen days after the friendly Allied occupation of the Faroes, Winston Churchill proclaimed: "All Faroese ships are to paint the Faroese flag on the side of their ships so that Allied forces can differ between the Danish ships and the Allied Faroese ships."'

Simonsen, an anglophile, mimics Churchill's unmistakeable tones. 'Twelve thousand soldiers came here,' he adds. 'As well as building the airport, the soldiers played a lot of football and there was a regular tournament between a united team of Tórshavn comprising of B36 and HB players and the various British brigades and divisions. It was known as the War Cup, except in 1944 when there was a shortage of footballs. They say that the Faroese game improved a lot during the war.'

In fact, the first Faroese league championship was held in 1942. 'Many Faroese people started listening to the BBC during the war and never stopped. They became interested in British football. Then the

Manchester United disaster and the great Liverpool teams of the '70s and '80s added to that interest.'

In Café Natur, Toreshavn's smartest bar, two hours after the derby, Jakob a Borg, the closest the Faroes have to a superstar, is notable by his absence. A Borg, who had trials with Watford and Liverpool, caused a stir when he moved from B36 to HB. It was so bad that B36 asked for the return of his club tuxedo. A Borg sells cars for a living and is a big fish in, well, a very small Atlantic pond. Everyone knows him, but then everyone knows everyone. When we speak the day before the game, *I* suggest meeting for a quiet coffee. A Borg smiles. 'We can have a few beers after the match tomorrow,' he says.

He clearly hadn't banked on a 6–0 derby defeat against his former club. His mobile rings and rings. It's understandable that he doesn't want to come, especially as the café is now B36 territory. Downstairs, victorious fans sit around two tables, while pretty girls fill the rest of the bar, perhaps hoping to catch the eye of the players sat upstairs. There's a dozen of them, honed semi-professionals slowly sipping beer.

One is Mikkjal Thomassen. When he's not playing in midfield for his club B36 against B68, EB, HB, or VB, or for his country against the likes of Michael Ballack, Thomassen is a detective in the Faroes police. He spends his days trying to unravel what few crimes the islands' 48,290 population manage to commit. Occasional sex offences – there's one story of a man who impregnated his daughter-in-law – and domestic disputes punctuate the quiet life on this eighteen-island archipelago where locksmiths go short of work. Football has been good to him. 'I've travelled all over Europe playing,' he says. 'But it's not my number one priority. My work and family are.'

His team-mates eschew a potentially dangerous third pint. All have jobs to go to in the morning, train four nights a week and have a trip to Malta for a Champions League qualifier in four days. They don't know anything about their Maltese opponents and don't expect to find out anything ahead of the game.

As the players head home for bed, it's still light outside. Watching them go, a B36 director beams from ear to ear. He can't stop thinking about the 8–2 loss a decade and a half ago. 'We've never avenged that defeat,' says one B36 director. 'Until today.'

How will he celebrate? I ask, hoping for sordid tales of debauchery. 'I think we'll have some coffee and play poker,' he smiles. 'But no more than that.'

Boys from the Black Country

West Bromwich Albion v Wolverhampton Wanderers, October 2006

Pride, derision, hatred, casual violence, and gang warfare: it's not always fun and games when the Baggies host Wolves.

It's a beautiful Sunday morning in the Black Country. The sun is shining, the birds are singing. It's the type of bright, fresh start to a day that makes you want jump out of bed, take the dog for a walk or stroll to the local corner shop to pick up the newspapers. Easy like Sunday morning. But today is going to be far from easy for the 600 officers of the West Midlands police force who have just arrived outside the Hawthorns, home of West Bromwich Albion.

At 8 a.m., four hours before the Baggies take on their arch rivals Wolverhampton Wanderers, the police are taking no chances. The line of riot vans stretches down Halfords Lane, as far as the eye can see, and next to each one, a team of men and women are readying themselves for action. First the stab vests go on, then the visors and truncheons are secured in their place, while the CS gas canisters are given the once over before being slotted back into their pouch.

Then, sheets of A4 paper are handed out with twenty-eight mug shots of mainly skin-headed men – photos of local hooligans currently on police banning orders. The officers are studying the pictures intently, as if cramming in some last-minute revision before an important school exam. The crackle of police radios and the muffled sound of dogs barking from inside the vans add to the feeling of unease. This isn't what Sundays were made for.

'Bloody hell,' remarks one passer by in a deep Black Country accent, 'there are more coppers here than there are troops in Iraq!' In the build up, the local media has been in derby frenzy, recounting matches from the past, speaking to players and ex-players from both sides, while in the offices and factories of the West Midlands, rival supporters have been baiting each other all week in largely good-natured banter. But more sinister taunts and threats have been made on some unofficial supporters' websites and, given the history of this fixture, the huge police presence is entirely justified.

The West Midlands isn't short of football rivalries, from Walsall in the north to Coventry in the south, there are six professional clubs, but today really is a special one. It's the 150th Black Country derby and the first time West Brom and Wolves have met in five years.

In the Hawthorns press room, thirty minutes before kick-off, the scene is a familiar one. Journalists are tapping away on their laptops, photographers are cleaning and tweaking their various lenses and when a plate of bacon butties and pies is brought out, it's like feeding time at the zoo.

Munching on a meat and potato pie and pondering today's match is a familiar face, comedian Frank Skinner, who's chatting to *Match of the Day* presenter and fellow Baggie Adrian Chiles. 'I honestly think we could humiliate them today,' says Skinner with a typically mischievous grin. 'I don't know,' says Chiles cautiously, 'The Wolves have still yet to get us back for doing them in 2002. One of these days they're going to make us pay for that, I just know it.' Chiles is referring to the climax of the 2001–2002 season in the old second tier when Wolves blew an eleven-point lead at the top of the table and missed out on promotion to the Premiership, while West Brom won seven of their last nine matches to secure their place in the top flight after a sixteen-year absence. Chiles refers to this as his greatest ever moment as a Baggies fan.

I politely interrupt the conversation to get these two West Brom 'legends', albeit of the celebrity variety, to give us their take on the Black Country derby. Given that Skinner once declared he'd like to buy Wolves' home ground Molineux and turn it into a car park and Chiles has been stuffing his Albion allegiances down the throats of television viewers for the past decade, it's unlikely to be an objective account. 'Basically, they're scum and we're not,' says Chiles sarcastically, before striking a more serious note. 'Roughly speaking, the northern part of Birmingham is predominantly Aston Villa, the south is largely Birmingham City, whereas the Black Country is interwoven with fans from both Wolves and Albion. They live together, work together, families are divided between the two teams, it's a big deal.

'I remember presenting the morning business show a few years ago and at the end I said, 'Just one football score for you, West Brom 1 Wolverhampton Wanderers 0.' It was juvenile, but I just thought, why not? Six or seven years later Wolves beat us and I got a random e-mail from an irate viewer saying, 'I bet you won't be telling people about the fucking score this time, will you Chiles?' He clearly hadn't forgotten how I pissed him off all those years ago and wanted to shove it down my throat. Fair enough I suppose.'

Skinner adds his twopenneth: 'I think when you move out of the area though, you do lose the feeling for the derby. I would take promotion to the Premiership over anything else, but I've got a mate who genuinely says he would rather do the double over Wolves, and he's not the only one. I just don't understand that. Also, for me, the big rivalry has always been against Aston Villa, that's what I remember, although my mate says that's because I'm a "foreigner", I don't live here any more, so I don't understand. Maybe he's right.'

Not necessarily. Skinner's view that Aston Villa are the main adversary of the Baggies is a widely held one – and not just because Villa Park is less than four miles from the Hawthorns, whereas Molineux is some thirteen miles away. John Homer is the chairman of West Brom's official supporters club and believes there is a generational divide between Baggies fans. 'The older generation of West Brom fans,' he explains, 'and I'm talking about people who are 45 and older, tend to see Villa as the main rival, whereas the younger supporters, those who first started watching in the 1980s, would tend to say it's Wolves.'

For West Brom, the 1950s proved a fertile period for rivalries to flourish with both of their West Midlands neighbours. In 1954, under progressive coach Vic Buckingham, the Baggies won the FA Cup and were heading for a historic double until Wolves, coached by former player Stan Cullis and captained by England international Billy Wright, pipped them in the league to claim their first ever championship.

Villa–Albion spats were also common in the 1950s. In 1957, Villa defeated West Brom in an FA Cup semi-final replay and went on to win the trophy for the seventh time in their history. Two years later, the Baggies got their revenge, humiliating their neighbours 4–1 at Villa Park, a result that contributed to the Villans being relegated from the top flight for only the second time.

Search even further back into the history books and it's the Villa–Albion rivalry that comes to the fore. In 1887, at the Kennington Oval, Villa won their first major trophy, beating West Brom 2–0 in the FA Cup final. In 1892 they met in the final again, only for their fortunes to be reversed, West Brom winning 3–0. And three years after that, a third FA Cup final between the sides was settled by a goal inside the first minute for Villa.

West Brom legend Tony 'Bomber' Brown certainly fits into the 45+ category John Homer refers to. Brown still holds the club record for appearances and goals, scoring 218 times in 574 matches between 1961 and 1980. He shares Homer's view that the men from Villa Park remain the team to beat. 'The Black Country derby is always special,' he says. 'One of my first derbies was at Molineux in 1967 in front of 50,000 fans. The atmosphere was amazing and the game finished 3–3, so it will always mean a lot to me. But for me, games against the Villa were always the big one. We played against each other so many times and historically we've played Villa more than any other team.'

That's true, but only just. The two sides have met 152 times, West Brom with fifty victories, Villa with seventy-one and thirty-one draws, while before today, Wolves and West Brom have locked horns 149 times.

Yet in more recent times, the Wolves–West Brom rivalry has taken on greater significance, and the most acrimonious and hostile of the Black Country battles took place in what are widely regarded in these parts as 'the Steve Bull years'.

Rarely has one player been so closely linked with the fluctuating fortunes of his club as Steve Bull (when we say 'his club', we are of course talking about Wolves, though he supported Liverpool as a boy). And never has one club regretted selling one player to a local rival as much as when West Brom sold Bull to Wolves. The boy from Tipton, roughly halfway between the two clubs, not only saved Wolves, he re-ignited their rivalry with the Baggies. 'Bully' joined the Baggies in 1985, but lasted less than a year at the Hawthorns, before being sold to the Gold and Blacks, along with Andy Thompson, for a combined fee of £64,000.

'I scored three goals for the Baggies in five games', he recalls in his harsh Black Country brogue. 'I was 21 at the time and felt I was just starting to prove myself in the First Division. Then Ron Saunders called me into his office and told me I didn't have a good enough first touch and he was getting rid of me. I was gutted. I arrived at Molineux and the place was a complete shit hole. Tiles were falling off the wall, there were cockroaches in the changing room and I just thought to myself "Jesus Christ, what have I come to here?"'

Bull's fall from grace mirrored that of the club he had joined. In the 1950s, Wolves were among Europe's elite. Real Madrid, Celtic, and Spartak Moscow all suffered defeats at the hands of Stan Cullis's side, but it was the December 1954 victory over Hungarian champions Honved that led the *Daily Mail* to declare them as 'Champions of the World'. That night, in front of 55,000 fans at Molineux, the visitors, who included five of the Hungarian national side that a year earlier had humiliated England 6–3 at Wembley, were beaten 3–2 thanks to two late Roy Swinbourne goals. Wolves went on to win the league title in 1958 and 1959 and the FA Cup in 1960, but the good times didn't last.

Twenty-five years later, after three consecutive relegations, Wolves found themselves in the Fourth Division for the first time in their history. But if 1986 was very much Wolves' nadir, it was also when Steve Bull joined the club and when the road to redemption began.

In Bull's first two full seasons he scored 102 goals as Wolves won the Fourth Division and Third Division titles. A year later, they narrowly missed out on a place in the Second Division play-offs and what would have been a unique third successive promotion, but the revival was complete.

'Imagine what would have happened if we hadn't sold Steve Bull to them,' says John Homer with a sincere sound of regret still piercing his voice. 'They were so close to oblivion, they were heading out of the Football League and Bully single-handedly saved them.'

Due to Wolves' protracted spell in the doldrums however, the two sides went without playing each other for nearly five and half years. That's not to say that sentiments surrounding the Black Country derby were being neglected. 'When Wolves had their massive lean spell,' says Homer, 'their supporters took some real ribbing from the West Brom fans and I think that caused a massive amount of ill-feeling. It was always going to be a massive game when we eventually met them again.'

That moment came on 15 August 1989 and, as expected, it was a defining moment in the rivalry. In his first game back at the Hawthorns, Bull inevitably scored in Wolves' dramatic 2–1 victory.

Five months later at Molineux, Wolves did the double over the Baggies. It was the start of a new and ugly phase of enmity between the two Black Country clubs.

The worst case of violence took place in 1994 after West Brom beat Wolves 2–1 at Molineux. Skirmishes between both sets of fans took place throughout the game and forty-six fans were thrown out and arrested. At the end of the match a mob of 400 Wolves fans blocked in Baggies supporters as they tried to leave the ground. Mounted police were called in to break them up, only to be pelted with bricks and stones. Several police officers were injured.

Rivalries between the various hooligan firms were particularly intense during the 1990s and are still going strong today. 'There's only two big mobs in the West Midlands – Wolves and Birmingham,' says 'Gilly' a member of Wolves' Yam Yam Army. 'You could write on the back of a postage stamp what the West Brom boys have done, they're nothing, even Walsall have done them a couple of times.'

Unsurprisingly, members of West Brom's Section Five firm disagree, 'That's rubbish and they know it,' says 'Kola' disdainfully. 'They're the type of firm that beat up tourists and disabled people, that's what they're like.'

'Kola' is referring to an incident in London on 2 October 2004. After a league match against West Ham, a gang of booze-fuelled Wolves hooligans, who hadn't even attended the game, went on the rampage through Leicester Square, attacking innocent bystanders. Passers by were chosen at random and punched and kicked to the floor. One of the victims was disabled. Fourteen of the perpetrators were later convicted and jailed for a combined total of eleven years.

The incident ensured that, for today's Black Country derby, the worst hooligans remain behind bars and out of harm's way. That's not to say the police are being complacent. 'A lot of the Internet message boards have had West Brom fans taunting the Wolves fans saying that all their "top boys" won't be there on Sunday,' says Mark Douglas from the *West Midlands Express & Star*. 'I think the fear is that the Wolves fans will see this as a challenge and they're going to come looking for trouble.'

With so much local pride at stake, you would assume the teams understand the importance of the fixture, but the truth is that not a single player from either of today's sides has played in a Black Country derby before. Wolves' on-loan winger Darren Potter admits that he wasn't even aware the game against West Brom was a derby until recently. Only three of his team-mates were born in the West Midlands, while West Brom are unable to boast any Black Country natives. The last local boy to score in a derby was Bull, a decade ago.

The two coaches, Wolves' Mick McCarthy and West Brom's Tony Mowbray, are also derby virgins. For the latter, it will be his first match in charge since leaving Hibernian, so unsurprisingly the words 'baptism' and 'fire' have been cropping up all week in the local press. Given that the teams are third and fourth in the league table, 'six-pointer' is another cliché doing the rounds.

That said, most people in these parts, including Bully, believe that Mick McCarthy's side have been achieving results above and beyond the ability that the sum of their parts would suggest. Wolves released fourteen players in the summer and, in his first press conference at Molineux back in July, McCarthy reminded people that 'the MM on my tracksuit doesn't stand for Merlin the Magician'.

West Brom, on the other hand, have largely retained the squad that was narrowly relegated from the Premiership last season, adding John Hartson and Kevin Phillips to their strike force. In the past, thanks to the money of owner Sir Jack Hayward, Wolves have always been regarded as the wealthy neighbour in these parts, but with the Baggies flush from spending three of the last four seasons in the Premiership, there's been something of a role reversal.

'Albion fans used to always go on about how we're big-time Charlies,' says Wolves fan John Lalley, who writes a weekly column in the *Express and Star*. 'They used to bang on about Sir Jack's money and how we think we've got a divine right to be in the Premiership, but if anything, it's the other way round now. What really rankles with me is that Wolves fans are criticised for being impatient and for having massive expectations, but since 1984 we've spent only one season in the top flight and in that season we were relegated before the smoke from the starting pistol had evaporated. So work that one out?'

Going into this clash, West Brom are clear favourites and inside the Hawthorns ten minutes before kick-off there's a buoyant mood among the home fans. The police have done everything they can to sanitise the atmosphere – the 12 p.m. kick-off, the banning of pubs from selling alcohol until 6 p.m. – but when the Wolves team is read out over the PA, ear-splitting whistles and boos let the 3,000 visitors know just how unwelcome they are.

The first five minutes of the match is typical derby fare, more a game of head tennis than football. West Brom's Jonathan Greening is booked after ten minutes for a nasty lunge on Rohan Ricketts and a minute later the former Man United and Middlesbrough midfielder further endears himself to the Albion fans, but in far more emphatic style. Jason Koumas picks up the ball on the left hand side of the penalty area and squares it to Greening, who takes a touch, then smashes the ball home from just inside the box. 'One-nil, to the Al-bi-on' and the one line of policemen that has so far sepa-rated the Wolves fans from the rest of the crowd quickly becomes two.

Sixteen minutes later the scoreline also doubles, Diomansy Kamara heading in Martin Albrechtsen's right-wing cross. Cue the Baggies' famous 'Boing, Boing' celebration, which sees the vast majority of the 26,000 crowd bouncing up and down dementedly. It's an impressive, gleeful sight.

Wolves dominate the second half, but fail to make any clear-cut chances. Then, with twenty-five minutes to go, striker Nathan Ellington is replaced by John Hartson. Seeing the former Welsh inter-national play these days is like watching widescreen TV, but Hartson is always up for a piece of the action, especially on derby day. Within ten minutes of coming on, he clatters Rob Edwards and then, when Kamara is brought down by Mark Little in the penalty box, wrestles the ball from the Senegal international and smashes it in from twelve yards: 3–0. Boing, Boing; Boing, Boing.

It's not quite the humiliation Frank Skinner was predicting, but it's enough for many Wolves fans to make an early exit. Just before they do though, there's enough time for Baggies fans to throw in a quick 'Are you watching Stevie Bull?' He's not, as it happens: claiming that he 'didn't want any hassle', he's chosen to stay at home. Given the final scoreline, the most he would have got from the Albion fans is a heap of good-natured piss-take, similar to that which will be replicated throughout the workplaces of Dudley, Tipton, Bilston, and beyond in the coming weeks.

'The third goal gave the scoreline a bit of a gloss,' says Mick McCarthy after the game. 'The West Brom fans are the ones who can go to work tomorrow and have a good gloat. But I thought it was a great match, a great atmosphere and that's what football should be all about with a full stadium and lots of passion.'

At full-time, a section of Wolves fans rip up some seats in the away end and, in all, thirteen arrests are made, but given the fears leading up to the fixture, the police operation can only be deemed a success.

'I think it was a good thing that we didn't play each other for five years,' reflects Wolves fan John Lalley. 'It needed the sting taken out of it because things were getting really nasty, but the match was played in a great atmosphere, there was hardly any trouble and I thought it was a triumph for the fixture. Maybe now we can move back to 3 p.m. kick-offs.'

Or maybe not. That there was little trouble was in part down to the 'Leicester Square Fourteen' being holed up at Her Majesty's pleasure. Police surveillance and other covert operations have also successfully clipped the wings of the various hooligan groups. 'It's like *Big Brother* now,' says 'Kola' of West Brom's Section Five firm. 'There's surveillance everywhere and you can't get away with anything. You can get put inside for conspiracy to cause trouble these days. I'm 38 with three kids and the stakes are just too high.'

'Gilly' of Wolves' Yam Yam Army firm is convinced the police have a 'talker', an informant inside one of the firms, such is their ability to anticipate potential flashpoints. 'A couple of years ago we'd arranged to meet up with a rival gang in a pub on the Birmingham Road, but the cops were there waiting for us. You can't go looking for trouble these days because you won't find it, your best chance is to just stumble across it.'

Any notion that suggests the spectre of hooliganism is a fading force in the West Midlands should quickly be dispelled, however. The overcrowding crisis which has hit the UK prison service means the 'Leicester Square Fourteen' will all be released by the New Year, less than four months after being convicted and having served less than half their original terms. All of them, and the large majority of known hooligans in the Black Country, are subject to banning orders which prevent them from attending any football matches, but there are ways and means to avoid detection and most trouble usually takes place away from the stadium anyway.

And that's not all. 'We've got some good young ones coming through,' says 'Gilly', and he's not talking about the Wolves youth team. 'We've got some lads who are as young as 15 who are right lunatics. They've got no fear and they showed that when we went to Cardiff the other week.' It doesn't bode well for the future, or the return fixture at Molineux on 11 March.

For the majority of fans though, they're just happy to battle over local bragging rights. The only problem for Adrian Chiles tonight is that there aren't many Wolves fans in BBC Sport's London office. Just as well then, that eight hours after West Brom's comprehensive derby victory, he's presenting *Match of the Day 2* with an audience of a couple of million. At the end of the show, pundit Alan Hansen asks Chiles 'Anyway, why are you so happy tonight?' in a sardonic, stilted tone.

'Well,' says Chiles with a smug grin, 'my team won today, West Brom beat Wolves 3–0.' Let the abusive e-mails flow.

Love and Hate
Hajduk Split v Dinamo Zagreb, September 2006

Teams from Belgrade were once the common foe, but the break up of Yugoslavia left Croatia's big two having to hate each other. It didn't take them long …

It's like a scene on the French Riviera. Expensive yachts, drenched in sunshine, bobbing up and down in the bay in front of the palm tree-lined promenade, with its packed cafes and their overworked espresso machines. But this isn't the Cote d'Azur, it's the Riva in Split, Croatia, a cheaper, less pretentious version of France's Mediterranean coast.

Take a closer look at the people sipping cappuccino and sparkling water and you'll notice that an inordinate number are wearing football shirts: Hajduk Split shirts to be precise. From pensioners walking their dogs to babies in prams, the crisp white jersey with the club's distinctive red-and-white chequered crest is everywhere. Not many of the people enjoying their Sunday afternoon on the Riva will be going to tonight's match, however. Instead, they'll be watching on the dozens of big screens that the cafes have had specially installed – it's the safest place to be when Hajduk take on their bitter rivals Dinamo Zagreb.

A five-minute walk in the direction of Hajduk's Poljud Stadium shows why. The Stari Plac is the club's old ground and today houses the headquarters of the Torcida, Hajduk's hardcore supporters. The contrast with the atmosphere on the Riva couldn't be starker. Five hours before kick-off, 500-plus fans are already gathered, drinking beer, lighting flares, and burning blue shirts with the letter 'D' on them. The singing is loud too, though there's little variety, the words 'fuck', 'Dinamo', and 'Zagreb' appearing in virtually every chant. A donkey draped in Hajduk colours is paraded around the sweaty, beer-sodden street, as fans cheer and maul the poor animal like a stripper at a stag party, yet despite the raucousness, there are few police present – the majority are at the stadium, awaiting the arrival of 2,000 Dinamo Zagreb supporters.

I ask one Hajduk fan if he's expecting trouble. 'Yes,' he says hopefully, 'I think so', and given the recent history of this fixture, his optimism is well founded. Few derbies in the Balkans, arguably anywhere in Europe, are as explosive as Dinamo versus Hajduk, with violence marring every single match. But it wasn't always so …

Slaven Bilic is in an awkward position. As head coach of Croatia, the former Everton and West Ham defender has to be diplomatic about the biggest match in the domestic calendar, but given that he joined Hajduk at the age of nine, it's not easy. That said, when Bilic played against Dinamo before the break-up of Yugoslavia in the early 1990s, matches between Croatia's two most successful clubs were one big, patriotic, love-in. 'The games were like a big celebration,' explains Bilic, in his intriguing half-Scouse, half-Cockney English accent. 'It was the only chance Croats had to make an expression of our nationality. The fans sang the same songs, it was fantastic.'

Back then the enemy was Serbia and anyone and anything that emanated from Belgrade, particularly Red Star and Partizan. Indeed fans of Hajduk and Dinamo, in an expression of allegiance with their Croatian 'brothers', would often attend each other's matches if they were playing opponents from the Yugoslav capital. Supporters from both clubs enlisted in the Croatian Army and Police Force and fought and died in Croatia's War of Independence between 1991 and 1995, while both sets of fans claim to have acted as a catalyst in the move towards civil war.

Early in 1990, with nationalist fervour simmering, Hajduk were at home to Partizan Belgrade. With ten minutes to go, the hosts went 2–0 down. 'At that time,' explains Bilic, 'the mood in the country was very difficult. Yugoslavia was on the verge of breaking up and tensions were very high. After we conceded the second goal, hundreds of our fans broke down the perimeter fences and ran onto the pitch. They chased the Partizan players, but they didn't beat them like many people said.'

Far more violent, and significant, was the match between Dinamo Zagreb and Red Star Belgrade on 13 May 1990. For many, the events that day symbolised the start of the disintegration of the Yugoslav Federation. Two weeks earlier, Franjo Tudjman had been elected as President of Croatia on a fiercely nationalist ticket, vowing to lead the republic to independence. For Red Star's visit to Dinamo's Maksimir Stadium, violence seemed inevitable. In fact, much of what happened seems to have been pre-meditated: rocks had been stockpiled, while fans used acid to burn away security fences. It's widely believed that Red Star fans actually started the trouble by ripping up seats and throwing them onto the pitch, but when the Serb-dominated police force failed to take action, Dinamo fans invaded the pitch and running battles with the law ensued.

As the police laid into the Dinamo supporters, the players were enraged, none more so than Zvonimir Boban. Amid the chaos, the Dinamo captain simultaneously jumped up, kicked and punched a policeman before being dragged away. Red Star players had to be rescued from the rioting by police helicopters, while a total of 138 police officers and fans were injured. Boban's actions earned him legendary status in Croatia and a six-month ban from the Yugoslav national team, causing him to miss the 1990 World Cup, but he insists he has no regrets: 'It was the best thing I've ever done. I had to defend our people and I wanted to fight the injustices that were being done that day. The frustrations that had built up for so many years just exploded.'

After all they had been through as allies – on the football pitch and the battlefield – how did Dinamo and Hajduk become such bitter enemies? One theory suggests that after the break-up of Yugoslavia and the formation of independent football leagues, the two clubs were left with no obvious enemy, so a new rivalry had to be invented. With Dinamo and Hajduk accounting for fourteen of the first fifteen Croatian championships, football was the obvious hook to hang it on, but very rarely does a rivalry based solely on football produce such bile and bitterness. Other factors are usually at work, and this case is no exception.

'When Croatia became independent,' explains Split-based jour-nalist Zdravko Reic, 'Zagreb became the capital and we reverted to the old-style communist system of centralist government. So we went from centralist control from Belgrade to centralist control from Zagreb. If you want to get a good education you have to go to univer-sity in Zagreb, if you want to get a good job you have to go to Zagreb. I pay my taxes here in Split and all my fucking money goes to Zagreb, that's what pisses us off.'

Socio-economic data would appear to back up Reic's claim – nearly a quarter of Croatia's 4.5 million population lives in Zagreb and unemployment there is low, whereas Split's two major industries, tourism and shipbuilding, suffered immeasurably as a result of the war. Reic's final argument, though, takes some beating. 'In 2005 Croatia hosted the World Beach Volleyball Championships,' he says, indignantly. 'So, given that the Adriatic coast has some of the most beautiful beaches in the world and Zagreb is 100km from the sea, where do you think they hosted the tournament? In fucking Zagreb! They took the sand from Split and flew it up to Zagreb – unbeliev-able!'

Unsurprisingly, the perception of centralist rule from Zagreb has also affected the politics of the national team. The President of the

Croatian Football Federation is Vlatko Markovic, a former coach of Dinamo Zagreb, and the main reason why Croatia haven't played a competitive home match outside the capital since 1997. Markovic is on record as saying the players prefer playing in Zagreb and, given that they've never lost a competitive match in the Maksimir Stadium (England being the latest victims), it's a stance that is difficult to argue against. Even so, it irks the football-loving public of Croatia's second biggest city. To appease them, four months before Croatia were to take part in Euro 2004, the national team played a friendly against Germany in Split's Poljud Stadium, but the Torcida asked locals to boycott the game and demanded the Federation start hosting some competitive matches outside Zagreb. Only 12,000 fans turned up at Hajduk's 35,000-capacity stadium. Their demands continue to be ignored.

Journalist Dejan Bauer, a colleague of Zdravko Reic based in Zagreb, offers an alternative view. 'In Zagreb, we have a saying, "When it's raining in Split, Zagreb is to blame".' Bauer stops short of saying people from Split are lazy and have a chip on their shoulder, but the inference is clear. 'Let's just say Zagreb is near Vienna, everything is very organised and efficient, whereas in Split the people have a very "southern" or "Mediterranean" attitude.'

Slaven Bilic is one of the few people I meet who gives a balanced assessment. 'Both Zagreb and Split are great cities,' he says. 'Zagreb is more like London: it's big, people are busy, always working and you never get to see your friends. I live on the beach in Split and my assistant coach, [former Derby star] Aljosa Asanovic, lives at the other end of town. It takes me six minutes to drive to his house. When you live in Split you can see your best friends four of five times every day. The two cities are just very different.'

The merit and commitment of Hajduk's and Dinamo's hardcore support is another major source of antipathy. Derbies are as much about the Torcida and the Bad Blue Boys, Dinamo's hardcore support, as they are about the teams. Few clubs, though, are as closely associated with their city as Hajduk Split. If you believe local folklore, only three things truly symbolise Split: the Marjan hills which overlook the city, the Diocletian Palace and Hajduk. Indeed, it's impossible to walk through the streets for more than a minute without coming across graffiti relating to the club or the Torcida, both of which boast impressive histories.

The club was formed in 1911 by students returning from Czechoslovakia who had been blown away by the passion created by both Sparta and Slavia Prague and wanted their own team to support. Hajduk, named after a group of bandits who fought against Ottoman and Venetian rule from the Middle Ages onwards, won two Yugoslav league titles in the 1920s, but it wasn't until 1950 that the Torcida were created. So amazed were the Hajduk fans at the organisation and enthusiasm of Brazilian football fans at the World Cup that year, they named their own supporters group after them.

Like the Torcida gangs in South America, Hajduk's fans were trailblazers. In their first year, they provided the team with Rio-style support for the title decider against Partizan Belgrade, the first time torches, banners, and mass chanting had been seen in this part of Europe. Hajduk won the game and their third league title, but the football authorities were shocked at the frenzy of popular support on display. The Yugoslav regime, which regarded Hajduk as 'their' club, were horrified that supporters could organise themselves in such numbers without the leadership of the Communist Party. In response, Torcida founder Vjenceslav Zuvela was given a three-year prison sentence and Hajduk's captain was expelled from the Party.

Dinamo fans have also had their fair share of run-ins with the authorities, most notably in 1993 when club president Franjo Tudjman dropped the Dinamo name and re-branded them Croatia Zagreb. Tudjman's thinking was that Dinamo was a communist identity and Croatia Zagreb could serve as an advert for his new country in prestigious European competitions. For such a skilled populist politician, the renaming of his, the capital's, and the country's most popular club was a rare misreading of the public mood. The Bad Blue Boys immediately launched a vociferous campaign to abandon the change. It didn't happen until after Tudjman died in 1999 and his party was defeated in parliamentary elections a year later, but at the first game back as Dinamo Zagreb, the Bad Blue Boys celebrated by fighting police in the stadium.

The Torcida's HQ resembles a working men's club: smoky, badly lit, a bar, and pool table. 'Look at this shitty clubhouse,' says Torcida member Ivan Pupacic. 'The roof is leaking and we haven't got the money to repair it. Dinamo fans get financial support from the mayor of Zagreb and local government. We rely on money from our members, and you know what, we prefer it that way, because when politics and sport mix it always ends badly. That's what makes us real fans, not puppets for the politicians.'

Before long, the conversation inevitably turns to violence. 'The Bad Blue Boys have a history of using knives, whereas we're more old school, we just use our fists.'

Getting an alternative viewpoint is not so straightforward. 'I can't talk on the phone,' says Bogdan Urukalo of the Bad Blue Boys. 'The cops will be tracing this line. And I can't meet you in "Shit" either. The police will be on our trail and you won't be able to get near us. It's best if you meet us somewhere outside the city before we head to the stadium. I'll e-mail you.'

Three hours before kick-off, I am in a quiet café in a sleepy village twenty miles outside Split. Inside, Bogdan and three pals are drinking coffee and smoking cigarettes. 'This will have to be quick,' he says anxiously. 'We could be attacked at any minute. We've hired cars with Split number plates so there's less chance of the police trailing us, but you never know.'

Their fears are understandable. Three years ago, a convoy of Dinamo fans was ambushed by the Torcida. When Dinamo fans in one car refused to get out, flares were thrown inside, leaving them no option but to evacuate. Shocked and dazed, the four supporters were then badly beaten. But if ambushing cars is an increasingly common tactic – and it is – so too is pre-emptive action by the police. Driving back from our pre-match meeting with the Bad Blue Boys, the news on the radio is that twenty Torcida members have been arrested and detained in dawn raids. They won't be at the match tonight. Bogdan will and, in our brief interview, he sums up his thoughts on the derby. 'They're jealous of us. We've won more Croatian league titles than them and have more money than them.'

Dinamo's superior financial muscle has often lured Hajduk's best players to the capital, but the most notorious move between the clubs, in January 2005, saw Niko Kranjcar move the other way. Kranjcar was not just Dinamo captain, he was a product of their youth team and the son of famous Dinamo player and coach Zlatko. It's impossible to underestimate how much of a stink his departure caused. The Bad Blue Boys told the midfielder, now with Portsmouth, that he'd never be safe walking the streets of Zagreb and, just in case he didn't get the message, lit 200 blue candles in a 'D' shape outside Kranjcar's home with a banner saying, 'To us, you are already dead'.

Yet Kranjcar, who admits to 'getting really caught up in the rivalry', still believes the move was justified. 'Dinamo had been playing badly for six months and everybody blamed me,' he explains. 'I didn't agree and I didn't agree when they cut my salary. The vice-president then said I wasn't wanted anymore, so what could I do? I could have moved to Russia but it was two years before the World Cup and I wanted to keep playing in Croatia.'

In Split, 10,000 Hajduk fans turned up at his unveiling and Kranjcar was an instant hit with the Torcida. Yet as he reflects on his days in Croatia, Kranjcar puts his finger on one of the more intriguing elements of the rivalry between Hajduk and Dinamo. 'There's too much violence and hatred,' he says. 'We're the same people from the same country – I don't know why we can't have the same goals in life.'

Strip away the mutual hatred, and the Torcida and the Bad Blue Boys are very similar creatures. One common theme is an alarming level of anti-Semitism and racism. It should hardly come as a surprise given that sixty Croatia fans created a human swastika in the stands during a friendly against Italy last August, yet seeing the Nazi symbol daubed outside the Poljud Stadium and talking to members of the Torcida with 'Eighty-Eight 88' T-shirts on (the number represents the letters HH which means Heil Hitler) is still disconcerting. And Dinamo's supporters are just as bad. 'Hajduk are Croatian nationalists, they're right wing, just like we are,' says Bogdan. 'We don't care for black people, Arabs, Jews, or Serbs because thankfully they don't live in our country.'

His comments back up the theory that the rivalry is formed out of necessity rather than a genuine mutual hatred. You can't help thinking that if football reverted to an Adriatic League, as there is in basketball, comprising teams from the former Yugoslav state, the Serbs would return to being the enemy. Until then, the Torcida and the Bad Blue Boys will have to be happy hating and fighting each other. Torcida member Ivan Pupacic even admits he wouldn't want to see Dinamo relegated. 'They were almost relegated two seasons ago, but it wouldn't be the same without them. We just want to see them playing shit.'

With the best Balkan players playing abroad, interest in domestic football isn't exactly flourishing in this part of the world and even derby matches can fail to live up to their billing. A week ago, Red Star and Partizan contested Belgrade's 'eternal derby' in front of 21,000 fans, just half the capacity of the Stadion Partizana, while only 8,000 attended last season's cup semi-final between the two sides. But there are no such concerns 200 miles away in Split. Half an hour before kick-off, the 45,000 capacity Poljud Stadium is jammed solid. The only empty seats are either side of the 2,000 Dinamo supporters, flanked by two lines of heavily-armed police. The stadium is a sea of flags, flares, and banners and the noise is deafening.

Slaven Bilic is watching the game with his nine-year-old son, Leo, from the safety of the VIP area, but there isn't much to encourage the national team coach. It's a scrappy affair, blighted by mistakes and play-acting. Hajduk look particularly nervous, and who can blame them? Their fans may be renowned for their loyalty, but it comes at a price. The Torcida expect success. When Hajduk lost to Irish champions Shelbourne in a Champions League qualifier in 2004, fans broke into the Poljud Stadium, dug eleven six-foot deep graves on the pitch in a 4–4–2 formation and left a banner saying, 'Be league champions or you're dead'.

Tonight, the only players who seem capable of rising above the dross are Dinamo's Luka Modric and Eduardo da Silva. Every time Da Silva, a Brazil-born Croatia international, gets the ball, a chorus of monkey chants fill the air, but he seems oblivious. Meanwhile, the rest of the players are more intent on fighting than winning. Seventeen minutes in, a couple of hefty challenges prompt a ruck involving all twenty outfield players. Seven minutes later, the match explodes again with Hajduk's coach, Zoran Vulic, also getting involved. How nobody is sent off yet is anyone's guess.

Then, on the half hour, Hajduk take an undeserved lead from a dodgy-looking penalty, Mario Carevic converting from twelve yards. Cue the lighting of a dozen or so flares. Five minutes before half-time, the stadium still engulfed in smoke and the choking smell of sulphur, Da Silva waltzes past four Hajduk defenders and is up-ended in the box. Another penalty, another goal. Da Silva celebrates by kissing his Dinamo badge and running directly towards the Hajduk fans, who respond with more monkey chants and a hail of mobile phones.

In the second half, another twenty-man brawl ends in Carevic's dismissal and the visitors capitalise when Davor Vugrinec stabs home from five yards after a well-worked move: 2–1 to Dinamo.

Up in the VIP area, Dinamo staff are on the receiving end of torrents of abuse, including one skinhead accusing the club president of paying the referee, but with eight minutes to go, it's the Hajduk fans who are indebted to the referee, Drazenko Kovacic, when he awards their side's second dubious penalty. The Poljud Stadium is said to be earthquake proof and it needs to be when Pablo Munoz converts the penalty. The whole place tremors and the fireman whose job it is to put the burning flares into buckets of water is soon working overtime.

As the final whistle blows and fans stream out into the streets, I reflect on a classic derby, low on quality but with four goals, three penalties, and one red card, played in an electric atmosphere. In the next day's newspapers, the game enjoys front and back page coverage. Almost as prominent as the scoreline is the arrest count – 'Torcida 30, Bad Blue Boys 9' reads one headline. The only major off-field incident occurs when a bus carrying Dinamo fans is pelted with bricks and stones, smashing all its windows, but according to Torcida member Ivan Pupacic, this is 'nothing special' for derby day.

On the field, the result means the sides stay level on points at the top of the Croatian championship. Going into the winter break, the title race is, again, between the country's big two. There will be a lot at stake when the sides meet in Zagreb on 24 February. Bogdan Urukalo, for one, has the date ringed in red in his diary. 'We wait the whole year for this match,' he says, excitedly, like a child talking about Christmas. 'I'm already thinking about what we will do for the next derby, it's in my head all the time, I can't wait.'

Birds of a Feather
Tenerife v Las Palmas, March 2007

They might be seen by many as merely a destination for sun, sea, and sangria, but the Canary Islands is home to some of the most passionate fans in world football.

A sweating yellow mass is moving steadily from the sea to the stadium. It emits the noise of a tweeting canary – 'Pio! Pio! – Pio! Pio!' – as it climbs through the streets of Santa Cruz de Tenerife. Two thousand Las Palmas fans have ignored the plea of their club president not to travel to rivals Tenerife for fear of trouble.

Flanked by the flashing lights of police vans, ambulances, as well as police in riot gear – some of whom have been flown in from the Spanish mainland to control the crowd at the biggest Canary Islands' derby – the visiting fans are in high spirits and happy to stretch their legs after ninety minutes crossing the Atlantic on a ferry between the islands of Gran Canaria and Tenerife.

With a population of 250,000, Santa Cruz is the size of Plymouth, yet this busy port city escapes the radar of the 3.4 million northern Europeans who holiday in Tenerife annually. Most consider Tenerife's football culture to be little more than Lineker's Bar, ads for televised Premiership games or the replica shirts worn by holidaymakers, yet football is serious business in the Canaries.

The noise of the visitors reverberates around the deserted streets. It may be a warm Saturday afternoon, but the shops are shut and the closed shutters of the apartment blocks indicate that residents of the island's capital are indulging in siesta, rather than abusing their island neighbours.

As the Las Palmas fans close in on Club Deportivo Tenerife's Heliodoro Rodriquez Lopez Stadium – a typically graffiti-ridden steep-sided Spanish city-centre venue of exposed concrete stands overlooked by apartments – their confidence and its accompanying tweeting swells. 'Pio! Pio! – Pio! Pio!' Some Las Palmas fans let off flares, others gesticulate at the few Tenerife fans brave enough to yell back. Lord Nelson would have envied such limited Spanish resistance.

What happens next is as comic as it is unbelievable. From a back street a group of eighty Tenerife supporters surges towards the visiting fans. They hurl abuse and taunt. A few make a charge, prompting the police to draw batons. The Las Palmas fans watch in amazement, not because they didn't anticipate trouble, but because they are being charged by Tenerife-supporting British ex-pats accusing them of being homosexuals – in Spanish.

The scene is surreal. Some of the Las Palmas fans are hooded wannabe hooligans, but they appear uneasy when faced with one English lad, resplendent with a Tenerife tattoo on his leg, hollering: 'Come on then you c*nts!' – this time in English – before being pushed back by police. 'I fucking hate them pio bastards!' he says in a caustic Essex accent as he returns to a bar where a bottle of beer costs less than a pound. This is the world of the Armada Sur (South Army), the well-organised international Tenerife supporters club that is comprised largely of British ex-pats who live at the opposite south end of the island around garish resorts like Playa de las Americas.

As the Las Palmas fans are finally escorted into the away end, members of the Armada Sur in their 'Tenerife: Pride-Passion-Loyalty' T-shirts, led by Aldershot-born Chris Todd, hang a stuffed yellow canary (the Las Palmas symbol) from a tree. A fuse projects from the bird's backside, which is then lit. The group stand back as the bird explodes, its singed feathers floating slowly down to the baking pavements as observers cheer. A group of local girls on the opposite side of the road look across when they hear the explosion. 'Get your tits out for the lads!' some of the ex-pats bellow, pointing to the girls. They walk on, confused. They probably weren't taught that one in their high school English classes.

'Until the 1990s, the rivalry with Las Palmas was relatively friendly,' ventures Todd. 'Then there was a game when it kicked off between the two sets of fans and it has been bitter ever since.'

'Las Palmas, Segunda B!' the Armada Sur continues, hoping that Las Palmas will be relegated to what is Spain's regional third division. When the two biggest clubs of the Canary Islands met as recently as five years ago, both were in the top flight, with Tenerife managed by Rafa Benitez and former Spurs midfielder Vinny Samways starring for Las Palmas.

Formed in 1922, Club Deportivo Tenerife had spent most of its existence in Spain's second tier until gaining promotion to La Liga in 1989. After barely surviving their first season, they gradually improved their league position over the following five years. They made their biggest headlines when Real Madrid twice lost the league title at Tenerife on the final day of the season – effectively handing the title to Barcelona on both occasions.

In 1992, Madrid let a 2–0 half-time lead slip and were beaten 3–2. Spain's leading sports paper *Marca*, always hungry for a conspiracy theory, dedicated the next day's entire front page to accusing the Galician referee of being 'bent'. Incredibly, the next season Real Madrid again lost the league at Tenerife on the final day of the season, losing 2–0 as their players wilted under the heat of the sun and the islanders' hostility. Tenerife were managed by the erudite Argentinian Jorge Valdano, who told his players to take up the challenge of defeating a team that had 'all the prestige of history on its side' before the game. They did, but then the result wasn't a huge surprise as Valdano had crafted a side containing the brilliance of a young Fernando Redondo, a team good enough to finish fifth and qualify for the UEFA Cup where they were knocked out by Juventus.

Despite causing Madrid double heartache, Valdano's success ensured he was destined for a bigger club. Perhaps to prevent him taking the title off them a third time, Madrid signed him, and he promptly won the league at the first attempt in 1995.

Tenerife's heroics were not finished, however. Valdano's replacement was the highly respected German, Jupp Heynckes, who achieved another fifth-placed finish and led Tenerife to the semi-finals of the UEFA Cup after beating Maccabi Tel-Aviv, Lazio, Feyenoord, and Brondby, before losing 2–1 on aggregate to eventual winners Schalke 04. Against Lazio, Tenerife overturned a 1–0 away deficit and came from a goal down in the home leg to win 5–3. That night at the Heliodoro remains the highlight for many fans.

Like Valdano, Heynckes ended up at the Bernabeu, where he won Madrid's first European Cup in thirty-two years in 1998. Saddled with underperforming players on big contracts, Tenerife's fortunes faded and the club went on a downward spiral which eventually led to relegation in 1999. Struggling to pay the lavish salaries they had offered when they were in the top flight, they slipped into a debt still carried today. But it hasn't been all bad. Benitez was appointed and in 2001 he led to promotion a side featuring future Spanish internationals Luis Garcia, Curro Torres, and Mista.

True to the pattern established by his predecessors, Benitez left for a bigger club, this time Valencia, and his trio of stars jumped ship too. Tenerife were relegated in 2002 and haven't got close to returning to the top flight since.

Las Palmas, as their fans like to remind those from Tenerife, have spent thirty-one years in the Primera Liga and are 18th in the all-important all-time Spanish league table ahead of teams like Mallorca, Villarreal and, crucially, Tenerife who are 23rd with twelve top flight seasons. Las Palmas may have been playing in the third division when

Tenerife were playing in Europe in the mid-1990s, but with players like locally-born Juan Carlos Valeron, they rose through the second division, reaching the top flight in 2000.

Despite the efforts of Vinnie Samways, who achieved such cult status that one supporters' club was named after him (at the time, Samways picked up more red cards than any other player in the history of Spanish football), Las Palmas were relegated after two seasons. Showing ambition, a new 32,500-seater stadium was built, but it was often two-thirds empty as the club was relegated to the third division in 2004. Only in 2006, when they returned to the second tier, could hostilities be resumed with Tenerife.

Football in the Canaries isn't limited to the big two. Tenerife and Las Palmas may average 10,000, but Vecindario, another Gran Canarian team, rose to the second division for the first time in their history in 2006. With average crowds of just 1,000 and a measly £1 million budget compared to Tenerife's £6 million, and Las Palmas' £3 million, Vecindario were relegated in May 2007. Interestingly, both Tenerife and Las Palmas fans look upon Vecindario favourably, almost as if they are a little brother from the same Canarian family. They did likewise with another team from Gran Canaria, Universidad de Las Palmas, who rose to the second division for one year in 2000–01 – some achievement considering they were only formed in 1997.

Almost every away game from the Canaries necessitates an air trip to the Spanish mainland and a flight of two to three hours. Away support is largely comprised of Canarians living on the Spanish peninsula; students from Tenerife who live in Madrid will watch the away game at Real Madrid Castilla, Madrid's B team, for instance.

Or there is Andy Woolley, a 57-year-old trade union official who lives in Somerset and supports Stoke and Tenerife. Like many others, Woolley started supporting the club when he holidayed on the island. In the fourteen years since, he's watched Tenerife around five times a season, including away trips against the likes of Espanyol, Toledo, and Almeria.

Woolley started the club's first website www.andywoolley.zen.co.uk, prompting curiosity from local fans and the club to launch its own official website. 'When [Dutch striker] Roy Makaay played for us [1997–99], his brother-in-law used to email me for updates,' says Woolley.

It's twenty minutes before the 5 p.m. kick-off and long queues twist through the turnstiles at the 24,000 capacity Heliodoro. All the tickets are sold for a league game – the first time since the days when Tenerife were in the Primera Liga. Most fans are inside the ground when the bizarre club anthem crackles through the public address system. ¡Riqui-raca-sumba-raca, sin-bon-ba! ¡Ria Ria Ria, rian-pun-ta! Written by Los Huaracheros, a popular island group in the '60s, its popularity endures. The lyrics would be displayed on the scoreboard, had it not stopped working at 2.15, 'sometime in 1997'.

Behind one goal, the Frente Blanquiazul (white and blue Front) are well organised. A stream of banners are unfurled from the upper tier to read 'CHICHARREROS' – a nickname for Tenerife fans. When Santa Cruz was a fishing village, its population were renowned for eating little fish (chicharros). Other Tenerife inhabitants used 'Chicharreros' as a pejorative, but the people of Santa Cruz turned it into a term of affection.

The majority of the Armada Sur, who pay just £150 for their season tickets, stand with the Frente Blanquiazul, making a din. If you're going to go bare-chested at the match, it's better to do it in Tenerife than on Tyneside. There appear to be several Scotland flags, but that's because the saltire of St Andrew is also the flag of Tenerife. One fan bangs his drum so hard that he puts a hole in it. A shirtless man shouts '¡Pio, Pio maricon!' into a megaphone and soon the whole ground is following him, 18,000 Tenerife fans united in their belief that every Las Palmas fan is a homosexual.

'The Frente love us, and appreciate our support,' explains Chris Todd, 39, who has lived on the island for eighteen years. 'They know we love the island, love football, and support the club. They call us the "Frente Hooligans" – The Hooligan Front. They think that all English are hooligans, but we're not. We have a few songs in English, but we sing most of the others in Spanish. We might not be from Tenerife originally, but plenty of us have been here a long time and we've followed Tenerife through thick and thin. When two of our members died in a car crash, the club held a minute's silence, the captain brought flowers and the Frente blacked out a section of seats as a mark of respect.'

Todd formed the Armada Sur in 1992. 'Quite a few Brits travelled to games in cars,' adds Todd. 'I started running a bus and it grew from there. When we played Real Madrid two years ago in the cup we took four coaches.' Tenerife need the Armada Sur. 'Around 800,000 people live in Tenerife, but a lot of people support Barcelona or Madrid which is quite sad. Tenerife have a hardcore of 9,000.'

The Las Palmas fans, packed tightly at the opposite side of the ground in the upper tier, unfurl a series of flags that read 'Puta Tenerife' (Tenerife whores) and 'Anti-Chicha' (short for 'anti-chicharreros', the nickname for Tenerife fans).

Given the distances involved, away fans are a rarity in Gran Canaria and Tenerife. But because of the proximity, the main Las Palmas ultra group – the Ultra Naciente – is well represented. Pablo, one of their members, is one of the few Las Palmas who hasn't travelled by boat and is easily spotted in the terminal because he's singing 'Ole Amarillo' (Brilliant Yellow) alone at the bar. He explains what he thinks of Tenerife. 'Gran Canaria is the authentic Canary Island with the best girls,' he says, slurping his lager and munching on a hot dog. 'Tenerife is full of groups of drunken tourists, whereas the people who come to Gran Canaria have more class.'

Pablo's assertion of superiority is dubious. Although Tenerife's population has risen a staggering 23 per cent in the last decade, largely down to sun-starved Brits in football shirts, Gran Canaria also boasts several resorts attracting exactly the same kind of clientele.

Back at the game, the politics of the two sets of supporters becomes more apparent. Tenerife's Frente Blanquiazul are more left-wing, anti-Spanish, and supporters of the limited movement for independence for the Canaries. 'Canaries is my nation,' they sing. 'Long live the three-coloured flag [of Independence]. All the Spanish are sons of bitches.'

The majority of Canary Islanders are happy with the status quo. They are an autonomous region whose local government has significant powers. Santa Cruz and Las Palmas share the status of co-capital of the Canaries and have the clout to restrict any over-development of the islands. They are virtually powerless, however, to prevent West African illegal immigrants arriving on boats that wouldn't be considered safe on a millpond, let alone the Atlantic. The African coast is just 150 miles away.

The rivalry between Santa Cruz and Las Palmas goes beyond football. Both are by some distance the biggest cities in the Canaries – the ninth and tenth biggest in Spain. Both boast that they have the best carnivals in a country where such a statement matters. Gran Canarian residents drink Tropical beer, Tenerife's go for Dorada. Both claim the other tastes like rat's urine.

The stadium explodes after four minutes when Tenerife edge a goal in front. The scorer is Iriome, a local boy and Spain U21 international who is seen as the club's brightest prospect. Fans are pleased at his progress, but worried he'll be snapped up by a bigger club like so many of their heroes of yore. The Las Palmas fans are furious and flares spill onto the pitch from the upper tier, as well as invective towards the lineswoman: 'You slut! You've slept with the whole Tenerife team!' Iriome then makes it 2–0 on twenty-nine minutes, prompting more scenes of delirium among the home fans.

After a rare spot of rain on the hour that inspires utter disbelief among the locals, Las Palmas pull a goal back. Some of their more energetic supporters rip out seats and hurl them towards the pitch. The police, who have stood by and watched as the two sets of fans trade insults, fly into action, charging into the crowd, batons swinging.

The drama continues on the field when Tenerife earn a penalty. The fouled player goes down as if shot and rolls around the floor in frantic death throes. Stretchered off as the penalty is taken, he miraculously springs to his feet to join in the celebrations as the chance is converted to make the score 3–1. British crowds may not accept these theatrics, but in Spain it's part of the show.

The win lifts Tenerife to the safety of mid-table, while Las Palmas remain just one point above the relegation zone. Both teams have decent enough support and stadiums to compete in the top-flight, but, as so often is the case in Spain, boardroom instability, over-spending and rampant egos lead to constant changes in personnel. Tenerife bought thirteen new players last summer and sold sixteen, while Las Palmas saw eight new arrivals and five departures.

After the game, the Armada Sur meet in a bar close to the stadium and wait for the away fans to pass. Kids are encouraged to move to the back of the bar in case of trouble, but there's a buzz among this lot. Do they not find it strange, you wonder, to cheer for an obscure Spanish side when they grew up supporting the likes of Crewe, Leicester, Man United, and Liverpool? 'My 88-year-old father, who's a lifelong Stoke fan, is worried I'll give up supporting Stoke, but I think I can support both teams,' says Andy Woolley. 'Until we meet in the Champions League Final, of course. Then I'll have to choose.'

The Colombian Connection

Deportivo Cali v América de Cali, April 2007

Take a city bloodied and divided by two sets of fans. Add a sprinkling of passion, drugs, and violence. These are the ingredients for Cali's explosive derby.

The threats began before I had even arrived in Colombia. It had taken four months of delicate negotiations with the Frente Radical Verdiblanco (FRV), Deportivo Cali's *barra brava* – one of Colombia's biggest and most highly organised hooligan groups – before we were permitted to accompany the leaders of this 3,000-strong group into battle against city rivals América de Cali.

'You must be trustful and reliable or YOU WILL HAVE PROB-LEMS IN YOUR FUTURE,' warned one of the many e-mails from our contact 'Johnny'. 'You have to understand we are in a country full of conflict and we have to take precautions.' Despite a vastly improved safety record and considerable rise in tourism, Colombia is still a country at war. For more than forty years government forces, left-wing guerrilla groups and right-wing paramilitaries have been waging a bloody three-way fight for power killing thousands of people. Mix in the fact that Colombia is the biggest producer of cocaine in the world and you have a very explosive cocktail.

'There is a serious risk of kidnapping and crime throughout most parts of the country,' advises the UK Foreign Office, adding dark warnings of 'a high threat of terrorism' and 'lives being lost on an almost daily basis'.

The Cauca Valley and its capital Cali, is no exception. Set in the heart of guerrilla-controlled countryside, it is home to the Norte de Valley cartel, the biggest drug-trafficking organisation in the world, whose leader Diego Montoya is currently starring in the FBI's Ten Most Wanted list.

It is against this violent backdrop that Deportivo Cali and América de Cali came to despise each other. Their first game, in 1931, ended with América banned from all tournaments for a year. Last year saw the murder of one of the FRV's leaders and, in 1982, dozens died in a stampede at a meeting of the two teams. It was Colombia's Heysel Stadium disaster. Like almost everything in this beautiful yet blighted country, Cali's derby is inextricably intertwined with death and drugs. But it is also famed for the fiery Latin passion that fans of both teams bring to the terraces.

The very centre of the north terrace in the Estadio Pascual Guerrero is strictly reserved for the upper echelons of the FRV. Anyone else who tries to enter this zone is fiercely held back. At least, that's usually the case. Today, though, I stand amid the heaving throng. In the middle is Franklin, the leader, *El Don*. Tattoos and cuts scar his heavy frame, long bedraggled hair hangs loose over his torn t-shirt, his eyes are bloodshot from beer and poppers. From this privileged position he conducts his rambunctious and ramshackle orchestra of drums, trumpets and 3,000 coarse voices. He constantly barks orders: 'different song', 'sing louder'.

The stand bounces along with the fans to the beat of five bass drums. A couple of snares tap out a pattern while the trumpets guide the melody. The noise is deafening. And then comes a goal. Bodies and arms flail everywhere, the racket doubles, green smoke is blasted out over the pitch, streamers fall from the sky, the concrete floor sags.

Suddenly the whole stand is covered by a giant flag decorated in the team's green and white colours. It's like sharing a tent with the 3,000 nuttiest fans you've ever met. And then the sky appears again and the game, well under way, can be glimpsed through the flags. The exhilaration is literally breathtaking.

On the opposite terrace, thousands of América's *barra brava*, known as Baron Rojo Sur, are briefly silenced before redoubling their efforts and spitting hatred back north. The atmosphere is as oppressive as the uncomfortable heat.

Colombia's third city sits in the southwest of the country, bathed in sweltering heat. Two great mountain ranges cut through the mist, the Cordillera Occidental and the Cordillera Central, flanking the city and its endless sugarcane plantations. It is a dramatic setting for a place in which high drama is part of daily life (appropriately, and a touch disconcertingly, on my arrival, the taxi's radio started blaring *Highway to the Danger Zone* as we hurtled into the city).

Central Cali is not a pretty place. Modern monoliths have eaten up most of the colonial architecture, but that doesn't seem to bother the *caleños* who are strikingly friendly and cheerful. They also pride themselves on being Colombia's biggest party animals. Salsa is the soundtrack to Cali and from early evening the bars and clubs down the main strip fill with scantily-clad women and smartly-dressed men, ready for a night of knocking back *aguadiente* – a potent aniseed-flavoured drink made from sugarcane – and dancing off the effects. By morning they return to the teeming streets, passing stalls selling a bewildering array of fruit and avoiding the manically-driven colourful *chiva* buses. There is always time to chat with a neighbour, or sup down a strong *tinto* made from Colombia's primary export, coffee. The centre feels safe, and it is; only heavily armed police and newspaper headlines hint at the violence and poverty that still permeate the more rural regions of the province and Cali's poor shanties.

It is one of these less than salubrious areas, in a dimly-lit park below an underpass, that I can be found the night before the game, supping beer with forty or so members of the FRV who are putting the finishing touches to their derby plans.

Our contact, the baby-faced Johnny, explains how the FRV is broken down into seven 'legions' around Cali, each with a leader who reports to Franklin. The bespectacled Calvo is one young legion leader with an encyclopaedic knowledge of European hooligans. 'The Headhunters of Chelsea, Millwall Bushwackers, Inner City Firm of West Ham,' he reels off. 'We are pioneers in Colombia. We model ourselves on the ultras of Italy and the hooligans of England, not the *barra bravas* of Argentina. We are different, very organised and very disciplined.'

Andres asks if we have seen their 'bibles', *Green Street Hooligans* (the one with Elijah 'Frodo' Wood), and *The Football Factory*. Hector, another legion leader, joins the conversation. 'We were the first ultras in Colombia, starting in 1992. We were radical then because we were more than just waving a flag or singing a song. We live the game everyday. Nothing is more important to us than winning, lifting our team as much as we can.'

They boast about fights they have had with other fans, but also lament the loss of a fellow *verdiblanco* at the hands of, they claim, Baron Rojo Sur. It was almost a year ago when 22-year-old Stevenson Galeano Rivera was shot through the forehead during a clash between the two groups. 'We don't want any more violence,' one legion head insists. 'We had a national congress with all the other *barras* of Colombia so there wouldn't be any more trouble at national games. We still support our teams fanatically but it's not worth the death of a young man.'

Then Franklin stands up and the assembled members hush. 'This is the big one. We all need to be there; no excuses, singing together, jumping together,' he shouts to cheers. 'I was talking to the players today,' Franklin continues over a chorus of hoots and whistles. 'They said they need you to support them. We can change the course of the game, you give them confidence. This is a *clasico*, and we simply can't

DRUGS AND FOOTBALL: COLOMBIAN STYLE

Drugs and football are inter-twined in Colombia – with some-times horrific consequences. Drug cartels, also involved in gambling syndicates, were blamed for gunning down national team defender Andres Escobar in a bar in Medellín after he scored an own goal in the 1994 World Cup.

The boss of the Medellín Car-tel, the notorious Pablo Escobar, was renowned for his passion for football. He built stadiums for the poor areas of Medellín, and also became heavily involved in Atlético Nacional. In 1989, a ref-eree admitted that he was threat-ened by Escobar's cartel after a particularly biased game against Millionarios in 1989. 'Fortu-nately,' the referee said, 'Nacional won 6–0.' In the end, the 1989 Copa Mustang was abandoned after one official was kidnapped and another mur-dered for making a mistake against Nacional. In 2006,

lose.' The throng start to chant: '*Come on Deportivo/We are going to win/These fans will never leave you/We'll never stop encouraging you*'.

As we walk out into the night, Andres hands out a fourteen-page song booklet produced for the game and distributes the latest copy of their glossy monthly magazine *Ultra Verdiblanco* which features an interview with Deportivo manager Omar Labruna, a eulogy to their lost friend and an advert posted by a local politician seeking to curry favour with the FRV.

Like all great footballing rivalries, the two sets of fans are separated by more than just a whimsical affection towards their team. A deep cultural and economic divide separates the generally middle-class *los Azucareros* of Cali (named after the region's ubiquitous sugar-cane) and the working-class *los Escarlatas* of América (after their fire-engine red jer-seys). These disparities of wealth have characterised the region since the Spanish conquistadores overwhelmed and enslaved indigenous tribes of the Cauca Valley in 1536. Quickly recognising the cash bonanza in sugarcane, the Spanish imported thousands more slaves from Africa, a legacy still represented in the faces of the population today. Cali steadily grew in importance, attracting both sugar and coffee magnates and poor farm workers, but it was when the railroad rolled in at the beginning of the 20th century, the city began to flourish.

At this time sons of the wealthy tycoons returned from studying in Europe with a new game and formed Cali Football Club in 1912. In contrast, América originated from literally the other side of the tracks. Established by Pablo Manrique, a sports teacher at a poor college in the southern shanties, on behalf of the city's workers, it took nine years and three name changes (Júnior, Racing and Independiente) before the club was officially founded on 13 February 1927.

In 1931, América finished top of the second division and, wanting to test themselves against a team from the top flight, organised a 'friendly' against neighbouring side Cali. It turned out to be anything but. By now called 'Deportivo', Cali took an early lead, but América quickly replied with two goals, both, according to América's official history, disallowed for offside. A furious América published flyers denouncing the 'irregularities' of the match and the Federation of Colombian Football reacted by suspending the team for a year.

---

second division Deportivo Tuluá was accused by the US of being a front for the Norte de Valley cartel and placed on the Clinton List alongside América de Cali.

Meanwhile, the players have also found themselves involved. René 'scorpion kick' Higuita was jailed for his involvement in a drug cartel's kidnap plot. The kidnappers reputedly demanded that Higuita acted as their negotiator only because they wanted to meet him. He was released after seven months without charge.

In 1948, though, América became the first professional team in Colombia, quickly followed by Millionarios and Santa Fe in Bogotá, then Cali. And in September of that year the two Cali teams played their first professional derby. Cali won 4–3 but journalists admiringly noted América's penchant for aggressive and passionate play, and described them as playing like devils. The tag stuck and the club adopted the devil logo as their own – apart from twelve years in the '80s and '90s, when the coach banned it for religious reasons.

At first neither team had great success in Colombia's premier tournament, the Copa Mustang. Cali finally broke the deadlock in 1965, but América had to wait until the appointment of Gabriel Ochoa Uribe as coach in 1979 to win their first Copa. Then the floodgates opened. During Uribe's twelve years at the helm, América won the Copa Mustang seven times and finished second in the Copa Libertadores, the South American Champions League, three years running. As always, however, it was the derbies that were most fiercely fought.

Abel Da Graca, an Argentine, who is now director of Cali's youth teams, remembers playing in *clasicos* between 1971 and 1977. 'The city was divided,' he says. 'América and Cali fans wouldn't even speak to each other. Once I hailed a taxi with a little devil hanging from the mirror. As soon as he recognised me, he swore at me and drove off. It was the most important game of the calendar. You remembered who hit you, who knocked you over, so you had to get your own back. This is lost now because players move around so much.'

On 17 November 1982 the rivalry came to a horrific conclusion after América and Cali drew 3–3 at the Pascual Guerrero stadium. Reports tell of drunken thugs urinating on enemy fans below causing a stampede. Twenty-four people died and 163 were injured. It was one of four fatal incidents at games around the country in the early-'80s that killed a further forty-seven fans. Despite the violence that marred the period, it is remembered as a golden era by fans of América. In contrast, Cali won no silverware at all throughout the

'80s, even with national legend Carlos Valderrama bossing their midfield. Still they trail, with eight championships to América's eleven. América's supremacy, however, was to come crashing down in an instant.

In a luxury apartment in Cali's Ingenios neighbourhood, on 9 June 1995, Gilberto Rodríguez Orejuela was found by police crouching in a cupboard and arrested. Known as 'The Chess Player', Rodríguez Orejuela was the head of the Cali Cartel, Colombia's most violent drug smugglers. According to the US Drug Enforcement Agency the Cali mafia at one point controlled 80 per cent of cocaine exports to the US earning $20m ... a day. It was discovered that Rodríguez Orejuela spent his money on fine clothes, luxury mansions and a football team. The football-loving *capo* bankrolled América; partly due to his enthusiasm for the game and partly in order to field a team to clash with Atlético Nacional, a club backed by his arch-enemies the Medellín Cartel.

Months after Rodríguez Orejuela's arrest, Corporación Deportiva América was placed under scrutiny by Executive Order 12798 by the US government, along with all the other companies in Colombia suspected of having links with the cartels. This is commonly known as the Clinton List, after the president who inaugurated it. As a consequence, all América's assets (estimated to be $1m) were frozen and no company has been allowed to do business with them since.

Accusations of pay-offs, bribery, money laundering, and corruption have tarnished the club's image. Twelve years on, América are still on the Clinton List and still fighting for survival. 'We are stigmatised by the List,' América's spokesman Alvaro Almeida complains. 'We haven't had any official sponsor for four years and many of our best players are here on loan, so we take the best from the lower leagues.'

Considering their dire financial situation, América have managed exceptionally well with Copa Mustang wins in 1997, 2000, 2001 and the Copa Merconorte (now Copa Sudamericana) in 1999. Last year, however, they experienced their worst ever league run, narrowly avoiding relegation after spending much of the season at the bottom of the table. It prompted club president Carlos Puente Gonzalez to publish an open letter to the people of Cali urging a positive outlook: 'We are survivors, shipwrecked, financial lepers and we have to resign ourselves to our unjust stigma,' the letter complains, before signing off, 'In 2007 this provincial team will be 80 years old, we have to fight with goodwill, because where there is goodwill there is life.'

Almeida cites numerous examples of how the club is turning around. 'We are about to become the most diplomatic club in Colombia. The fans will be part of the club, they can help us as much as we can help them. It is a new, positive era and we can prove we shouldn't be on the Clinton List.'

Nevertheless, going into their 258th meeting with Cali, América are loitering in 15th place out of 18. They must win. Cali, in second position, are the favourites, but having missed out on the play-offs last season for the first time in years, they have something to prove.

'I'm pleased with the team,' says Cali's new manager, the former River Plate star Omar Labruna. 'We won't be changing our strategy today but this is the *clasico* and it will be what the word means: classic. There is a deep rivalry and the players are very enthused. They will go in with their teeth bared.'

It's 10 a.m. on the morning of the game and I am being bought beer by FRV leader Franklin in a car park several kilometres from the stadium. As the booze is knocked back, a stolen América flag is blown up with firecrackers, to the glee of the 300 FRV assembled members and the consternation of the neighbours. A couple of hours later, Franklin summons the troops and the three-mile march to the stadium commences, fuelled by alcohol, poppers, and more than a pinch of Colombia's finest. The police escort stops traffic to let the all-singing, all-dancing entourage past. Leading the group is a van full of flags and fireworks, balloons and banners which they hope will make their entrance more spectacular than ever before.

As the parade arrives at the stadium, América's ultras, the Baron Rojo Sur, are spied. A handful of the FRV chase them throwing stones and bottles. Caught in the middle are riot police who don't take kindly to being showered with glass and initiate a baton charge attacking whoever happens to be under their cosh. I narrowly avoid a whipping thanks to the swift action of one member of the FRV who manages to drag us to safety.

From the other side of the barriers, the Baron Rojo Sur scream obscenities and make all sorts of aggressive gestures. Leaving the protection of the FRV, we head round the other side of the stadium where the scarlet shirts of América are congregating. 'You'll see the difference between the fans inside the stadium,' boasts Jhon, a tattooed member of the Baron Rojo Sur. 'Cali are nothing to us. They are just kids. We are a much bigger *barra*.'

From pitchside in the stadium the number of red and green shirts seem equally matched, as does the terrific noise they are making. Then as the teams run onto the field, firecrackers are let off, increasing the decibels ten-fold. Ticker tape turns the sky momentarily white, before being cast green to the north and red to south as the *barras* blast smoke out of adapted fire extinguishers.

Through the still-clearing smoke, América kick off the 258th Cali derby. Cali's players currently earn around five times as much as their rivals and they dominate from early on, but it is a typical derby game: scrappy, ill-tempered, and passionate. The crowd of 35,000 'oooh' and 'ahhh' every near and not-so-near miss, while the *barras* rattle through their chant repertoire. Only some great saves by América's acrobatic keeper, Rolando Vargas, keeps out voracious attacks from Cali's star forward Sergio Herrera.

At half-time I head to the centre of the terrace where the FRV leaders are relaxing with a spliff. Drunken fans grab at our camera, but those who recognise us bustle us through the throng. It's an intimidating atmosphere. Sensing our fear, Franklin places a reassuring paw on our shoulder and advises, 'Stick with us and no one will touch you'.

As the teams run out for the second half the drums strike up, Franklin demands a song and the 3,000 fans begin to jump. It's like being in a mosh pit; unexplained scuffles break out constantly and a couple of times we're knocked flying. It's both terrifying and exhilarating. We desperately want to get out, but the adrenalin buzz keeps us wanting more.

And at last, the game is as break-neck as the scenes on the terraces. Man-of-the-match Herrera puts Cali ahead with a skilful flick round the keeper on fifty-six minutes. I am hugged, pushed, punched, and kissed as the giant flag smothering us causes claustrophobic pandemonium.

The goal is too much for *los Escarlatas* defender Perdo Tavima who lunges at Herrera and is sent off. Minutes later and it's Cali midfielder Johnny Vazquez, still angry at Tavima's foul, who is expelled after an altercation. A third red card in five minutes is shown to América's Pablo Armero after yet another violent quarrel and the game is sealed in favour of Cali. Only dodgy finishing prevents *los Azucareros* from finishing the game off. Then, in the final minute Cali's centre-forward Armando Carrillo blasts one in off the post and, in a calculated yet bizarre gesture, runs to the red corner flag and stuffs it in his mouth. The following day the image is plastered across the local newspaper's front page beneath the headline: 'Top class Cali devour suffering América'.

As the final whistle blows on a 2–0 victory for Cali, the players hurtle towards the north terrace to celebrate and 3,000 fans go berserk. For América it's a disaster, yet through the bedlam the singing of the Baron Rojo Sur can still be heard defiant and resolute. 'We are used to suffering,' explains Jhon later. 'It only makes the *barra* stronger'.

After the game, I grab a spicy kebab outside the stadium with our FRV hosts. They are thrilled with the win as the team are now well on their way to the play-offs. 'We have fulfilled our role as the 12th player,' says Franklin. Would it have mattered if Cali won or lost? 'Of course we are happy when they win, but the most important thing is the passion,' he admits with a grin. 'We only see the team every seven days but we are the *barra* every single day of the year.'

Dutch Courage
Ajax v Feyenoord, February 2007

The enmity between Holland's two biggest clubs is long-standing, resulting in some of the most sophisticated security operations in Europe to keep rival fans apart.

An angry crowd awaits the arrival of the two double-decker trains carrying the 1,600 travelling Feyenoord fans to the Amsterdam ArenA. Preventing the couple of thousand baying Ajax fans from making contact with their hated foes is a security operation of immense proportions.

Up in the leaden skies, a police helicopter surveys the scene while, above that, a 747 makes its final descent into Schiphol Airport. Ajax fans are gathered between the stadium, their team's lush training pitches and a train station which has a tunnel linking the platform with the away end. In front of them, two lines of police wait, poised in RoboCop gear, their batons and shields ready for the inevitable. One has a fire extinguisher attached to his back, others restrain agitated dogs. Behind them, a line of police horses creates a further barrier. Add in two phalanxes of police vans, assorted security officials and officers with surveillance cameras and you get a good idea of the measures in place to keep fans of Holland's two biggest clubs apart. A clutch of plain-clothes officers loiter nearby. Every few minutes they identify a problem fan and close in, before dragging him into a van where they administer their own form of justice. Most fans cover their faces with scarves in an attempt to preserve their anonymity yet one seems determined to attract police attention, clad as he is in a gas mask and white boiler suit with a Feyenoord cockroach (Ajax call Feyenoord 'cockroaches') painted on his back.

It's an hour before kick-off and the maelstrom that surrounds Ajax v Feyenoord, the biggest, angriest and most eagerly anticipated game in Dutch football, is raging.

That Amsterdam and Rotterdam are different becomes obvious as soon as you leave the latter's central station. The buildings are newer, taller, bolder, and construction cranes are everywhere. Rotterdam has been a building site since the war and while some of the developments have been lauded, others are loathed. It's a hard, predominantly working-class city, the second biggest in Holland (metropolitan population 1.1 million to Amsterdam's 1.5 million) and it boasts the largest port in Europe; globally, only Shanghai is bigger.

Rotterdam has the highest percentage of non-western foreigners in Holland, with nearly half the population not native to the Netherlands or with at least one parent born outside the country, and the cities are increasingly polarised politically, Amsterdam remaining liberal to socialist as Rotterdam becomes more right wing (though the city has always been a labour party stronghold). The controversial politician Pim Fortuyn, who was assassinated in 2002, set up his anti-immigration party here.

Rotterdam's inhabitants believe that civic pride matters more here and the locals are proud of their home city's industry. As the Dutch sayings go: 'While Amsterdam dreams, Rotterdam works'; 'Amsterdam to party, Den Haag [The Hague] to live, Rotterdam to work.'

Unlike Amsterdam, which has one Eredivisie club, Rotterdam is a three-team city, with Sparta Rotterdam and Excelsior currently playing in the top division. While relatively modest clubs like AZ Alkmaar and Twente Enschede have challenged the powerful Ajax–PSV–Feyenoord triumvirate, it's an achievement for the smaller Rotterdam clubs just to be playing top-flight football. The smallest, Excelsior, are on friendly terms with Feyenoord, but many conservative Sparta fans prefer Ajax to 'the people's club', with Ajax gleefully reciprocating the feeling by singing 'Sparta is the club of Rotterdam'.

Waiting in a bar by the station is Danny, one of the main Feyenoord lads and part of the SCF (Sportclub Feyenoord) firm. He has been arrested for hooliganism, but was released without charge. Now in his forties and working on the docks, Danny has followed Feyenoord all his life. He doesn't like Ajax or Amsterdammers 'and their stupid accents', but he acknowledges that Ajax have the edge when it comes to winning trophies and playing beautiful football: the Ajax board's policy statement commits the club to 'creative, attacking and dominant football.' 'And yet,' says Danny with a smile, 'their utopia is to be like Feyenoord – a real football club with real fans. When it comes to supporters, we eat them for breakfast. Ajax talk about the F-Side and Gate 410 being noisy. That's two sections. The whole of De Kuip is noisy.' Talk to Ajax fans and most will actually concur – the one area in which they respect Feyenoord is the atmosphere at De Kuip.

'Ajax is the team of celebrities, the media and phonies,' continues Danny. 'Their main stand has more executive boxes and posh seats. People go there to be seen; people go to Feyenoord to support their team. Everyone hates Ajax's arrogance in Holland and the media bias towards them.'

As he speaks, Rotterdam-based lawyer Erik scribbles Feyenoord's anthem on a piece of paper. A Manchester United fan who has travelled to over 300 United games since 1978, Erik's no anorak, but he's also seen games at all ninety-two Football League grounds, plus twenty-eight league grounds in Scotland.

'Here,' he says, passing over the sheet of paper. It reads:

'Hand in hand comrades,
Hand in hand for Feyenoord,
No words but action,
Long live Feyenoord!'

Danny has brought along hundreds of photographs of Feyenoord fans. He points them out and explains the stories behind them. There's one of the Feyenoord mob who travelled to Amsterdam by a boat which left Rotterdam at midnight. 'We had a house party with DJs on board,' he recalls. 'Everyone was drugged up and dancing, but when we arrived in Amsterdam in the morning the police were waiting for us.'

He's got pictures of a game at De Meer from the early '90s, when Feyenoord fans threw a home-made bomb into the Ajax section, causing injuries, some serious, to eighteen fans. And he's also got pictures of a wrecked television studio after a TV station invited both Ajax and Feyenoord fans to a live show in Hilversum, near Amsterdam. Fighting before the show meant the programme was never recorded. Violence, it soon becomes apparent, is part of the fabric of this fixture.

The enmity between Holland's biggest two clubs is long-standing. Ajax have four European Cups, but Feyenoord were the first Dutch team to win the big cup, beating Celtic in 1970 under the Austrian Ernst Happel, whose pre-match talks famously amounted to one sentence: 'Gentlemen, two points.' Then Ajax's Rinus Michels adapted the catenaccio style of Happel, called it 'totaal voetbal' and Ajax won three successive European Cups.

That scenario is typical of a history in which Feyenoord have enjoyed only brief interludes of one-upmanship. In 1983, Ajax legend Johan Cruyff controversially moved to De Kuip. Aged 37, he led Feyenoord, with a young Ruud Gullit, to the double. 'He was the conductor for our orchestra,' Danny says. 'And we had a beautiful orchestra with a superb defence.' The message is clear – Cruyff was a genius but Feyenoord also had a great team around him that year. Yet to Ajax fans, it was their man who led Feyenoord to glory. Even when

Feyenoord last won the league in 1999, Ajax beat them 6–0 in one of the final games of the season.

As is so often the case, the rivalry is defined by prejudice. But there are many similarities, perceived and otherwise, between these bitter rivals. Both clubs claim support from well beyond their city boundaries; there are even 1,100 Ajax season-ticket holders living in Rotterdam and 400 Feyenoord in Amsterdam. Ajax fans have been known to make life difficult for celebrity Feyenoord fans living in their city, painting 'Ajax' on the front of their houses.

Like bickering brothers, the clubs attempt to outdo each other at all levels. In the late-1990s, the Costa Rican player Froylán Ledezma flew into Schiphol to sign for Feyenoord, but because Ajax had better airport contacts, the Feyenoord representatives were left waiting in Arrivals, while Ajax officials were allowed to meet Ledezma directly from the plane. He signed for Ajax leaving Feyenoord furious that their foes had kidnapped the player, though they had the last laugh when Ledezma failed to shine in Dutch football.

In truth, though, the story represents a brief comic interlude amid the violence. Three years ago, for example, Feyenoord midfielder Jorge Acuña was hospitalised after Ajax hooligans attacked him at a reserve-team match. This season, Feyenoord bought Ajax's fourth-choice striker Angelos Charisteas, scorer of Greece's winning goal at Euro 2004. At his initial training sessions, he needed two security minders having outraged some Ajax fans by claiming that Feyenoord was a 'warmer club'.

Fears about the safety of players and fans en route to each other's stadium can usually be allayed by bumping up the security, but hatred sometimes finds a way. And a decade ago in Beverwijk, the mutual loathing became lethal. In a field by a motorway intersection between Amsterdam and Rotterdam, the two firms clashed in a pre-arranged meeting. The precise numbers are disputed but, like a scene from *Braveheart*, hundreds moved towards each other carrying bats, knives and poles. There were few police and it became known as the Battle of

Beverwijk. Feyenoord outnumbered their rivals and as Ajax retreated, a heavy-set asthma sufferer called Carlo Picornie was stranded. Picornie, 35, had once been a prominent hooligan, but by 1997 wasn't usually active; however, he had come out of his hooligan 'retirement' that day, telling his partner that he was going to get something to eat. Picornie was beaten to death in a muddy field. Another Ajax follower who saw what was happening went back to help him and was stabbed twice in the lungs.

The death stunned the Dutch. Some Feyenoord fans paid for an advert in a leading national newspaper offering their sympathy and stating that it was never meant to happen; others simply celebrated the death. At the first Feyenoord–Ajax game afterwards, the majority of Feyenoord fans bellowed 'You left your friend on his own' and held up inflatable sledgehammers. All Dutch fans felt the repercussions as Picornie's death led to a nationwide campaign: 'Football: don't mess it up'.

Now, if you want to travel away with Ajax or Feyenoord, you have to go through more identification checks than an MI5 job candidate. You can only travel on supervised trains, which are often delayed by the police. Flouting the frequent alcohol bans can mean an immediate €450 fine, while police infiltrate ultra groups and have legal powers to phone-tap suspects. And when the visiting fans finally reach the opponents' ground, they are accompanied and met by enough security to satisfy a third-world dictator.

The first of the yellow trains appears on one of several elevated rail lines that surround Ajax's gleaming home ground. An angry roar goes up, firecrackers explode and bottles are thrown towards the police. The crowd surges towards the formidable line of security in the vain hope of reaching the Feyenoord contingent, before police horses charge straight into the group, scattering people everywhere. Eleven fans are arrested and three officers wounded.

The train doors open and the Feyenoord fans spill onto the platform. The forty-three-mile journey between the two cities should take an hour, but football trains deliberately travel more slowly with the heat turned on full and the windows closed to make the occupants drowsy.

Undeterred, and invigorated as the fresh air hits them, the Feyenoord fans immediately begin hurling abuse at the Ajax supporters, eighty metres away. For decades they have traded insults via the media and websites, but only twice a year do they see the face of the enemy. One Feyenoord fan unfurls a Palestinian flag. 'Hamas, Hamas – Jews to the gas,' chant some of the Feyenoord fans. 'We are Super Jews,' retort Ajax fans brandishing a Star of David.

'They're just kids, the real lads aren't there,' says 'Longy', an Ajax lad observing the scenes, 'because if they did anything they would get nicked straight away and their photos would be on television tomorrow.'

Instead the hardcore Ajax hooligans are drinking in a bar at the opposite end of the ArenA, close to the cluster of glass skyscrapers that house international blue-chip companies. As with the stadium, they were built to gentrify Bijlmer, the poor area of blighted '70s housing projects south of Amsterdam.

'It's like Kinshasa over there,' says, one pointing to the housing on the other side of the rail tracks. 'But it produces good footballers.' As with many new developments it's a cold, sterile environment – but there's a buzz today because Feyenoord are in town.

Longy knows everyone in the bar. His peers, ranging from 17-year-old lads to granddads with gnarled faces peering out from between their Stone Island jackets and Aquascutum caps, let on as they sip beer from small plastic glasses. The smell of cannabis is omnipresent. They know that, since Beverwijk, the police operation is so sophisticated that they won't get close to Feyenoord.

Ajax's main firm is the F-Side, founded in 1976 and named after the section where their hardcore used to stand at Stadion de Meer, their home between 1934 and 1996, where Johan Cruyff's mother washed the shirts. With a capacity of 22,000, it was less than half the size of

Feyenoord's iconic De Kuip [literally, 'the tub'] and hardly a suitable home for the 1995 European champions.

'De Meer stank of lager, piss and burgers and was an unsafe dump – but it was home,' recalls Longy. The move to the ArenA was difficult, with fans who'd stood together for years spread around the stadium and bemoaning a new type of middle-class Ajax fan. The suspicion was that Ajax had deliberately diluted their most problematic support.

'After seven games we went to the club and told them that the F-Side had to sit together again or there would be problems,' claims one fan. 'Nonsense,' counters a source who was a senior director at the club. 'It's very dangerous to be influenced by fear and we weren't. We had given all the fans a chance to sit together.' Whatever the truth, the F-Side soon regrouped.

'Fuck Rotterdam!' shouts a lad in English by the turnstiles. A family walk by, dad clutching a plasma screen television bought from a shop close to the ground. They couldn't look more incongruous among the F-Side if they tried. What's striking about the Amsterdam ArenA is its height. Whereas some of the greatest venues in the world like the Nou Camp and Old Trafford have pitches below ground level, lessening their visual impact outside the stadium, the 51,000-capacity ArenA's pitch is positioned ten metres above ground level, on top of two floors of parking.

Sitting with the F-Side, I'm using a season ticket from another fan. His photo's on the credit card-style season ticket and, frankly, he looks as scary as anyone we've seen so far, but when you go through the electronic turnstiles the operator checks your passport, not your season ticket, against a list of banned fans. The list is eight pages long.

It costs €15 (£10) to sit behind the goal – less than at many Conference North/South games in England – and for that you get an uninterrupted view from the lower tier, which is today bedecked in a fifty-metre long flag reading 'Amsterdam – No Bullshit'.

'There's fuck all in Rotterdam,' sing the 6,000-strong F-Side from behind the moat which separates them from the pitch, in reference to Feyenoord's chances of success this season. Feyenoord have been thrown out of the UEFA Cup for crowd trouble at an away game in France. Had they stayed, they would have played Spurs, who recorded the first ever incident of overseas hooliganism by an English club in Europe in 1974, in a match against Feyenoord.

Despite the Sunday morning kick-off and the closure of the bars belonging to the Ajax fans as yet another security precaution, the atmosphere positively crackles. As kick-off approaches, a flag is unfurled close to the away fans. Above the phrase 'Bloody Sunday', it shows the Rotterdam skyline and a German Messerschmitt bomber dropping its payload, as ninety of them did in the carpet-bombing of Rotterdam in May 1940, killing more than 800 and rendering 70,000 homeless. (Holland immediately surrendered to Hitler, sparing Amsterdam from the same treatment.) At the same time, firecrackers explode behind the goal as if to re-enact the bombing and the whole stadium holds up red, white and black cards. Then, to the tune of 'Tulips From Amsterdam', they chorus:

> *'When the spring is coming, we'll be throwing*
> *Bombs over Rotterdam,*
> *Thousands of big ones and lots of casualties, more dead than alive,*
> *What the Luftwaffe don't destroy, the F-Side will.'*

As if such a fixture requires further stoking, today marks the first appearance of a returning warrior hero: sixteen years after his Ajax debut, local boy Edgar Davids is back. His popularity has never waned and his return is celebrated on several flags; some are in English, like many around the ground – 'Red & White Fighters', 'There Can Only Be One'. There are many chants, too, imported from Britain, and as thousands sing 'If you all hate Feyenoord clap your hands,' a giant Union Jack below the away end reads 'Ajax Can't Be Stopped'. Some ascribe this to the extraordinarily high numbers of English-speaking Dutch people (85 per cent of the population has at least a basic knowledge of the language). Others mutter darkly about an underlying fascination with old-school English hooliganism.

When the game finally kicks off, as if on police request, the players do their best to release the off-pitch tension. Once the smoke clears, it takes barely half an hour for second-placed Ajax to surge into a 3–0 lead against fifth-placed Feyenoord. Davids is tenacious, but the star is playmaker Wesley Sneijder. 'Always look on the bright side of life!' chirp the Ajax sections. The travelling fans, hemmed in by security, three-metre-high walls and glass shields at the front of their section, are devastated. Even without their best player, the suspended Jaap Stam, Ajax canter to a 4–1 victory.

While most of the home fans leave after the Ajax players have completed a lap of honour, the majority of the fans in Gate 410, close to the away fans, stay put. They're Ajax's second fan group, mainly made up of younger, more enthusiastic members than the F-Side.

'We model ourselves more on the tifosi of Italy, or the fans of Greece or Argentina,' explains one of the 410 leaders, who spends the match with his back to the pitch orchestrating the chants. The abuse becomes more vicious. 'You left your friend on his own,' sing Feyenoord, in reference to Picornie. 'Wherever I've been in the world, I've never seen so many Jews as in fucking Amsterdam,' they add.

There's a reason that these songs start after the game. If they are sung during it, the referee has the power to stop the match and the authorities will impose further measures, such as banning away fans or forcing games to be played behind closed doors. And nobody wants that, no matter how vocal their hatred.

The Ajax fans then head back into town, first to a bar called Henry VIII opposite Amsterdam Centraal. Posters of former Ajax teams adorn the walls, with pride of place given to one commemorating the 1995 European Cup winners. With names such as Kluivert, Seedorf,

Rijkaard, Overmars, Litmanen, Van der Sar, De Boer, Reiziger, Kanu, Blind and Davids, it's not hard to see why.

'Van der Sar got married in Amsterdam last year,' explains Longy, who also watches the ex-Ajax goalkeeper, who plays for Manchester United. 'So 100 Ajax Ultras waited for the wedding boat to pass along the canal. When it did, we let off flares. Van der Sar is a down-to-earth man who understands the fans. The boat stopped and they passed us all a beer.'

Longy goes on to confess that he hates Feyenoord so much that if he sees a Feyenoord book in a shop he bends the cover so that it can't be sold and that if he sees a car with a Feyenoord sticker then he sprays the words 'Ajax' on it.

'Feyenoord say that we're arrogant,' he spits, 'but we support a better team. We have beaten them in their own stadium more times than they have beaten us. They are obsessed by us far more than we are by them.'

The lads move onto the Back Stage, a small bar in the busy red light district. In the street outside, a sympathy card hangs on a ribbon, marking the spot where a Middlesbrough fan was tragically stabbed to death by a drug dealer before his side's game against AZ Alkmaar in November 2005.

Some fans are coked as well as boozed up, but all are buzzing because they've just beaten Feyenoord. Dutch pop music drowns the commentary from Tottenham against Manchester United on a big screen. Many fans of both Ajax and Feyenoord travel to England to watch their second clubs. Liverpool, Manchester United and West Ham are all mentioned. What's strange is that while the Ajax lads know that some of their Feyenoord counterparts travel, they've never met them in England.

'Today was brilliant,' explains one refreshed fan as the night draws to a close. 'Fuck Feyenoord, fuck Rotterdam.'

As with all great rivalries, Ajax–Feyenoord will continue to rage. PSV could win the league for the next twenty years, but they're dismissed by fans of the big two as a factory team (for main sponsor Philips) with an appalling away following.

Some wish their enemies dead. In Holland, the situation became so bad that their wishes came true. But Picornie's death has had a positive legacy, and families can now feel safer watching football there. The situation has been improved, but only by implementing the most sophisticated security operations in Europe to keep rival fans apart. Italy take note.

Ajax and Judaism

Ajax's Jewish connection is a source of some dispute. Some say it's because fans used to pass through a Jewish area on the way to De Meer; during World War II, most of Amsterdam's Jews were sent to concentration camps, from where they didn't return. There are records of Ajax being known as 'Joden' [Jews] even before that, and what was initially and crudely used as an insult was quickly adopted by Ajax fans as a badge of honour; the Star of David is represented on many badges and scarves, huge Israel flags are often unfurled and it's not uncommon to hear thousands of F-Siders chanting 'Joden, Joden'. However, the more vocal opposition fans have taken to reacting by imitating the hissing of the gas chambers, performing the Nazi salute, waving Palestinian flags and singing songs about Hamas.

In January 2005, in the wake of a startling rise in anti-Semitic acts against a background of unstable social attitudes to multi-culturalism after the assassination of anti-immigration politician Pim Fortuyn, the KNVB (Dutch FA) published a list of words and sounds which, if heard by the referee, would justify the abandonment of the game. The list includes hissing, jungle sounds, sheep sounds, the word 'Hamas' and everything referring to prostitution, genitalia, disease, religious faith and ethnic groups.

Played for both sides

The most famous man to cross the divide was Johan Cruyff who started his career at the De Meer in 1964, bagging 190 goals in 229 games on the way to successive titles from 1970–73. After eight years abroad, he returned in 1981, only to leave in a fit of pique after being refused a new contract and sign for Feyenoord, where he helped them to the title in 1984.

Winger-cum-forward Johnny Rep played his first game for Ajax in 1971, winning a league title in his first season before scoring the only goal of the 1973 European Cup Final against Juventus. After moving abroad, he too returned to the Eredivise, linking up with Cruyff in Feyenoord's championship-winning season.

At that time Ronald Koeman was at Ajax. He guided them to the title in 1985, but, after stints at PSV and Barcelona, he made his way to Rotterdam in 1995 where he linked up with fellow international Robert Witschge. Witschge had already won the league with Feyenoord in 1993, but he, too, had started at Ajax, where he won two domestic cups and a Cup Winners' Cup.

And yet inter-club interaction isn't confined to the players. In 1997, Ajax's chief executive began an affair with his female equivalent at Feyenoord. It caused such a stir that Feyenoord relieved their employee of her duties … but she successfully sued the club for unfair dismissal and the pair are now happily married.

It's Just Not Cricket
East Bengal v Mohun Bagan, February 2007

India may be minnows on the international stage, but football in the world's second most populous nation can attract enormous crowds, particularly when Calcutta's 'big two' are going toe to toe.

Salt Lake Stadium is a huge, drab slab of concrete that sits, like some wayward Cold War relic, in a northern suburb of Calcutta rather grandly named Salt Lake City. It's suburbs such as this where that Indian economic miracle you've been hearing about is beginning to assert itself, announced in the glittering glass towers and five-star hotels that join the stadium on the skyline like altogether more fashionable and affluent residents.

It's a couple of hours before kick-off and the crowds are already gathering inside the stadium. Hindi songs crackle from the PA system, the sound of drums rises up through the thick, mosquito-infested air, and fans let off bangers so loud they rattle the spine. The spectrum of colour moves from red and yellow through to maroon and green; the former belonging to East Bengal, the latter to Mohun Bagan, both Calcuttan sides, and the oldest and greatest rivals in Indian football. Given that Salt Lake Stadium can hold about 120,000, their numbers look sparse amid the grey spartan stands, yet over 60,000 are expected here to watch what is an inconsequential league game, Mohun Bagan being well off the pace so far this season. If it had been something as significant as a cup semi-final, as it was in 1997, 131,000 would be crammed in here, and the noise, awesome even now with the stadium half-full, would have been deafening.

Just over twenty-four hours ago, flying into Calcutta from Delhi, neither myself nor my photographer, local Bengali Anamit Sen, had managed to secure press accreditation, despite spending weeks wading through the quagmire that is Indian bureaucracy. As the plane began its descent over small tufts of tropical forest, the leaves of palm trees bursting skywards and the late afternoon sun forming an orange disc on the horizon, reflected in the water of flooded rice fields, I dwelt on the fact that I might not have a story to do once I got here.

For all that, the prospect of being in Calcutta itself was motivation enough for making the trip, and I was buoyed up by this surprisingly idyllic arrival. This is a city, after all, whose grim reputation is hardly the stuff of glossy travel brochures. Comments down the years describe it as being like 'a corpse on which the Indians feed like flies', a place full of 'the hot stench of the slow-decaying poor', 'a squalid sump-hole of filth and poverty' and 'a city pursued by nightmares'. Winston Churchill said 'I shall be glad to have seen it, namely that it will be unnecessary for me ever to see it again', while people are ritually warned not to even think about going anywhere near the tap water – 'Brush your teeth with cola if you have to,' they are told. It's not exactly going to have you rushing down to Thomas Cook …

Yet beneath this wretched first impression, many visitors have discovered, as Anglo–American journalist and author Christopher Hitchens put it, a 'fantastically interesting, brave, highly evolved and cultured city which has universities, film schools, theatres, bookshops, literary cafes, and very vibrant politics.'

And, what he failed to mention, a fanatical devotion to football. Calcutta was the first city in India to take up the sport, and it remains its emotional heartland, encapsulated by the derby match. When you first hear about this, it comes as something of a shock. Mention 'India' in word association and people respond with 'curry', 'Taj Mahal', 'Shilpa Shetty', 'cricket' ... But football?!

Yet when India gained independence in 1947, most people expected football to become the national sport. It had already been thriving for the previous fifty years, it was cheap to play and it permeated all levels of India's highly-stratified society, appealing to all classes. It would also have been a more appropriate vehicle to promote the new sense of nationhood, a chance for India to introduce itself to, and compete with, a greater number of countries than cricket ever could. And yet, the reasons why it didn't happen are, in part, the same reasons why Mohun Bagan v East Bengal still attracts so many fans; football here is still essentially about regional, rather than national pride. This extends to the governing bodies – the game's history is awash with incidents of in-fighting between states that have prevented a coherent national agenda from ever emerging.

The Indian Football Association, founded in 1892, was the first indigenous institution established for the sport. Its founder, Nagendra Prasad, is regarded as the father of subcontinental football.

It's to the IFA's offices that we're immediately heading. With little time to get things arranged, most Indians would have thrown in the towel by now. The local media normally has to set things in motion months before hand if it wants to get accreditation for a game like this. We have hours.

But we have two advantages: I'm white and representing the UK press, phenomena that are about as common in Indian football as Thierry Henry warming the subs bench. Anamit remains confident that my presence alone will be enough. After making our way through the pressing heat of the central Calcutta crowds, shirts stuck to our backs, we arrive at the IFA HQ which, despite the illustrious heritage, is a ramshackle collection of poorly lit rabbit warrens tucked down a backstreet not far from the giant park that dominates the city, known as the Maidan.

We're here to meet Shri Subrata Dutta, the Honourable Secretary of the IFA, who has yet to arrive, so we're ushered into an empty office and told to wait. We do, for an hour. Given his status, Dutta can afford to be late. Indians love hierarchy and Dutta's position makes him a demi-god in this world, a man with enough power to make the wheels turn that bit faster for a chosen few. Eventually we're called to another room where Dutta is sitting expansively behind a desk, his bald head shining beneath the fluorescent strip lighting. He apologises for being late and is enormously helpful, promising to make sure we receive VIP passes for the game and the necessary IDs in order to take action photographs. 'It's a good job you were here,' says a relieved Anamit.

It's a neat illustration of how the colonial past still impacts upon the present, often expressed as an exaggerated defence to Westerners. Yet it worked the other way in the past, the game giving the local population the first means by which they could compete with their 'masters' on equal terms, a chance to assert their opposition to occupation. 'War by other means,' as George Orwell put it.

The British brought the game here with the expansion of trade under the East India company. As the British capital at the time, Calcutta was the first city to be exposed to football, games being played as early as 1854, teams made up mainly of the military classes or industrial workers. Despite the creation of the IFA in 1892, the football league was the exclusive reign of British teams until 1914. Nevertheless, Indian teams were free to play in cup competitions, and it's here that Mohun Bagan established their reputation as an emblem of national self-esteem, when in 1911 they beat a British side in the final of the IFA Shield, the first native team to do so.

After the victory, the ecstatic indigenous press reported how 'the Bengalees were tearing off their shirts and waving them around their heads'. If that sounds curiously contemporary, another report is even more so, stating 'it would fill every Indian with joy and pride to know that rice-eating, malaria-ridden, bare-footed Bengalis have got the better of beef-eating, Herculean, booted John Bull'. It could almost be a blueprint for the notorious Norwegian commentary after their victory over the English in 1981: 'Margaret Thatcher, Princess Diana, Winston Churchill – your boys took one hell of a beating!'

With the bureaucracy finally dealt with, we head out for a taste of Calcutta nightlife. Mother Theresa may have led us all to believe that there was nothing here but misery and deprivation, but walking past brightly lit modern bars and restaurants in a trendy part of town, it's easy to see how such a view is offensive to many Bengalis. What depravity there is comes via whispered offers of opium, marijuana, and 'college girls, full naked'.

I end up in a bar where a band is playing convincing covers of well-known samba tracks. The vibe is loose and easy-going, with everyone just the right side of drunkenness. It's easy to see how, when the World Cup comes around, Calcutta transforms into a Brazilian outpost, cheering on their adopted side with all the reverence and fanaticism of those in Rio or Sao Paolo.

The love affair with Brazilian football stretches back to 1977, when 100,000 people made a pilgrimage to the Maidan to see Pele juggling a ball. During the 2002 World Cup, crowds gathered on the platforms of the much-celebrated metro system to watch Brazil on the screens there. In the excitement following one goal, a commuter was pushed in the path of a train and died.

A few more mojitos later, the last of the revellers leave the bar, give up the sense of Latin abandon and make their way home, the incessant sound of car horns providing the familiar lullaby.

Come match day and repeated 'No's down the phone line make it clear that we won't get access to the players prior to tonight's game. They will go for the ritual 'puja' (prayer) and then be kept away from the media until after the game. Instead I meet up with Raman Vijayan, a striker for Calcutta's other major side, Mohammedan Sporting, who made a habit of humiliating British clubs in the 1930s, and have remained a major force.

Vijayan is a rangy 33-year-old but looks ten years younger and played for East Bengal for four years in the mid-'90s. He explains how important it is for players to get sponsorship from a company who will provide them with a job after they retire. Consequently, clubs are often named after the companies and institutions that finance them, like JCT Mills or Mahindra United. East Bengal players are on an average yearly contract of around £17,000 – good money in India, but not enough to save for a life outside the game. There are plenty of stories of former greats reduced to selling street food, while some reached a level of destitution that led to suicide.

Vijayan didn't kick a ball until he was 12, when he joined a sports school. He played his first professional game at 20 and was called up to the national side two years later, subsequently earning eighteen caps and becoming one of India's all-time top scorers. So what sort of condition does he think Indian football is in? 'In 1996, when the NFL was introduced, things got better. More sponsors have come into the game, like Vijay Mallaya, owner of Kingfisher beer and Kingfisher airlines, who now sponsors East Bengal. These sorts of people will finance the teams but don't feel the need to interfere with the coach's work.'

Unlike some people. Politicians and bureaucrats have used football as a tool to advance their own careers and the game has suffered as a result. What's more, corruption in India is endemic and football is no exception. A friend in Delhi once told me how he used to get picked for the national youth team over better players because of his influential father.

Globalisation has led to more familiar problems. 'One of the issues at present is the number of foreign players here,' explains Vijayan. 'Indian coaches have so little respect for their own players that they just assume foreigners will be better. Sometimes that's not the case but they play them anyway because of how much they cost, so their reputation depends on it. Part of the reason people think like this is from watching foreign games – mainly the Premiership, but also La

Liga and Serie A – which are now on TV. Lots of people would rather pay to watch cable than support local teams.'

As Boria Majumdar and Kausik Bandyopadhyay observe in their book on the history of Indian football, *Goalless*, 'Any failure on the part of cable operators to show important European matches has often resulted in their employees being beaten up and their offices ransacked.'

Such violence surrounding football is not uncommon here, particularly between Mohun Bagan and East Bengal. The rivalry took a more violent turn after Partition in 1947, when refugees flooded into the city from East Bengal. It was exacerbated further in the 1970s when the war for the independence of East Pakistan resulted in the creation of Bangladesh. Once again, refugees from the East poured into Calcutta. While both sets of supporters are mostly Hindu, sharing a common language and cultural heritage, Mohun Bagan fans regard themselves as more urbane and metropolitan than the 'bumpkins' from the East. That has changed as new generations have grown up without the sense of cultural division. These days, it's not uncommon to find an East Bengal-supporting son to a Mohun Bagan father.

Yet there are some remarkable stories of the intensity with which fans treat the encounter. In the 1975 cup final, East Bengal defeated Mohun Bagan 5–0. One fan was in a state of such ecstasy after the fourth goal that he had a heart attack and had to be taken to hospital. A tragedy all the more bizarre befell 25-year-old Mohun Bagan fan, Umakanto Palodhi, who was so dejected by the defeat that he committed suicide that evening, leaving a note saying, 'I wish to take revenge for this defeat in my next birth by returning as a better Mohun Bagan footballer.'

In 1977, after another defeat, one Mohun Bagan fan poisoned himself by devouring a bottle of pesticide, while matters came to a head in 1980 when a stampede claimed sixteen lives and injured hundreds.

'Do you think there will be violence tonight?' I ask Anamit, as we pogo over the potholed road en route to the stadium. He shakes his head but jokes about getting hold of a helmet just in case. At least it's mostly a joke... 'I remember going to meet my father after a derby when I was a boy,' he says, 'and seeing him emerge holding a blood-stained handkerchief to his head. He'd got caught in the crossfire.'

Tonight, Mohun Bagan are ravaged by injury, former Bury striker and India captain, Baichung Bhutia, among the absentees. East Bengal will field their new Brazilian, Edmilson Pardal, who got off to a good start two games ago, scoring twice against JCT Mills. Both coaches are foreign; the experienced Carlos Alberto Pereira da Silva for East Bengal, and the fresher Nigerian, Chima Okorie, who was a big star as a player here in the 1980s.

Dutta's VIP stamp gives us access to everywhere in the stadium except the changing rooms so we wander around the gloomy interior in search of a bar. But facilities inside prove to be every bit as low-rent as the exterior would suggest and we find nothing. What luxury there is consists of a block of seats sealed off behind lengthy panes of glass, into which cool air is pumped via air-conditioning units to stop Calcutta's great and good from sweating. The stiff, austere demeanours of the people taking their seats here are in marked contrast to the fans arriving in the stands, animated faces tribally painted, extravagant hats and banners on display, all manner of instruments tucked under their arms to help generate a suitable din.

Pitchside, India's press corps are positioning camera tripods, hooking up laptops and smoking with the zeal of relapsed quitters. Bangers increase in frequency and the Bollywood tune reverberating through the PA is increasingly drowned out by the rising chants of opposing fans, the noise creating ghostly echoes in the empty upper tiers. The opposing players emerge onto the pitch and line up for the national anthem and the derby gets under way to an almighty roar.

Nerves account for some, but not all, of the dodgy first touches and misplaced passes that set the tone in the opening ten minutes. It's a scrappy affair, the general level of quality akin to Conference football. One or two players display moments of skill; there's some typically Brazilian flair from Edmilson, but like the rest of the outfield players, he lacks any decisive pace, and the whole game runs at about 70 per cent of the speed of your average Premiership match. East Bengal chairman, Swapan Ball, had touched on this earlier in the day: 'The principle problems are stamina and strength. After 70 minutes, the players are flagging.'

On fifteen minutes we get a goal. East Bengal striker and Indian, Saumik Dey, breaks free to slot the ball home and is greeted by a wall of noise. More bangers go off, flares are lit and the East Bengal fans erupt in a mass of red and yellow. The drama is maintained by the constant pressure from Mohun Bagan's enthusiastic youngsters as they search for an equaliser, but they are denied by a few near misses and some outstanding saves from East Bengal keeper, Abhra Mondal. The final whistle goes and the East Bengal fans begin their celebrations. Tonight and tomorrow they will be eating a fish known as Hilsa to mark their success, pushing the prices up in the local markets. Had Mohun Bagan won, prawns would be costing over the odds now. But the Mohun Bagan fans are philosophical about the result, encouraged by the gutsy performances that may help them rise above mid-table this season.

The only violence comes from the scuffles among the press as they jostle for interviews afterwards. When interviewed, Mondal displays an unselfconscious boastfulness that many Indians seem prone to, crowing, 'I am my own hero'. Perhaps he was getting carried away in the moment, as happens literally a short time later, when he is held shoulder high by fans and led out of the stadium with a police guard in tow.

In contrast, East Bengal coach Da Silva strikes a rather forlorn figure, despite victory. As the fifth estate clambers over each other, arms and microphones thrust towards him, he looks like foreigners often do here in India, exasperated and exhausted by the cheerfully irrational and chaotic nature of the culture.

For the football fan, Calcutta is a revelation. If the city's intellectual life is personified in artists like filmmaker Satyajit Ray and Nobel prize-wining poet Rabrindranath Tagore, football is the barometer of its irrepressible spirit. This is a city that has taken the worst that history has thrown at it and survived, its character not only intact but enhanced. The enduring passion for football captures something of that.

But whether such enthusiasm can be channelled into a successful commercial future is less sure. The dilapidated condition of both teams' stadiums suggest neglect born of a stifling bureaucracy, not to mention a threadbare budget. But with India's cricketers returning from the World Cup in the West Indies in shame, maybe people will once again turn to the game that gave them their earliest memories of sporting national pride.

'You're Not Very Good'
Elgin City v East Stirlingshire, September 2007

If losing is a habit then Elgin City vs East Stirling is akin to two hopeless addicts scrapping in the gutter. I went to see Britain's worst game so you don't have to.

Welcome to, statistically speaking, the worst game in British professional football. Elgin City, currently propping up the Scottish Third Division, are playing host to East Stirlingshire, who have held that honour for the past five seasons. Both clubs have become a standing joke, their average gates are the lowest in Scotland (730 between them) and their (often inevitable) results are read out long after most fans have switched over to *Harry Hill's TV Burp*.

Yet the home dressing room is a mix of happy house music and upbeat banter, an incongruously buoyant blend for a team who have only just recorded their first win of the season after losing the first five.

Elgin manager Robbie Williamson slams the dressing room door and tells the players to sit down and listen. Williamson's nickname as a tough-tackling midfielder was 'psycho' so the semi-professionals, who earn between £75 and £175 a week, do exactly that. 'This is Andy,' he says. 'He was in Lisbon watching Manchester United on Wednesday night and tomorrow he'll be at Old Trafford to see Chelsea. In between, he's come here to see some quality football. Be as helpful as

you can, but the deal is that *when* we win, we throw him in the ice bath.'
I expect to stay dry, but don't say so.

Soon after, I leave the dressing room, appreciative of the access granted at Britain's most northerly senior football club.
Unfortunately, the hearty welcome is not replicated by rivals East
Stirlingshire. I introduce myself to a clutch of East Stirlingshire directors.

'I spoke with your director Paul Marnie this week and he was very
helpful. We're doing a big feature on your club and Elgin City.'

'You won't be doing anything on East Stirlingshire until after the
game,' is the curt reply. 'Understand?'

With that, the dressing room door is slammed shut. With 'the Shire'
bus scheduled to leave straight after the match, that won't be easy. I'm
stunned, given how co-operative the club have been in the week leading up to the game, but perhaps a suspicion of the media is understandable.

In 2005, Jeff Connor wrote the access-all-areas book *Pointless: A
season with Britain's worst football team*. Although rightly commended
in reviews, several Shire personalities felt that it made them look
stupid. The team were already so bad that they were attracting nationwide publicity. Sky's Jeff Stelling used to highlight their results on
Soccer Saturday. 'And East Stirlingshire have only lost by four today,'
he'd announce, grinning. Though much has changed since, some of
the club's directors clearly aren't comfortable talking about the upturn
in fortunes.

A day earlier, Williamson had picked us up from Inverness airport.
Now 38, he grew up in Merckinch, the closest Inverness has to a ghetto,
and supported local side Clachnacuddin – one of Inverness's three
Highland League teams at the time – and Rangers.

'I had trials with Rangers in 1987,' he says, 'Graeme Souness spotted me in a pre-season game, but I was disappointed and disillusioned
that they didn't take me.' A career of lower-league football followed,
most of it at Ross County who awarded him a testimonial against

Coventry City in 1998. 'By that time I'd broken my right leg on three occasions. That was the price for always giving 100 per cent and I expect the same from my players.'

In 2001, Williamson became manager of Clachnacuddin. 'Mum was delighted because she went to every game. I loved the club (he has a "Clach" tattoo) and we won our first Highland League title for 30 years. I was a local managing the team I'd supported. I knew all 300 fans by name.' But by 2004–05, the dream had started to turn sour. 'Wages were cut to £10 per player per week and I started losing men to better payers down the coast. I told the board my feelings and left. It broke my heart.'

After a year out, Williamson took the job at struggling Elgin, thirty-eight miles east of Inverness, in January 2007. 'Everyone said I was mad because Elgin were bottom and hadn't won a game,' he says. 'When I arrived I was fitter than half the players and had to clear the training pitch of dog shit, syringes, and broken bottles. It was a significant achievement that we didn't finish bottom.' That honour was left to East Stirlingshire, but more of them later …

Located five miles from the sea of the Moray Firth, Elgin is a handsome city, even viewed through persistent drizzle. Daniel Defoe described its cathedral ruins as 'magnificent'. Today its centre consists of grand buildings and unpretentious shops that do exactly what they say on the tin: newsagent, fish bar, pet shop, optician, Polish deli. Indeed, the Highlands have a burgeoning Polish population and manager Williamson has even put a flyer up in factories where a lot of Poles work in the hope that he'll pick up a stray ex-Legia Warsaw player.

Elgin is also located between two of the RAF's biggest bases, Kinloss and Lossiemouth, which provide an unorthodox source of football talent, such as forward Darren Shallicker, 33, a bomb and missile technician from Manchester. He joined the RAF at 22 and has represented the Combined Services team around Europe. A Manchester United season-ticket holder who makes the six-hour journey south when he's not playing, some have put Elgin's atrocious start down to Shallicker's – who signed in the summer – absence.

'I pulled my hamstring on my debut and then both my grans died so I had to go to funerals,' he says. 'Last week was my first game.' It was also Elgin's first win and Shallicker scored twice as they came back from being 2–0 down after eighty-five minutes to win 3–2 against Albion Rovers.

'I'm always on the websites and forums seeing what the fans are saying,' he says. 'Sometimes I'm tempted to reply to fans slagging us off, but then I stop myself.' Young striker Martin Charlesworth, the son of an RAF man, chips in: 'I'm sick of people coming up to me saying that I play for the worst team in Britain.'

While Elgin try to make the most of the local RAF talent, there is competition from other Highland clubs Ross County and Peterhead, both currently riding high in the Second Division, and in general geography is a hindrance.

'Most footballers in Scotland come from the central belt (the east-west line between Glasgow and Edinburgh that accounts for 70 per cent of Scotland's five million population) and we have trouble enticing them four hours up the A9,' explains acting Elgin chairman Graham Tatters. 'Some teams in our division train in the central belt, away from the towns in which they play. We don't want to do that as we see Elgin as part of the community.'

Yet a sense of community seems to be seriously lacking in Elgin's clubhouse. It's 8 p.m. on a Friday night and the place is virtually empty. 'That's part of the reason we're struggling,' says Tatters. 'A few years ago it was far busier, but we're trying to compete with pubs who sell beer at prices cheaper than we buy it. Older members have passed on. Younger guys want something different, but if we played loud music the older men wouldn't like it.'

On the club's message board, Tatters receives much of the blame for Elgin's predicament. 'I get pelters,' he says. 'It's frustrating because much of it is personal, anonymous and not constructive. I'm trying to do my best for this club, but I can't do right for doing wrong at times.'

Another former RAF man who served for thirty-one years after joining up in 1966, Tatters is amicable and those who question his commitment should see his house, which has a room full of Elgin mementos. In the past week, he's mowed the pitch, put the goals up, repaired the nets, coached the under-19s team and driven the under-15s to Livingston, 'because I'm the only one at the club with a licence to drive the bus'. He preceded Williamson as manager and his son played for Elgin. 'Made his debut at 16,' he says, his accent hinting at his Geordie roots. 'He got a bus to Greenock Morton and nobody spoke to him for 10 hours. That annoyed me.'

It's 11 a.m. on the morning of the match. The East Stirlingshire coach left Falkirk (it's often wrongly assumed that East Stirlingshire are from near Stirling) three hours ago and they're still two hours from Elgin.

Ian Ramsey, a 44-year-old electrical assembler, is the chair of the Shire Trust. A Falkirk lad, he began supporting the Shire 'To be different from my mates. I wanted to support the least fashionable club.' He didn't have to look far. 'I've seen some good and many bad times,' he says, of watching a club that gave 32-year-old Alex Ferguson his first managerial job in 1974. There were only eight registered players when Ferguson arrived. 'They were the worst senior club in the country,' Ferguson later wrote.

'He was a frightening bastard from the start,' said winger Bobby McCulley. Ferguson left for St Mirren 117 days later, having revolutionised the club and pushed them to the top of the table.

'Things really started to go wrong at the turn of the millennium when the people in charge behind the scenes changed,' explains Ramsey. 'Alan Mackin, a former player, took control and fans were suspicious of his motives. He introduced a £10 per week wage for all players which meant we lost most of our best ones. He was unpopular, rarely attended games and it didn't seem to bother him that we were getting huge amounts of negative publicity for failure on a grand scale.'

The club began to decay. Firs Park, East Stirlingshire's home, was given a safety capacity of just 750. The capacity of a roped off football pitch with no stands is twice that.

Ramsey is personable, intelligent and articulate, the antithesis of the anonymous internet warrior who rights the world's wrongs from the safety of his bedroom, but he doesn't mince his words about Mackin and his fellow East Stirlingshire directors. 'Those bastards have done this to us. We didn't blame the players because they gave it their all. The low point came in 2003–04 when we were not just bad, but legendarily bad.'

That season, the Shire went on a twenty-six-game losing run. Pools companies stopped including them on their coupons, bookies didn't take win/lose bets. They were well on their way to breaking the twenty-seven-game losing streak British record until they beat Elgin 2–1 in the last game of the season.

'It was like winning the Champions League. We were jumping around like fools,' adds Ramsey. 'We'd achieved something at last – we'd stopped ourselves becoming the worst British team ever. We never thought about leaving, because without us there would be no club.' And, you would assume, nothing to stop the ground being sold.

But the situation didn't improve. 'We became so bad that in 2005, the Scottish League came up with the notion that any club could be thrown out of the league if they finished bottom of the Third Division four seasons in a row.'

It was a surprise then, that East Stirlingshire's shocking form attracted a possible saviour. Spencer Fearn, a Sheffield Wednesday supporting businessman, has put an estimated £40,000 into the club so far, helping The Shire break their infamous £10 a week (usually paid in coins) wage shackle. Ramsey hopes Fearn will take over the club, but for now will have to make do with his investment coinciding with the Shire winning four of their first five games of the season. 'But

The Lowdown
Elgin City

Population: 23,000.
Club formed: 1893.
Elected to Scottish League: 2000.
Average 2006–07 attendance: 423 (second lowest in Scotland).
Highs: Highland League Champions fifteen times, Scottish Cup quarter-finalists (v Celtic) 1968.
Lows: Losing to East Stirlingshire on last day of the 2003–04 season, sparing their opponents the indignity of breaking the British professional football record of twenty-seven consecutive losses.

Did you know?

– Celtic legend Jimmy Johnstone played for Elgin, as did 'super' John McGinlay, while Andy Goram did a half season.
– In 1991, when still in the Highland League, Elgin's average crowd was 1,300.
– In 2005, assistant manager Kenny Black saw a takeover bid thwarted by wealthy local builder Billy Robertson, who cleared the club's debts, but has offered little further investment, complain fans.

the job is only half done,' insists Ramsey. 'We want the luxury of mid-table obscurity.'

Ramsey has travelled up overnight to meet Andy Crerar, 42, a former RAF man whose work in logistics took him to Iraq and the Falklands, among other places. Originally from Greenock where he worked on the Morton Supporters' Trust, Crerar is now part of Elgin's Trust and hopes to learn some lessons from his Shires counterpart.

'There has been a noticeable improvement since Robbie Williamson took over, but we feel there's a lack of direction at the club,' he says, supping his pint in a pub on the High Street. 'We don't want to be anti-board, but we're owned by a builder and we have cordoned off grass terraces at both ends of the ground! There's a "them and us" situation, which is why I think every club should have supporter influence on the board.'

It works both ways, though. Tatters, for his part, is happy to speak directly to fans, but he's less inclined to communicate when people are consistently, and anonymously, sniping.

'Fans need a soundboard and that's all the websites are,' argues Crerar. 'It's no different to people talking in a pub.' The board would argue that it is very different, with the wider audience of the internet meaning opinion quickly becomes fact.

With both sides aiming for the same objective, such differences should be easily reconcilable. But there's little they can do about Elgin's residents travelling to Glasgow to watch Celtic or Rangers instead of supporting their local team. 'It's a pity but it's their choice,' says Crerar ruefully. 'The potential for greater support is here – we had 3,500 for a Scottish Cup game against Buckie Thistle only last season.'

Elgin's picturesque Borough Briggs ground is surrounded by greenery and handsome housing which overlooks the nearby river. The 478 black seats in the main stand came from Newcastle's St James' Park and sit opposite the archaic covered terrace that houses the majority of the 3,927 capacity – much reduced from the 12,608 who watched a Scottish Cup game against Arbroath in 1968. Such a privileged position by the River Lossie costs Elgin £500 a week in insurance. 'We've been flooded seriously twice in the last ten years,' says Tatters. 'That's a fortune for a club at our level. It's killing us.'

Williamson arrives at 12.45 p.m. after watching his son play football, soon followed by the 'Hey Jimmys' – the Glasgow car pool (Elgin

folk reckon that their Glasgow counterparts say 'Hey Jimmy' to everyone). Elgin have four players from the central belt who make the four-
hour trip north for home games. One, Paul Kaczan, 24, is a defender
from Hamilton who was with Hearts.

The Lowdown
East Stirlingshire

Population: 32,890 (of Falkirk, who are in the SPL).
Club formed: 1880.
Elected to Scottish League: 1900.
Average 2006–07 attendance: 307 (the lowest in Scotland).
Highs: Scottish Division Two champions 1931–32.
Lows: Finishing bottom of the Scottish Third Division in 2003–04
    with just eight points from thirty-six games, including a twenty-
    six-game losing streak.

Did you know?

- Following a goalless ninety minutes in a 1980 League Cup
  match against Albion Rovers, East Stirlingshire won the
  penalty shootout to progress. The referee, however, should
  have played extra-time. A replay was held and Albion
  won 4–0.
- A Shire fan club was set up in Norway after a feature on the club
  and their Norwegian-bred defender Carl Erich Thywissen
  appeared on Norwegian TV. It currently boasts 4,800 members
  – ten times their average crowd.
- There is no spectator accommodation behind one end of the
  East Stirlingshire ground. Instead there's a wall, which forms
  part of a Land of Leather store.

'We set off at nine for home games,' he says. 'The club hire us a car and it's usually OK, unless we get caught behind a caravan or lorry. During the week we train with Shorts, a junior [semi-professional] club. For away games we meet the rest of the lads at a service station or sometimes at the ground itself.'

Standing by the pitch are Robert Jack, 63, and Jim Wilson, 50, the Shire's kit man for twenty-five years. They've seen the downs and the downs. One of them cracks a gag to the referee, who is inspecting the lush pitch. 'You should have come up on the coach with us,' he says, knowing that the referee, like them, has driven from Falkirk.

It's implausible that referee Craig Charleston, 37, would have travelled with the visiting team, but even if he had wanted to, it would have been impossible. 'I was working until 9.30 a.m. this morning,' says the transport manager for a haulage company. 'I started at six, then drove north. I'll get back about 10.30 tonight.'

In the dressing room, meanwhile, Williamson is doing his utmost to ensure I get the threatened ice bath come the final whistle. 'We've got to win our home games,' he stresses. 'Their two centre-halves are not very good … their midfield like to pass the ball … work your fucking bollocks off.'

The photographer, who has driven up from Glasgow, takes a picture. 'For fuck's sake, I've not done my hair yet,' shouts Williamson. The comment raises a laugh, the mood still remarkably upbeat. Has one victory done this?

After a warm-up, the players return to the dressing room and change into their match kits. Charts on the wall show each player's body mass index – a fat count. The average is 10 per cent. Striker Shallicker's is 25.4.

'Focus, focus,' says Williamson. 'Deliver … If you don't put the ball into the box you can't score … we've got to dictate.' Someone burps loudly. Another player shouts: 'Come on, let's beat the c***s.'

Behind the goal stand twenty-six Shire fans, not so fresh from a five-hour coach journey. Entrenched in years of despair, they've travelled with genuine hope. One wild-looking man in a brown leather jacket is clutching a plastic bag. He continuously shouts instructions which are indecipherable even to those around him. His efforts are in vain, as Shallicker gives Elgin the lead with a 33rd-minute penalty. The football is of a similar standard to level eight in England – that's three below the old Conference – where the players earn the same. With the Shire down to ten men, Shallicker adds a second.

Everyone is elated in the dressing room at the break. Everyone, that is, except the bloke nervously eying the ice bath. Some players down water or Red Bull, while Shallicker lies on the physio's bed, where another RAF man, 35-year-old father of five Leigh Thomas, rubs handfuls of Deep Heat into the striker's lower back.

Williamson is happy, but berates striker Craig Frizzell for passing to Shallicker when he had a chance to score. 'I had a fiver on him to score the first goal,' comes the reply.

Shallicker gets his hat-trick seven minutes after the restart, and then leaves the field to a standing ovation. Borough Briggs is buzzing – if that's possible with a crowd of 399 – with laughter and smiles replacing the gallows humour. The faithful are not used to seeing Elgin win, let alone destroy opponents. Fans walk past the home dugout, all clenched fists and words of encouragement to the manager. Frizzell adds two more and Mark Nicolson another as Elgin win 6–0, each goal followed by The Proclaimers' *I Would Walk 500 Miles* on the public address system.

The incredible result (the headline on the club's website reads: 'Super Shelly grabs a hat-trick, Shire are atrocious.') lifts Elgin off the bottom for the first time all season and the players are euphoric. Watching me take my punishment is merely the cherry on top of the icing.

Williamson switches on his mobile as he gets in his car for the drive back to Inverness. He has twenty-five new messages, all of them congratulatory. 'If the score's right, Jeff Stelling will be having a fit,' reads one.

'Did you enjoy that?' asks Williamson as he rings his eldest son, seven-year-old Jake, who has been at the game. 'It was brilliant, dad. The best game I've ever seen. Is it too late to win the league now?'

The answer is probably yes, although at time of writing Elgin are unbeaten in five games and lie just one point behind East Stirlingshire, who have lost both their games since the unofficial clash of 'the worst two teams in British professional football'. As things stand, both have their wish of mid-table obscurity. But frankly, where's the fun in that?

Sheep Shaggers v Donkey Lashers

Preston North End v Blackpool, December 2007

It certainly isn't all quiet on the Preston front when one of Lancashire's fiercest rivalries is re-awoken after nearly eight years. Blackpool detest 'Nob End' – and the feeling is mutual …

'Sheep shagging inbred bastards. I can't wait until the morning.' Welcome to the Devonshire Arms in Blackpool's northern suburbs. It's a local pub, for local people – 'no tourists in here trying to take the piss' – and the reason tomorrow can't come soon enough for this Devonshire regular is that it will bring his beloved Seasiders face to face with bitter rivals Preston North End for the first West Lancashire derby in almost eight years.

'Preston was the first thing we thought about when we won the play-off final at Wembley in May,' concurs fellow Blackpool fan Gary Tate, who runs coaches to all the Tangerines' away games under the name Tate Independent Travel Services (TITS). His father, a Wearside miner, moved to the resort in 1965 in search of a better life, finding work in a factory making rock, making Tate one of many Blackpool residents who are second or third generation exiles from northern cities, or Glasgow. 'When the fixtures came out, we just looked down them until we saw the word "Preston",' he adds. 'For us, it's the biggest game.'

These sentiments are echoed sixteen miles east along the M55. 'In my time covering Preston the bad feeling has never gone away despite a spell of seven seasons apart recently during which time PNE's temporary derby rivals became Burnley,' says long-time *Lancashire Evening Post* reporter Brian Ellis. 'One Preston manager – Gary Peters – took it so seriously that he publicly refused to utter the name Blackpool, always referring to the Seasiders as "that lot with the tower". It almost earned him a good thumping when he was cornered on the car park outside Bloomfield Road after one game, but he faced them up and managed to get away unharmed.'

It's a far cry from the postwar years, when the two clubs enjoyed a more friendly rivalry in England's top flight in all but two seasons between 1946 and 1961.

'We always saw Blackpool as our main rivals and we had some great games against them' recalls Preston's proudest son Tom Finney, now 85 and still keeping a full diary, 'but there was none of the current nastiness from some fans. I can remember wanting the Blackpool side of Stan Mortensen and Stan Matthews to beat Manchester United in the 1948 FA Cup final,' continues the man who played 433 times for his hometown club between 1946–60 and won seventy-six England caps. Blackpool and Preston were joint favourites for the 1948 FA Cup, but United knocked out a Preston side featuring Finney and Bill Shankly in the sixth round, preventing a Preston–Blackpool final.

'The rivalry is mainly between the fans,' says Jimmy Armfield, the Radio Five Live pundit who played a record 568 times for Blackpool between 1952–71 and was capped forty-three times by England. 'It started with arguments over whether Stanley Matthews was better than Tom Finney in the '50s. What makes it so interesting is that it's a rivalry rich in goals. Derby games tend to be tight, but not Blackpool v Preston. I played in several high-scoring derbies – in my first season Blackpool drew 3–3 at Preston and lost 2–6 at home. Jimmy McIntosh scored five for Blackpool in one game in 1948.' That game finished 7–0 and is still Preston's record defeat.

Back in the Devonshire, talk is not of the distant past but of the immediate future. Many here will be among the 2,800 'official' away fans tomorrow, while others are prepared to pay over the odds to ensure they're also at Deepdale. 'I'd give £100 now for a ticket,' says one, and in a town where a night in a guesthouse including breakfast and evening meal is as cheap as £12, £100 goes a long way. 'But it has to be in our end. Can't risk going in with the Nobbers [as in Preston Nob End].'

Indeed, there's talk of trouble, but the Devonshire lads, who talk under a framed photo of Blackpool Tower – 'See that?' said one earlier. 'I don't ever want to live where I can't see that tower' – reckon the police operation will be sophisticated. 'There will be 200 of us on the train from Blackpool North at 11.15 [police insist the game kicks off at 12.30 to reduce the likelihood of trouble]. All the lads and the muckers.'

The what?

'The muckers – 18-year-old drugged-up mad heads who are game as fuck. We're meeting at a pub by the tower at 9 a.m.'

Peter Collins won't be travelling with them. 'It saddens me when violence comes into it,' explains the 73-year-old, who saw his first Seasiders game in the 1930s and finally realised his dream job – Blackpool secretary – in his seventh decade. 'I've always loved Blackpool, but before it became affordable to go to away games [Collins has since seen Blackpool play at over 100 grounds], I would catch a bus to Deepdale and watch the likes of Man United, Everton, and Liverpool play against Preston. There was no animosity because I was from Blackpool and I had a respect for Preston and great players like Tom Finney.'

Of more concern to Collins than Preston fans is the number of people from Blackpool who instead choose to watch one of the bigger North West clubs. The proximity of Liverpool and Manchester affects gates at both Bloomfield Road and Deepdale. This despite Blackpool's urban population being 261,000, just below Preston's 264,000, making

MATTHEWS vs FINNEY

Who was better?
Sir Stanley Matthews

Nicknames: The Wizard of
the Dribble
Position: Right-wing
Individual honours:
Footballer of the Year 1948,
1963; European Footballer
of the Year 1956; Awarded
CBE 1957; Knighted in
1965
Club honours: Division One
runner-up 1956; FA Cup
winner 1953, runner-up
1948, 1951
International honours: 54
England caps (11 goals);
played at 1950 and 1954
World Cup
They said: 'The man who
taught us the way football
should be played' Pele

both bigger than seven Premier League destinations: Wigan, Blackburn, Derby, Reading, Middlesbrough, Sunderland, and Bolton.

'There's some very loyal fans of the bigger clubs in Blackpool that I don't have a problem with them,' says Collins, 'but it's ones who never go to games that irritate me.'

Preston and Blackpool both have claims to fame that extend beyond the distinguished histories of their football clubs. Britain's first motorway was Preston's M6 bypass in 1958. Britain's first KFC was also in Preston, as was the last major battle in England – the Battle of Preston in 1715.

Blackpool attracts more visitors each year than Greece and has more hotel beds than Portugal. It consumes more chips per capita than anywhere on earth and boasts Europe's second most popular tourist attraction, the Pleasure Beach, only topped by the Vatican. 'Blackpool is ugly, dirty and a long way from anywhere,' wrote Bill Bryson in *Notes from a Small Island*, 'its sea is an open toilet, and its attractions nearly all cheap, provincial and dire.'

A planned supercasino seemed to offer salvation from such mockery but Manchester was awarded the project instead. 'We needed that casino,' says one local, 'needed some positive headlines. We're sick of the crap people write about Blackpool because it's not Blackpool folk who cause the problems but outsiders.' As the tourists deserted Blackpool for weeks on the Costas, so many of the B&Bs were filled with a benefit- and drug-dependent population. 'We picked up the scum from Manchester, Liverpool, and Glasgow. Blackpool people are decent and hard working, but nobody writes about them.'

While central Blackpool is run-down, its catchment area includes Lytham and St Annes, an area so prosperous and genteel that former resident Les Dawson said: 'Its so posh that when we eat cod and chips

---

MATTHEWS vs FINNEY

Who was better?
Sir Tom Finney

Nicknames: The Preston Plumber

Position: Right-wing, left-wing, inside-forward

Individual honours: Footballer of the Year 1954, 1957; Awarded OBE 1981; Knighted in 1998

Club honours: Division One runner-up 1953, 1958; FA Cup runner-up 1954

International honours: 76 England caps (30 goals); played at 1950 and 1954 World Cup

They said: 'Would have been great in any team, in any match and in any age, even if he had been wearing an overcoat' Bill Shankly

---

we wear a yachting cap.' The Football League headquarters moved to Lytham from Preston in 1959 and stayed there for four decades until re-locating to London.

Preston is faring far better – much to Blackpool's envy – boasting England's sixth biggest university, better transport links and a confidence brought about by its new city status. Plans for Preston to build an 'iconic' city-centre tower were recently objected to by Blackpool council, who feared it could damage the resort's own regeneration hopes.

It's in football though, that the rivalry has been most tangible. Preston North End were a founder member of the Football League in 1888 and were England's first league champions. Unbeaten throughout the 1888–89 season (only Arsenal, in 2003–04 have matched this feat), their 'Invincibles' became the first team to win the double.

Preston won the league again a year later, but they haven't won it since, although they finished runners-up in 1953 and 1958. They had further success in the FA Cup – victory in 1938 and another final appearance in 1954. But by the time they reached their next cup final in 1964, they had spent three years out of the top flight. They haven't returned since.

Blackpool joined the Football League in 1896 and were ever-presents in the top flight between 1937 and 1967. Losing FA Cup finalists in 1948 and 1951, they went one better in the 'Matthews Final' of 1953, when the Seasiders came from 3–1 down to beat Bolton 4–3. Blackpool finished runners-up to the Busby Babes in the race for the 1956 title.

The '50s was also the heyday for the West Lancs rivalry – with the pair meeting eighteen times in the First Division. Blackpool also supplied England with several internationals – four of them, including the great Stan Mortensen, for the famous 1953 Wembley defeat to Hungary. A statue of Mortensen now stands outside Bloomfield Road. Later, Jimmy Armfield was in the 1966 England squad alongside Alan Ball.

In 1970, Blackpool, then in England's second tier, went to Deepdale where, thanks to a Fred Pickering hat-trick, they won 3–0, sealing promotion back to the top flight and relegating Preston. 'The *real* rivalry started that night,' says Armfield, even though it put two divisions between the teams 'It was such a significant result for both teams. There were 34,000 in the ground – 15,000 of us with 3,000 locked out. Many walked back to Blackpool and our bus passed them on the way home, dancing and singing by the road.

After returning to Division Two, Preston appointed Bobby Charlton as manager in 1973, but he oversaw another relegation to the Third Division. Off the field, the rivalry carried on regardless. In 1978, fighting between fans at a concert in Preston led to a young Lillywhites fan being stabbed to death.

Big names like Nobby Stiles, Harry Catterick, and Brian Kidd could not stop Preston's rot. By 1985, they were in the Fourth Division for the first time in their history, finishing second bottom in 1986 and surviving relegation through re-election. A dilapidated Deepdale, now with a plastic pitch, needed as much work as the team and with areas of its once grand Kop fenced off, the capacity was cut from 41,000 to 19,500 – not that it was needed.

Solace came through lower league derby victories over Blackpool, with Preston fans still recalling the 1992–93 encounter when Tony Ellis scored a hat-trick in a 3–2 win at Bloomfield Road.

At Deepdale, inspiration came from long-time fan and graphic designer Ben Casey. When his plans for a new ground, modelled on Genoa's architecturally stunning post-modern Luigi Ferraris Stadium, were published in the local paper, they appeared a little too ambitious for a club in the Third Division. But, bit by bit, Preston have remained true to them, constructing four sleek new stands over thirteen years. The first featured Tom Finney's face picked out from the seats, while the gnarled features of Bill Shankly, another former great, adorns the Kop. In June 2001, the National Football museum opened at Deepdale. In 2005, Deepdale became the oldest senior football ground in continuous use in the world.

Preston's on-field revival started in 1996, a season after David Beckham's loan spell from Manchester United, with the third-tier title. That year saw serious disorder when the two clubs met at Deepdale. There were more than seventy arrests inside and outside the ground and pubs were trashed in the city centre.

David Moyes, a 34-year-old defender, became manager in 1998, guiding Preston to the second level as champions in 2000. Later, striker David Healy arrived from Manchester United for £1.5 million, an illustration of the club's progress. Thanks to him, Preston almost made it straight to the Premiership, but were defeated 3–0 by Bolton in the Division One play-off final. It was to become a familiar pattern.

North End were shrewd in the transfer market, often investing in Manchester United fringe youngsters. One, Jonathan Macken, cost £250,000 and was sold to Manchester City for £5 million. More recently, David Nugent was picked up from Bury for £100,000 and sold to Portsmouth for £6 million. Fans reckon Nugent's absence is a major factor in this season's struggle, but their club, under chairman Derek Shaw, has been a success story.

'If someone farts at Deepdale then Radio Lancashire have a special programme about it,' says one Blackpool fan, referring to a perceived media bias towards Preston in these parts. This smacks of an inferiority complex, born out of seven years of, well, inferiority. Given Preston's average home gate is also 5,000 more than Blackpool's, the coverage seems proportionate.

The last meeting in April 2000 was bittersweet for the Tangerines. Preston clinched promotion at Bloomfield Road and a Blackpool fan had to hand the victorious North End team a promotion flag at the final whistle. He deliberately gave it to them upside down.

By then, Bloomfield Road was the worst ground in the Football League, but at least the club was still in existence. In 1983, just twelve years after playing in the top flight, Blackpool faced the ignominy of re-election after finishing fourth from bottom of the old Fourth Division – not so much a rollercoaster ride, but a downhill slide in the famous fun house.

Local media tycoon, the flamboyant former actor Owen Oyston, saved Blackpool from ruin in 1988, only to step down when he was convicted of rape. His son Karl took over and remains chairman, but the Oystons divide opinion locally, with appreciation for their role in saving Blackpool from bankruptcy and keeping the club solvent tempered by concern. 'We've been promised more super stadiums than we can remember,' says one fan, 'and what we got were two stands that have already started to show their age. The ground looks awful.'

The unattractive stadium contrasts with the football on it. A superb run-in saw Blackpool make – and win – the 2007 League One play-offs under dynamic manager Simon Grayson, 38. Their second goal in the 2–0 victory over Yeovil was scored by Keigan Parker, another colourful character who'd sold his own kiss-and-tell story of a relationship with Jade Goody to a tabloid.

A week before the derby with Preston, courts fined the Scottish striker £275 after he kicked in the glass door of a Blackpool 'massage parlour' at 4 a.m., having been told to leave 'Desires' when he threw his bag of chips at one of the girls working there.

Blackpool were the division's top scorers last season, the football pushing average gates past the 8,000 mark in a stadium which holds 9,200. The bigger crowds weaken the Oystons' case for not expanding Bloomfield Road because of low demand. But are they even in charge? In May 2006, the Latvian businessman and Oyston business associate Valery Belokon became club president after making an undisclosed investment in the club which gave him a 20 per cent stake. Whatever, the biggest reward for Blackpool's promotion was a much-anticipated derby.

Match day starts in the Norbreck Castle, a famous Blackpool hotel where, in the 1960s, Manchester United would relax before big games. 'We thought it was dead posh,' recalls Paddy Crerand. It's not anymore. The clientele now consists mainly of elderly couples and brassy groups on cheap cabaret weekends. The night before, one lady in a tipsy gaggle even mistook my laptop bag for a record bag – 'The DJ's here.'

It's a vile December morning and rain lashes against the hotel's windows, obscuring the vista of the Irish Sea's heavy brown swell. Shelter is limited on Blackpool's famous promenade and shoppers scurry quickly to avoid the rain. The only people who appear to be doing a brisk trade, though, are newsagents selling derby supplements.

After meeting up early in a pub, Seasiders' fans make their way to Blackpool North train station for the 11.15 to Preston, where 'Good Luck Blackpool FC' appears on the information screens. Some wear tangerine shirts, others casual hooligan attire – a band of ageing brothers eager to go into battle against their oldest foes. Wisely, police don't let fans board unless they possess match tickets.

Those that do are greeted at Preston rail station half an hour later with airport-style security scanners to check for weapons. In 2006, the station was the scene of what police described as 'large-scale disorder' after Blackpool fans returning from their game at Millwall clashed with Preston fans returning from an England match at Old Trafford. Pubs in Preston have been told to stay closed before the game and visiting fans travelling by road are met by police as soon as they leave the M55 motorway (after passing under a 'Come On PNE' banner hung from a bridge near one of the villages between the two which has supporters of both teams).

At the train station, Blackpool fans are escorted onto a convoy of double-decker buses to prevent them walking through Preston city centre. Just an hour later, the *Lancashire Evening Post*'s website is reporting what happened next: 'Soccer hooligans went on the rampage, attacking a pub and smashing up a double-decker bus on a day of football violence in Lancashire. Blackpool fans ripped out windows and threw seats at police officers as they were ferried by bus from Preston railway station to Deepdale before the big derby clash with Preston North End on Saturday.'

Two days later, it reports: 'A mob of thirty Preston fans later attacked a Blackpool pub with bins and bottles in a "revenge" mission as staff and customers cowered inside. Nineteen people were arrested as more than 300 police officers were drafted in to keep both sets of supporters apart.'

Four Preston fans are waiting for me at Deepdale, not far from where some local wags have changed the 'Next Match – Blackpool' sign on Sir Tom Finney Way to 'Blackpoo'. Another sign now reads 'Next match – Donkey Lashers' – a reference to the donkeys on Blackpool's beach.

'Look where we were fifteen years ago,' says Wayne, a farmer from just outside Preston. 'We had a plastic pitch, a stadium that was falling down, crowds of 7,000 and watched the long-ball game under John Beck. Some critical Preston fans are disappointed with this season, but they've got short memories. This club has come a long way and we've punched above our weight and consistently challenged for the Premiership. We spent £1.5 million on two players in the summer, Blackpool spent £100,000.' And the rivalry? 'Blackpool is a dying town full of Glaswegian alcoholics. Preston is a proper city.' At least it has been since the Queen awarded it city status in 2002.

The game is a sell-out, the capacity limited to 17,807 while a new 6,000-seater main stand is constructed. The gap allows the wind and rain to swirl in from the Lancashire moors, but it doesn't dampen the atmosphere for this foot-of-the-table encounter. Preston fans magnanimously applaud Michael Jackson, the Blackpool captain who played 243 times for Preston as they rose through the leagues. Jackson is one of forty-six players to have represented both clubs, adding some heat to an already spicy match-up.

Typical derby fare songs reverberate and accusations of inbreeding are exchanged across a heavily policed six-seat buffer zone separating rival fans. Premiership official Mark Clattenburg oversees a pulsating match which Blackpool win following a cheeky, chipped, second half Wes Hoolahan penalty.

The three points lift Blackpool clear of the relegation zone, but this season will remain a tough one for both teams, with March's return game at Bloomfield Road set to be the proverbial six-pointer. Back in the Devonshire, they simply 'can't wait'. Again.

The Eternal War
Lazio v Roma, March 2008

Forget winning scudettos, the fans of Lazio and Roma are far
more concerned about going toe-to-toe with each other.

'There's blood on the bridge. Don't go there.' I have just disembarked
from a packed bus outside Rome's Stadio Olimpico. The blue flashing
lights of police riot vans add further chill to the cold night air. Armed
riot police sweep between the traffic, their batons poised. A cry goes up
from an officer and police swarm around a group of *ultras* (hardcore
fans), arrest a handful and then march them to a wagon holding
temporary cells.

Something sinister has also just taken place between the Tiber River
and the beautiful cypress trees which surround the stadium. Four
Manchester United fans appear. 'Don't walk there,' one says, pointing
towards the police vans. Another warns against going to the bridge, a
notorious ambush point of Roma's violent *ultras*. Several United fans
were stabbed there six months ago. You don't expect football violence
to be played out amid the granite statues, boulevards, and rich mosaics
at the foot of Monte Mario.

It's December 2007 and United are back in Rome. Lessons have not
been learned and there's more trouble, just as there always seems to be
when English teams play in the Italian capital. My mobile starts to

buzz with texts. 'Reports that five United stabbed,' says one. 'Be careful.' I was, but it was still very, very moody.

On a comedown at the hotel later, I hear: 'You think that was bad, go to a Roma vs Lazio game.' It's only from the receptionist, but the reputation of Il Derbi Capitale is ferocious.

'The Roman derby is the most intense in Italy,' states Aurelio Capaldi, football journalist for Italian state broadcaster Rai.

'Apart from the Old Firm, nothing compares with the derby of the Big Dome [St Peter's],' says former Lazio *ultra* and player Paulo Di Canio. Having played in five derbies, from Milan to London, he should know. 'Roma and Lazio fans care more about winning the derby than where they finish in the league,' he adds.

'Points matter in the Milan derby because Inter and Milan usually chase trophies,' Capaldi agrees. 'In Rome it's different. Only five *scudettos* have ever gone to the capital. It's all about the derby.'

There are other factors. While the Milanese derby is diluted by the existence of Juventus in nearby Turin – indeed, the Internazionale/Juventus clash is known as 'the derby of Italy' because both clubs boast nationwide fan bases – the Rome derby only really matters in Rome.

'Roma and Lazio focus on each other,' continues Capaldi. 'Football is serious in the eternal city and it affects Roman life. With good weather, Romans live outdoors far more than people in Milan or Turin. They talk about football in the squares, parks, and bars. Roma and Lazio fans always tease each other about the derby. The Romans' personality is suited to football – ironic and humorous. The Milanese character is far more reserved and the population of the north is diluted by many southerners who moved for work. In Rome, you are Roman. And you're either Lazio or Roma.'

It's Easter 2008. The winter gloom that enveloped the December trip is receding and Rome is full of tourists taking in world-class monuments like the Roman ruins of the Colosseum and the

Renaissance grandeur of St Peter's. Groups of appallingly dressed Americans follow uninterested tour leaders holding yellow flags. They talk of Bernini's Baroque fountains, the Spanish Steps and of hoping to see the Pope's Easter address. But there's another big event in town and I head in the other direction, towards Olimpico, the stadium Lazio and Roma share, for a league game. Back towards the bridge.

Lazio are mid-table in Serie A while Roma lie second. It's a Lazio home game, but 30,000 of the anticipated 70,000 crowd will be Roma, whose fans retain their *curva* (bank of fans) behind the south goal. Both clubs have suffered sharp decreases in crowds since the turn of the millennium, with Roma's average crowd dropping from 58,000 to less than 40,000 and Lazio's from 53,000 to 29,000. Three explanations are advanced: the proliferation of pay-per-view television meaning that more fans stay at home or in bars to watch their team; a decline in the standard of both teams – although Roma have improved greatly in recent years; and it is often unsafe to watch football in Italy.

It's two hours before kick-off and the fans crossing the bridge towards the blaze of Olimpico's lights wear the red and yellow of Roma. They have always been the better supported of the two clubs. One might assume that this is a designated entrance for their supporters until a light blue Lazio scarf is spotted, then another, the throng walking past the thousands of motorbikes that fans have left by the statues of former Olympians. Liverpool, Manchester United, and Middlesbrough fans have been attacked for wearing their colours outside the Olimpico, but for now the atmosphere is maudlin, not murderous.

The Lazio team bus cuts through the city's heavy traffic with a five-car police escort, but a horn would suffice, such is the indifference shown to them. A glance at the headlines in the voracious sport dailies explains why the mood is so different for a derby littered with a history of violence, corruption, and passion.

Rome based *Corriere Dello Sport* leads with: 'Emotion Derby.' In November, Lazio fan Gabriele Sandri, a 26-year-old DJ, was shot dead by police in an accident at a Tuscan motorway service station after Lazio and Juventus fans had rioted. That night, as Italian society attempted to comprehend another football-related death, fans rioted nationwide. Lazio fans blocked the bridge over the Tiber and torched cars.

If the hardcore fans hate anyone more than each other in Rome, it's the police, and for one game only the *ultra* groups of both clubs who wield significant power have agreed to pay their respects.

At an official level, a campaign name – 'Gimme Smile' – has been concocted, employing cartoon-like characters to promote goodwill. Few children will appreciate them. Italy may have an ageing population, but there are hardly any youngsters in the stadium. Besides, it's the *curva* who control the mood, not the authorities.

Flanked by both *ultra* leaders, Roma captain Francesco Totti and Lazio's Tommaso Rocchi walk towards the Lazio *curva* and a giant fan painting of Gabriele. Gabriele's brother stands solemnly between the two captains, their arms joined around the rival *ultra* leaders – stocky fortysomethings in baseball caps and army pants. The relationship between Italian players and *ultras* is complex. Such is their power that Totti, a living deity among Roma fans, will ignore media criticism and attend *ultra* meetings, funerals, and weddings.

The group are greeted by a respectful silence and the ambience remains sombre as the Roma *ultras* raise huge banners for their hated rivals at the other end. They read: 'IN THE LIGHT BLUE SKY, A STAR SHINES. CIAO GABRIELE'; 'TEARS DON'T KNOW PAIN'; 'GABRIELE. YOU ARE ALWAYS IN OUR HEARTS'; 'GABI IS ONE OF US.'

In the past, both fans have used the same sky theme in provocation. In 2000, a banner on the Roma *curva* read: 'Look up. Only the sky is bigger than you.' Lazio replied immediately: 'You're right, it's blue and white.' Lazio fans were waiting, literally, with a giant blank canvas and paint.

The mood changes before kick-off. Fireworks are let off from both ends, which are packed behind a moat and toughened glass screens to their 24,600 limits. They become a swirl of noise and colour but they lack the choreographies of past derbies.

'The Roma v Lazio derby is the best show in Italy,' says Rodrigo Cacho, a Roma fan lecturing at Cambridge University. 'The fans like to outdo each other with displays. As well as being friendly, outspoken, and convinced that they know everything, Romans are fixed with the idea that they are at the centre of the world – neither northern or southern – but special, living in the most beautiful city.'

A match ticket on the *curva* costs just £15 and despite the large gap to the pitch caused by the athletics track, there's hardly a spare seat in this section of the 80,000 capacity arena. In the main stand tickets cost over £100 and those who pay do so for the more refined company rather than better sightlines. There, immaculately attired men show off their elegant trophy females, none of whom concentrate on the game. Actors, politicians (there's an election approaching and candidates want to be seen to like *calcio*), and Roman socialites are there on view. 'She was the first black girl to win Miss Italy in 1998,' says our Italian translator Andre, a Milan fan and semi-professional footballer who has travelled down from Parma, pointing out one gorgeous woman. The Lazio fans can boast a longer history, in contrast to Roma's wealth and glamour.

Taking their name from the region around Rome, Società Sportiva Lazio was founded in 1900 by an Italian army officer, Luigi Bigarelli. They adopted Greek colours and between 1914 and 1931 played in wealthy northern suburbs like Parioli, close to their Rondinella home. Fascist leader Benito Mussolini was a fan and took his kids to games. Il Duce's plans for building a capital of the new Roman Empire included a football stadium. Before his grand scheme eventually saw Olimpico built, Lazio moved to the Fascist Party Stadium (the PNF) in 1931. The stadium staged the 1934 World Cup final but by this time Lazio had a rival.

Associazione Sportiva (AS) Roma were formed in 1927 from a merger of four small clubs: Alba, Fortitudo, Pro Roma, and Roman. Local patriot and Fascist politician Italo Foschi was the driving force. Pressure was also placed on Lazio to join the merger, forming a mighty Roma fit to challenge the northern giants from Milan and Turin. Mussolini wanted to promote Rome as the capital of a new rationalised Italy partly through football. Lazio resisted.

Roma played their games in the Campo Testaccio district to the south of the city, a working class district which is still an area of high Roma support. It was a glorious venue full of character and the *giallorossi* (red-yellows) lost just twenty-six games there in eleven years up to 1940 as Roma overshadowed their rivals and provided two of Italy's 1934 World Cup winners.

Il Duce took Italy into World War II and Roma reluctantly left their much-loved but too-cramped ground to share the bigger Fascist stadium with the *biancocelesti* (light blue) of Lazio. Older Roma fans declare that the club have been homeless from that day.

On the pitch they progressed though and won their first league title in 1941–42 – the first time it had gone south of Bologna – although it wasn't without suspicion. In a key derby game, a bizarre last-minute own-goal went Roma's way. In 1953, both clubs left the PNF stadium for the new Olimpico across the Tiber, built for the 1960 Olympics. Neither club troubled the trophy engravers much, though Roma won the UEFA Cup in 1961, and the Italian Cup in 1964. A British influence helped Lazio enjoy an upturn in fortunes in the early 1970s, and in 1974 they took a first league title, captained by the English-born Pino Wilson and with the Welsh-raised Giorgio Chinaglia firing the bullets.

Geographical divisions have blurred over the years, but traditionally Roma fans were more inner-city left-wing, while their neighbours were suburban right-wing and middle-class. By the early 1970s Lazio had attracted the first wave of *ultras*, fired up by the tense political climate and drawn from Rome's cramped southern housing projects, like Quarticciolo, where Paulo Di Canio was born in 1968.

'I have always felt a special affinity towards the weak, the disadvantaged, the unloved,' explains Di Canio. 'And I loved their symbol, the Lazio eagle.'

Lazio's *ultra* movement became focused on one group, Eagles Supporters, but they were usurped by the predominantly fascist *Irriducibili*. Member Di Canio once sprayed 'Roma is shit and their *curva* stinks' on a local wall. While a player in Lazio's youth teams, he would play on a Saturday then travel overnight to away first team matches with the *Irriducibili*, by then Italy's biggest *ultra* group.

'I kept the club in the dark about my travels. If they had known that I spent my Sundays with the *Irriducibili*, visiting far-flung corners of Italy, they would probably have kicked me out of the youth academy,' he says. He was spotted by the Lazio physio at one away game at Atalanta and warned to stay away, a warning he didn't heed. Di Canio was five yards away when the head of Bergamo's police was stabbed.

'What I loved about the *Irriducibili* was that we only travelled at night. We'd set off at 11.15 p.m. from Termini [Rome's railway station]. The trips were more eventful than the matches.' Di Canio never lost the *ultra* in him.

With such a following, Lazio were never far from tragedy. An *ultra* was killed during a 1979 derby game after being hit by a flare thrown by a Roma fan, two years after young midfielder Luciano Cecconi was shot dead in a jeweller's store. He was dressed as a robber for a joke. Then in 1980, both Lazio and Milan were relegated to Serie B after a scandal concerning illegal bets on their own matches. It wasn't the first or last time those clubs would be embroiled in corruption.

Roma's *ultra* thrived too, groups like *Commando Ultras Curva Sud* (CUCS) and Boys Roma asserting their dominance at various points. Over time, their left-wing sympathies shifted right.

Trophies continued to elude teams from the capital as Italy's big three dominated. A second *scudetto* came to Roma in 1983 with a side spearheaded by three-time Serie A top scorer Pruzzo, the Brazilian playmaker Falcao (who far-left Roma fans compared with Chairman Mao, partly because their names rhymed), winger Conti, and player of the year Vierchowod. *I Lupi* (the Wolves) reached the European Cup final a year later and, with the match staged at Olimpico, were strong favourites against Liverpool. Roma froze and lost on penalties to Bruce Grobbelaar's wobbly knees. Violence marred the game's aftermath, as Lazio handed weapons to Liverpool fans to defend themselves against Roma.

By 1988, a teenage Di Canio was in Lazio's first team and although he didn't last long in his first spell at the club before playing for Juventus, Napoli, Milan, Celtic, Sheffield Wednesday, West Ham, and Charlton, he did score in a derby.

'I just ran straight towards the *Curva Sud*, where the Roma fans were sitting,' he recalled. 'The roar at my back, from Lazio's *Curva Nord*, was spurring me on. I ran under the fans, finger raised, face contorted in a mixture of ecstasy, relief, and fury.'

The Olimpico was remodelled for the 1990 World Cup, but the Fascist entrance still stands, Mussolini dedications and all. The *Azzurro*, the Italian national team, plays every third home game there.

By the early '90s, both Roma and Lazio had acquired serious backers as presidents. Roma won the UEFA Cup in 1991. At Lazio, Paul Gascoigne and 'Beppe' Signori, were bought by the financier Sergio Cragnotti. With Alen Boksic, Karl-Heinze Riedle and Aron Winter (who was abused by his own fans for being a 'black Jew') Lazio became top-five regulars.

Both spent big, creating cosmopolitan and powerful squads and trying also to mimic the commercial success of big British clubs. Lazio became the first Italian club to go public and in 1998 Roma asked Edward Freedman, the merchandise maverick who revolutionised Man Utd's fortunes to do the same for them.

'I knew it wouldn't be easy because I'd already dealt with Lazio,' says Londoner Freedman. 'At Tottenham, I was a part of the egotiations to sell Paul Gascoigne. Their merchandise operation was on-existent; they'd never even seen a t-shirt with club colours on ntil we suggested they printed 10,000 Gascoigne t-shirts. They sold ut.'

Roma president, industrialist Francesco Sensi, flew to London to meet Freedman. 'Sensi ran everything there,' remembers Freedman. He picked the team and decided which players to buy, often off the ack of a video. English coaches have it easy. There was no forward hinking in Rome. Nor were there match programmes, club stores or fficial merchandise. We couldn't replicate what we had done in Manchester because the market was not mature.'

Rome's football battle continued, but it wasn't until Lazio ppointed Sven-Göran Eriksson that they turned into winners, lifting he 1999 Cup Winners' Cup and the league and cup double in their entenary a year later with players like Juan Sebastian Veron, Pavel Nedved, Sinisa Mihajlovic, Alessandro Nesta, Diego Simeone, and £35million Hernan Crespo. At the turn of the millennium, Rome was Italy's political and football capital. Buoyed by success, Cragnotti upped the ante spending £28million on Gaizka Mendieta, who played ust twenty games. As their wage bill soared, form dipped. Salaries vent unpaid, stars left, and debts mounted.

Cragnotti eventually went bankrupt and was arrested on charges of alse accounting and fraud, then a new Lazio president cut a deal with he government to pay off back-taxes over twenty-four years.

In 2001, a Roma side managed by Fabio Capello won their first cudetto for almost two decades with a side including Gabriel Batistuta, Vincent Candela, Vicenzo Montella, Aldair, Cafu, Emerson, and a young Totti. Capello is not popular among Roma fans. 'He betrayed Rome,' says *ultra* Francesco. 'He said he would never go to Juve. And then he went …'

Roma's impetus could not be maintained, FIFA blocked them from buying players and, like Lazio, they offloaded their talent as normal ervice resumed and the big three up north again dominated.

When Lazio made the headlines, it was usually for the right-wing behaviour of their fans. A banner at one derby read: 'Team of blacks, *curva* of Jews.' Other banners included: 'Your home is Auschwitz.' That Roma didn't possess a significant Jewish support didn't appear to register. Roma fans booed black players too.

The derbies remained in the news. A 2004 match was suspended when false rumours were spread among fans that a boy had been killed by the police. A year later, both teams were in danger of relegation and were happy to take a point from the derby. Which is exactly what both teams got. With minutes left, all fans began to sing 'Suspend the game' and 'Why did we bother?' *La Gazzetta Dello Sport* refused to award players a mark for their individual performances.

The players were booed off the field, though Di Canio, then 36 and by this time back at Lazio having taken a large cut in wages, threw his shirt at the *curva* to show that it was covered in sweat. Di Canio was not averse to the fascist salute and opined that Mussolini was 'misunderstood.'

Roma went through five managers in one season before settling on studious Tuscan coach Luciano Spalletti, who joined in 2005 and had improved them on a limited budget. In his first season, they equalled Milan's record of 11 consecutive wins, matching the feat with a 2–0 victory over Lazio. Three Roma players – Totti, Daniele De Rossi and Simone Perrotta – were 2006 World Cup winners. At Lazio, the controversies continued. They were embroiled in Italy's match-fixing scandal and removed from the UEFA Cup, but still finished third in 2007 behind Roma.

The derby gets underway, with no police present because fans have promised that for this game they will behave. Such is the power of the *ultras* – and the threat of violence if the police should enter the stadium – this vow is taken seriously.

'Derbies should not be like this,' says Roma fan Francesco, as he sips a cold, tiny Caffe Borghetti. 'We are supposed to hate, not respect

They are from the outskirts, they are not real Romans. They should fuck off and leave the city to us.'

Roma take the lead. 'Daje!' shout the Roma fans nearby – 'Get in here!' with a Roman twang – as their curva explodes. Lazio equalise just before half time and go ahead 12 minutes into the second half. News arrives that Inter have only drawn and Roma push forward, Perrotta making it 2–2. A win will take Roma within four points of Inter.

I make my way onto the Lazio curva for the final minutes, passing stalls selling unofficial merchandise controlled by the *ultras* inside the stadiums. It's so packed that it's dangerous, despite being seated. Two minutes into injury time the stadium moves, literally, when Lazio get their winner, not a welcome sight for any health and safety officials, as fists punch the smoky air.

Lazio have won another battle . . . but Roma will always believe they are winning the eternal war.

Two Languages, Two Peoples … and Two Countries?

Real Madrid v Barcelona, May 2008

El Gran Clasico remains probably the most emotionally-charged yet glamorous domestic club fixture in world football, even allowing for the enormous gulf in success between these two historically ferocious rivals.

The elderly Catalan on the new high speed AVE between Barcelon and Madrid doesn't realise he has an audience as he calls his friend i Madrid.

'Luis,' he shouts, loud enough for people in the adjoining carriage of the sleek train to hear. 'It's Jordi. I'm nearly there. Are you still sleeping? You lazy Madrid arsehole. Not a good day's work in any of you.'

Fellow passengers giggle and while it's only possible to hear on side of the conversation, they're able to decipher that Jordi's daughte has treated him to a trip to Madrid to see his old friend and his belove Barça play Real Madrid. And that Jordi is suspicious of Luis's clair that he's only been sleeping because he's been celebrating Madrid Spanish league title at the fountain of Cibeles for three days.

There's more laughs as stereotypes are traded, with Luis retortin with something about Jordi not paying for his train ticket himsel because Catalans are parsimonious. However, the rivalry betwee Barcelona and Madrid is not always expressed with such good humou

It's May 2008. Just two years ago, Barcelona were champions of Spain and Europe. Ronaldinho, Samuel Eto'o, Carles Puyol, Deco, Xavi, Iniesta, Henrik Larsson and Lionel Messi all shone in a world-class team coached by Frank Rijkaard. They deserved every superlative lavished on them as they stayed true to Barça's attacking 4–3–3 beliefs, playing incisive, passing football topped by the individual talents capable of deconstructing even Milanese defences. Barça remained hated in Madrid, but respected. When they demolished their arch-rivals 3–0 at the Bernabéu in November 2006, Ronaldinho wheeled away after scoring a superb individual goal to unprecedented applause from Madridistas. David Beckham looked crushed, like he had joined the wrong team. Yet in the summer of 2003, when Madrid beat Barcelona to sign Beckham, Barça fans could only shrug their shoulders. Such was the depressed state of their club that few in Catalonia could muster any outrage. There was a huge gulf in success between Spain's two biggest clubs and historically ferocious rivals.

The Spanish media are obsessed by the changing cycles of Real Madrid and Barcelona's dominance. Everything is black and white; it's victory or failure, boom or bust, first or second. And for Barça or Madrid, when second constitutes failure, the line between love and hate is fine. That November 2006 triumph saw Barcelona's fortunes peak, for in the five games which followed with Rijkaard as coach, they would not beat Madrid again.

Yet the Barça–Madrid rivalry has always run deeper than results. Far deeper. The clubs represent two languages, two peoples and, in the view of many Catalans, two countries. And each of those two countries invests enormous national pride and vast sums in their flagship clubs. Which is why the game they call the *el gran clasico* remains, whatever the relative positions of the two sides, probably the most emotionally charged yet glamorous domestic club fixture in the world.

It's 7 May 2008, three days since Madrid won their 31st Spanish title (against Barça's 18) and not even the heavy rain dampens spirits in Europe's highest capital. White Madrid flags hang limply from apartment windows and the headlines in the Madrid supporting *Marca* and *AS* sport papers are joyous. Both are excited at the humiliation about to be heaped on the Barça players who will form a guard of honour to applaud their hated enemy as the new champions.

In my hotel room on Gran Via, Madrid's main thoroughfare in this fast growing city of four million, I watch the local channels. Spanish television is routinely awful, but the interview with Mariano Rajoy, the right-wing leader of the opposition, is amusing. One minute he is being asked about politics, the next for a score prediction of tonight's game.

'Two-one, Madrid,' Rajoy, a Madrid supporter, says confidently. Rajoy has lost the last two Spanish elections to left-wing José Luis Zapatero, the first democratically elected Prime Minister of Spain to declare himself a Barça fan.

The channel cuts to a group of actors wearing Barcelona shirts outside the exit to the Santiago Bernabéu metro. Forming a mock guard of honour, they applaud passengers. Given that the Bernabéu sits on the wealthy Paseo de la Castellana (formerly the Avenida del Generalísimo Franco), a wide, leafy thoroughfare lined by skyscrapers in the heart of commercial Madrid, they greet suited uptown girls enthusiastically – less so the male northern European tourists in replica shirts. Madrid, like Manchester United, Liverpool, Chelsea, Barcelona and Milan, are clinical in exploiting the tourist dollar. And given it's only really tourists and kids who wear replica shirts to games, they change them every year.

The actors have long gone by the time I leave the same metro station three hours before kick-off. Instead, I'm greeted by stalls selling pro-Madrid and anti-Barcelona merchandise. 'This is Spain,' announces one slogan over a map of the country, 'If you don't like it, go!' Catalan nationalists would not approve.

The Madrid team bus nudges through the crowd to rapturous applause. 'I saw Robinho!' screams a girl to her boyfriend. There's no such warm welcome when Madrid visit Barcelona, even though Madrid is the second most popular team in Catalonia, because hundreds of thousands of Madridistas fans from all over Spain were encouraged to move to the region in search of work – and to dilute the Catalan identity – between the 1950s and 1970s.

'Once we got to Barcelona, it was mad with thousands of fans at the airport and up all night outside our hotel,' recalls former player Steve McManaman. 'We had so much security but the bus windows get smashed in every time on the way to the ground. Everyone got out of the window seats. We closed the curtains and edged into the middle with some in the aisle but there wasn't room for all of us there. If you stood you knew what was going to happen. I was never hit and thankfully the windows were reinforced. They had two layers so if the outside smashed, the bricks didn't come through.'

Glamorous television presenters loiter outside the Bernabéu with microphones hoping to grab a word with smiling celebrities. But they are celebrities of a lower order and spend most of their time posing for photos with fans. Madrid's home crowd are largely middle class, but their profile is very different just a hundred yards away in a street of nondescript mid-rise apartments. There, lads in Londsdale and Harrington jackets, snide tight jeans and Doc Marten's boots stand around drinking the local brew, Mahou, and singing. The road has been blocked off by the Policia Nacional (the national police force who are not allowed to police Camp Nou for their own safety) as members of the extreme right-wing Ultras Sur set off fireworks, drink alcohol and sing anti-Catalan songs. The humid air smells of stale sweat. Some Ultras wear paramilitary regalia and caps that wouldn't look out of place on a traffic warden. They also sing 'Que Viva España' and one Ultra swings the blue and white scarf of Español, Barcelona's local and historically non-Catalan rivals. There's a black van with their neo-fascist logo on the side, brought to transport their paraphernalia of flags, banners and flash bombs, which regularly puncture the air.

On my last visit there, I met Pablo, a Madrid socio for 40 out of his 41 years. 'Barcelona are like the shit from a dog that sticks in your shoes when you walk in it by mistake,' he told me. 'Sometimes we have to shake it off.' Asked for his view of Barça, Pablo's father said: 'They don't see themselves as Spanish and reject anything that comes from Madrid because it's the capital. I know Barcelona is very pretty and that most of the people are fine, but others have an inferiority complex about Madrid. We supported and contributed to Barcelona's Olympics and we were proud that they took place in Spain, but they are against Madrid's bid for 2012. Why?'

Madrid has tried to replicate Barcelona's Olympic games success by staging their own. Alongside Paris, they were favourites for the 2012 games, but were beaten by London. You can now buy 'Madrid 2012' t-shirts in Barcelona.

Having divided his time between Barcelona and Madrid for over a decade, Lancastrian Michael Turner has an interesting perspective. 'Even people who know nothing about football will watch the Barça v Madrid game. If it was between two countries it would be called racism, but because it's between two regions it's called rivalry. Catalans believe that Madrileños are superficial and too big for their boots. They believe that Barça players are playing for an ethical cause, unlike those who play for Madrid. They consider themselves better educated and superior beings. Catalans think they embody the upright nature somebody like Gary Lineker or Bobby Robson demonstrated – that's partly why they were thought of so highly.

'Barceloneses are proud of their city, whereas Madrileños tend to complain more about the local administration, the traffic,' adds Turner. 'There's actually a lot of respect in Madrid for the way in which things are managed in Barcelona. The dislike is definitely more from the Catalans and that's because of the political history of repression. That said, the majority of Catalans are reasonably happy with their lot. They would like respect within a federal framework and a little more autonomy, but not complete autonomy from Spain.'

'I will always hate Madrid. There's just something about them that gets up my nose. I would rather the ground opened up and swallowed me than accept a job with them. In fact, I really do not like speaking about them because it makes me want to vomit.' Not the words of a febrile Barça Ultra, but of Hristo Stoichkov, the tetchy Bulgarian striker whose sublime skills thrilled Catalunya for much of the 1990s. The 1994 European Footballer of the Year tells it like he sees it. And how he is loved for it. Wearing Barça's proudly corporate free carmine and blue striped shirt (the club pay UNICEF £1.6 million a year to show their logo), he backed up his words with the type of unflinching commitment every fan demands. Against Madrid, he scored extravagant last minute winners and received two yellow cards, not to mention a two-month suspension for stamping on a referee's foot. Stoichkov didn't disappoint. To this day he remains a hero.

Stoichkov has been honoured by two of Barça's 1,828 penyas (supporters' clubs) taking his name. Just eight of the club's many foreigners have been granted this honour. Gary Lineker has one – he became an instant hero after scoring a hat trick in a 3–2 win over Madrid in his first season, 1986–87. And despite being played as a winger, he also netted in Barça's win in the Bernabéu later in the season. Ladislao Kubala, often rated as the best ever Barça player has two. Only Johan Cruyff – the man who revitalised Barça on the field in the 70s and did even better as manager in the '90s when his 'Dream Team' won four successive championships and the European Cup – has more with three.

There was another foreigner with two, but Luis Figo was quickly dropped after events in the summer of 2000. Figo's move to Real Madrid still has repercussions. Easily Barça's best player and European Player of the Year in 2000, he moved for a then world record £38 million fee after signing a speculative deal with Florentino Pérez, a Bernabéu presidential challenger. Given that Madrid had just won their eighth European Cup under the incumbent club president, few gave Pérez a chance, but the influential construction magnate promised the impossible: vote for me and not only will I clear this club's preposterous £200 million debt, but I'll also deliver the best player from our rivals. Pérez was soon president, each year delivering to Madrid another franchise player – Figo in '00, Zidane '01, Ronaldo '02, Beckham'03.

Figo first returned in November 2000 to a welter of abuse. Every time he strayed close to the edge of the pitch – which, given that he played on the wing, he was inclined to do – a rubbish truck seemed to empty its contents in his direction from above, including, among the bottles and oranges, five mobiles, unused credit and all. 'It was impossible to concentrate,' sighed team mate McManaman as Barça won 2–0.

Figo wasn't the complete traitor that the Catalan media portrayed. Barça officials were sending him mixed signals about a new contract, and he called their bluff. He claims that the media and certain Barcelona officials conspired against him and that he still has happy memories from his time in Catalonia. Figo returned to the Camp Nou for a second time in November 2002. Most expected the hatred to have eased. It hadn't.

Locals joke that the Camp Nou's loudest noise comes at half time when Burberry-clad ladies unwrap the tin foil from their cured ham sandwiches. Either that or when news comes through that Madrid are losing. The Camp Nou does match the hype a couple of times a season, though. When the Catalan national side plays one of its non-FIFA recognised matches, the stadium is a feverish amphitheatre of Catalan flags. The other occasion is when Madrid comes to town. Watching Real Madrid walk out at the Camp Nou is one of the great moments in world sport. Resplendent in all white, their starting 11 run out to the centre circle and applaud the crowd, prompting further anger. When Figo returned, that anger was multiplied – hell hath no fury like a football club whose star player has defected to its most hated rival.

With 16 minutes left and the game goalless, Figo attempted to take a corner in front of a sea of contorted young faces – the Boixos Nois (crazy boys) Ultras. Objects were hurled towards him, a barrage of beer cans, lighters and plastic bottles rained down, plus an empty glass bottle of J&B whisky – the company were later said to be delighted with the free advertising – and a pig's head. Television showed several Barça directors laughing, grins which faded as the players were led off the field by the referee to 'cool things down'. Barcelona were ordered to close their ground for two games, a ban that was never enforced.

In Barcelona there's a widespread conviction that the Madrid-based authorities, both regional and national, have assisted the club because they see them as a major draw for the city. To clear Real's £200 million debt, Florentino Pérez, the president who oversaw the *galatico* era (as in they must be so talented that they are from another galaxy), called on his contacts in high places. He negotiated a deal to sell their prestigiously located training ground, which they'd acquired from the local council for next to nothing 30 years before. Admirable council support or unfair assistance? Barça, of course, have at times enjoyed an equally cosy relationship with the Generalitat, the Catalan autonomous government, as well as Catalan banks who would never close their lines of credit.

Whilst Barça have long pleaded persecution, there's a history of hostility going the other way. In 1916 there were reports of Madrid players being showered with missiles in Barcelona. In 1930, Madrid played a Cup final against Athletic Bilbao in Barcelona, the Basques and the Catalans combining to vent their derision of all things white. Madrid had a perfectly legitimate winner disallowed by a Catalan referee and Bilbao won the game in extra time, the Madrid players pelted as they returned to the changing rooms. In 1936, just a month before the Spanish Civil War broke out, Real Madrid met Barcelona in the Cup final in Valencia, Real's Catalan goalkeeper Zamora pulling off one of the greatest saves in Spanish football history in his team's 2–1 victory.

In the 1936–9 Spanish Civil War, Barcelona was a Republican stronghold, Madrid the base for Franco's eventually victorious Falangist rebels. After the war, Atlético Aviación, the air force team later to become Atlético de Madrid, initially benefited more from Franco's rule than Real. But not for long. Madrid's official history lists the club's biggest domestic cup win as an 11–1 victory over Barça in 1943. It describes the result as 'majestic' and the players that day as 'heroes'. What it doesn't say is that having lost the first leg 3–0, before the second leg Barcelona's players were treated to a terrifying changing room visit from Franco's Director of State Security who ominously reminded them that they were only playing due to the 'generosity of the regime'.

Barça's whole identity has been shaped by its persecution by Madrid. For 40 years under Franco, Catalonia was repressed, its language and culture outlawed. In those dark times Barça embodied the spirit and hope of Catalans. It had a club president executed by Francoist troops and the team banned from playing for six months after the fans booed the Spanish national anthem. Barça's Les Corts stadium and later the Camp Nou became a focal point for Catalan nationalism, a vehicle for a powerful collective identity in defiance of a dictator, one of the few places where the language could be spoken without fear of repression. Barça and Catalonia have been inseparable ever since. As former coach Bobby Robson put it, 'Catalonia is a country and FC Barcelona is their army.' In the light of history and its legacy of pride and resentment, Barça's motto 'mes que un club' (more than a club) is no exaggeration.

Real Madrid as we know it today only began to take shape when Santiago Bernabéu took up his post as club president in 1944. Bernabéu had fought with Franco's forces and aligned the club with the new regime, although his first act as president was to send a telegram to Barça saying he hoped for good relations with them. And yet the story of how Real's greatest player, Alfredo Di Stéfano, came to be at the club still causes arguments. Barcelona agreed a deal to take the Argentinian in 1953 and Madrid entered a counter-offer but was too late. At Madrid's request, the Spanish Federation intervened and Franco's General Moscardó passed a law banning the importation of foreign players. Barça were forced to relent until Moscardó brokered a deal for the two clubs to 'share' the player.

Barça were outraged, and washed their hands of the whole affair. Real got Di Stéfano and in his first season won the league for the first time in 21 years, going on to win its first five European Cups. Real Madrid became standard bearers for Spain at a time when the country was relatively poor and treated as a pariah abroad because of its dictator.

Barça had a fine 1950s team too, but government control of the media meant their exploits were overshadowed by Madrid's – another cause for resentment. Despite its standing as a beacon of Catalan pride, many of Barça's greatest managers and players have been foreign. Indeed the club was actually founded in 1899 by two expatriate businessmen, a Swiss, Hans Gamper, and an Englishman, Arthur Witty, who wanted to formalise their weekend kickabouts.

In recent decades players like Ladislao Kubala, Diego Maradona, Gary Lineker, Hristo Stoichkov, Rivaldo, Ronaldinho, Eto'o, Deco, Messi and Johan Cruyff have joined a list of successful foreign coaches including Helenio Herrera, Rinus Michels, Terry Venables and Frank Rijkaard. In Madrid, meanwhile, a mostly homegrown team lead by outstanding imports (in the 1950s Di Stefano of Argentina and Ferenc Puskas of Hungary) is a formula that has been successfully revived again and again.

Fans are loathed to admit it, but Barça and Madrid have more in common than they don't – like a propensity to dispose of successful managers. Both teams benefit from an obsequious media and both are expected to beat all who have the audacity to turn up against them. The flip side is that when either side loses, the media seldom credit the victors, but would rather magnify the mistakes of the losers.

Madrid's 2002 centenary year was a cringe inducing, backslapping celebration. Barça's, three years earlier, was not dissimilar. And both are similar in structure too, with fierce rivalries contested in basketball, ice hockey and handball sections along with many other sports. However Madrid have prided themselves on a level of consistency that Barcelona have been unable to match. Barça have frequently had the more stylish attacking teams, but they won the league just once between 1960 and 1984. Madrid won it 14 times over the same period.

Just as signing Di Stéfano was crucial to Madrid, signing Johan Cruyff was vital to Barcelona. (Cruyff's transfer fee from Ajax was financed by the Banca Catalana – so much for Madrid's unfair advantage.) Madrid had tried to sign Cruyff after he had destroyed them playing for Ajax in April 1973, but he reportedly resented the right wing connections and was seduced by the idea of living in and playing for Barcelona, where he still lives, the power without a position behind the Barça throne.

In Cruyff's first game for Barça in the Bernabéu, he scored one and set up three of the other four as his new team won 5–0. Madridistas refer to it as the Black Night and Barça were champions that year. Still, Real Madrid won five of the next six league titles with their 'Ye-Ye' team of Santillana, Pirri, Camacho, Ángel and Del Bosque. Madrid hated Cruyff. He called his son Jordi – ostensibly because he liked the name – but when he went to register the birth he was refused as it was an outlawed Catalan name. Authority backed down when they realised they couldn't really afford to upset the most popular man in Catalonia – which only made him a bigger hero.

In the 1980s, it was Real's 'vulture squad' who dominated. Emilio Butragueño, Michel, Martín Vásquez, Manolo Sanchís were all products of Real's youth system, with foreigners Hugo Sánchez and Jorge Valdano brought in to score the goals. Despite domestic success, they couldn't progress beyond the European Cup semi-finals, which they reached three times. And when Cruyff became manager in 1988,

Barcelona achieved the kind of consistency that Madrid had become famous for.

On this rain-soaked May evening there's a party atmosphere in the Bernabéu, with its tighter, steeper, vortex of seats than the Camp Nou. Despite having 23,000 fewer seats, the Bernabéu appears more imposing as it towers into the Iberian sky. It's from the inside that both stadiums impress, their outer exposed tiers of concrete contributing little of aesthetic note. Barça plan to change that with the English architect Lord Foster having won a competition to cover and remodel the stadium, expanding the capacity to a dizzying 104,000.

The Barça players have to soak up the Bernabéu atmosphere as they form a guard of honour for Real Madrid. The home players emerge from the tunnel, but don't take their opportunity to rub their foes noses in it, instead shaking hands. The Ultras Sur holler their anti-Catalan insults – 'Separatist bastards', 'Polish shits' (they class Catalans as a mongrel race) – which are drowned out by the rousing club anthem Hala Madrid a grandiose effort more opera house than stadium. Officially, the Ultras Sur are self-financing, but rumours persist that they receive tickets and travel assistance from club officials. The same was true of the Boixos in Barcelona until president Joan Laporta cut all assistance, receiving death threats for his troubles. The Ultras argue that without their presence, the atmosphere would be far flatter in the stadium, although there's little chance of that tonight as Madrid celebrate their league title triumph in style by crushing Barça 4–1.

It's the first time Madrid have done the double over Barça in 24 years and a result which helps deprive the Catalans of an automatic place in the Champions League. Despite every goal being greeted by awful rock music and a public address announcer in love with his own voice, the 78,000 crowd create a party vibe and love seeing Barça reel.

They sing 'El Viva Espanya!' and 'Barça, you twats, salute the champions!' When Barça won the league in 2005, striker Samuel Eto'o sang the same song, only with anti-Madrid sentiments. The 800 Ultras behind the goal then offer fascist salutes before singing 'campeones' and songs against Laporta, but at board level, both clubs enjoy cordial relations.

An otherwise dire Thierry Henry finishes superbly to net Barça's consolation goal, but there are just six Barça fans in the stadium to celebrate according to the club officials. And Jordi from the train, of course, who will have slipped under any figures. While Barça and Madrid fans claim with some justification that it would be unsafe for them to go as away fans to either ground in any serious numbers, their arguments mask an embarrassing truth: their away support is minimal. Different reasons are given. There's the theory that in buying a ticket for an away ground you are financially enriching a rival club. Then there's the distance argument. Barcelona to La Coruña, for instance, is 16 hours by road. English teams regularly take ten times as many fans to Europe as Barça or Madrid.

Still, in the 1990s, Barça's Boixos Nois obtained tickets and organised coaches for the Bernabéu. 'The police stopped us on the outskirts of Madrid and told us that they were going to protect us,' remembers one who made the journey. 'They led us into a trap where we were stoned with bricks and bottles. We travelled back with no windows through the freezing night. It took eight hours.'

As Luis Suárez, one of Spain's leading historians says of *el gran classicó*: 'It feels as if we are reliving the arguments that generated the civil war all over again, with the politics of nationhood and regional aspirations influencing a football match in a way that should best be kept outside the stadium.'

A Question of Ships and Coal

Newcastle v Sunderland, April 2008

Kevin Keegan once said of a typical blood-and-thunder Newcastle v Sunderland match, 'You don't get an atmosphere like that anywhere in the world.' Perhaps that's not surprising when you consider the rivalry between these two north-east giants has its roots in the English Civil War of the 1600s.

A topless overweight youth walks by surrounded by a feral posse of disciples, his Newcastle United shirt tucked into his jean pocket. He's gripping a large orange traffic cone, which he's looking to launch towards the 200 Sunderland fans on the other side of a formidable police presence. The ominous whirr of the police helicopter mixes with sirens and barking dogs, dominating the area in front of the neoclassical façade of Newcastle's Central Station. Bus passengers look terrified at what they witness – hundreds of alcohol and adrenaline fuelled youths punch the air shouting *'Toon! Toon!'*

The youth throws the cone into the path of an approaching car, an act which sees him become one of the seven arrests made in the vicinity. Nearby, a police dog sinks its teeth into the thigh of another lad. Its handler eventually pulls the dog away as a pair of shredded jeans fall away like tender roast lamb off a bone, leaving him semi-exposed in front of hundreds of onlookers.

It's 90 minutes after Newcastle United have beaten their arch rivals Sunderland in the Tyne–Wear (or Wear–Tyne if you are from Sunderland) derby, a lower mid-table Premier League encounter which is largely greeted by indifference and viewed as parochial outside the North East. Yet to the populace of both cities, the derby matters and is cherished, with Middlesbrough, the region's other Premiership club, sneered at and excluded from any true rivalry.

'It's the most intense rivalry in English football,' says Sunderland fan Andy Fury. 'Anything you can think of for a rivalry, it's there. And such is the animosity, it's not unusual for someone from Sunderland to have never visited Newcastle in their life. Translate this rivalry away from football into contention on the pitch and it's pretty tasty.'

Right now, the taxpayers' money is being spent escorting those travelling Sunderland fans who have definitely visited Newcastle. Trying to get at them are hundreds of gloating Geordies, many hoping to re-enact battles between the rival cities which pre-date football by centuries. If they do, there could be a repeat of the scenes in March 2000 when more than 70 rival hooligans took part in some of Britain's worst football-related violence. Sunderland's 'Seaburn Casuals' clashed with Newcastle's 'Gremlins' after boarding a ferry over the Tyne to North Shields. They fought for five minutes with knives, bats and bricks. One man was left permanently brain-damaged. Thirty-nine were arrested and several jailed after the jury were told that the violence had been like a scene from the film *Braveheart*.

Kevin Keegan's Newcastle have beaten Roy Keane's Sunderland 2–0, prompting Keegan to say proudly: 'You don't get an atmosphere like that anywhere else in the world. You can go round the world twice and you won't get that. Not in Liverpool, the Nepstadion, Budapest, the Maracana or at Boca Juniors. The derby match up here is very, very special.'

And it is.

'In the absence of us challenging for trophies, the rivalry with Sunderland becomes something to hold on to,' says Mark Jensen, long-time editor of Newcastle fanzine *The Mag*. 'When we pushed for the league in the mid-90s, fans considered Man United to be our biggest rivals. That wound Sunderland fans up even more, because we considered them insignificant. We were there, until the idiots running the club blew it. Now, everyone would say Sunderland are our main rivals.'

It's six hours earlier, an April Sunday morning under heavy grey skies in Newcastle upon Tyne, the centre of Britain's fifth biggest urban area. Alcohol has yet to be taken as the mood builds in the city centre. The cliché that all Newcastle fans wear shirts seems wide of the mark, judging by the Adelphi pub by the Georgian splendour of Grey Street – voted the best street in Britain by BBC Radio 4 listeners – where rum lads gather around Newcastle memorabilia and a large Newcastle United flag.

Newcastle has many faces, from the empty spaces where the terraced streets of the West End once tumbled down towards the Tyne, to fancy apartment buildings overlooking the magnificent vista of the Tyne bridges. A city famed for its nightlife, it has countless wonderful old pubs, often uneasily juxtaposed with the terrible cheesiness associated with the Bigg Market and more recently the Quayside bars.

'I couldn't believe it when I went up there,' says the Dutch forward Patrick Kluivert. 'I lived in some big open-minded cities like Amsterdam, but to see the way the girls dressed in the middle of winter on the Bigg Market left me with my mouth wide open.'

The previous night, Sam Jacks, a neon bar that forms part of a new entertainment complex of chain bars and American style restaurants, was packing in gaggles of scantily clad girls, all fake tan and exposed breasts. This morning, it advertises 'NUFC v Macems [sic]. *Toon's* busiest pre match shows: 34 screens and topless dancers'.

It's full of the type of jester hat wearing characters that Sky Sports likes to interview, people who will say that they don't eat bacon because it resembles Sunderland's colours. But that's only one side of Newcastle.

Elsewhere, fans fill the city centre pubs, with St James' Park, the best-situated stadium in Britain as it towers over the centre, an iconic structure, its new stands visible for miles around the Tyne valley like a standard bearer for this one-club city. In the 'Three Bulls Head' pub the shaven heads drink and talk football. There's barely a Newcastle shirt in the entire pub. A fresh-faced student starts singing, *'Proud to be a Geordie.'* Few join in. They are nothing like the fans in Sam Jacks but all are waiting to congregate in the broad church of the St James football cathedral.

Closer to the stadium, by a giant Chinese arch, business is brisk in the Back Page bookshop, Britain's only specialist football bookshop following the closure of Sportspages in London and Manchester. Joint owner Mark Jensen chats with customers as they eye up t-shirts with slogans like, 'Have you ever seen a Mackem in Milan?' or 'SMB' an abbreviation of 'Sad Mackem Bastards.' That's Newcastle's reply to Sunderland's 'FTM', either 'Fuck the Mags' or 'Follow the Mackems'.

Lifelong Newcastle fan Lee Clark was photographed wearing a 'SMB' t-shirt at Wembley before Newcastle's 1999 FA Cup final against Manchester United. This wouldn't have been a problem, except he was captain of Sunderland at the time. He was immediately transfer listed.

Outsiders struggle to decipher the code. 'Mag' short for Magpies, is one of Newcastle's nicknames. 'Mackem' (and 'Geordie') originate from aspects of the shipbuilding and coalmining industries on which both Sunderland and Newcastle thrived. Mackem is derived from the phrase 'Mak(e) 'em and Tak(e) 'em' and was invented by Tyneside shipbuilders to insult their counterparts on the River Wear, who would build the ships and have them taken away by the rich. Geordie comes from the Tyneside coalminers who preferred George Stephenson's 'Geordie' safety lamp to the more popular Humphrey Davy lamp.

A booklet called *Let's all laugh at Sunderland* is on sale. Boasting facts like, 'Sunderland have only beaten Newcastle at home once in the last 40 years', it exudes a smug air of superiority as it mocks Sunderland AFC for low crowds, poor teams and the city of Sunderland for being unsophisticated, inbred and backwards. Given that Newcastle produced *Viz* magazine, it's not hugely surprising that the fanzine scene in the North East is among the strongest in Britain, including the excellent Sunderland's *A Love Supreme* and Middlesbrough's esoteric *Fly Me To The Moon*.

I walk towards the stadium with Michael Martin, editor of the wily Newcastle fanzine *True Faith*. 'That's our left-back,' announces Martin, when he spots a suited José Enrique outside a pub, standing in front of his 4x4 Porsche looking flustered. I hear the £6 million rated Spaniard saying: 'I don't know where they are, I've lost them,' to whomever he is calling on his mobile, while passing fans admire his motor or take photos of him. The pub's half-dozen bouncers know who he is but can't communicate with him.

'He doesn't speak English,' says Martin. I tell Enrique that I speak Spanish and ask if he's OK. 'Not really,' he replies. 'I've run out of petrol. And I needed the toilet so I went in the pub and I've managed to lose my car keys.'

'I'm ringing my girlfriend, who has another key for the car, but there's no petrol and I'm already late.' He looks like a little boy lost. I explain the situation to Martin, who rings two contacts within the club; assistant manager Terry McDermott immediately dispatches two security lads to sort the problem out. Enrique later plays 90 minutes.

There's also a reference to keys on the other side of the ground, up by Town Moor where Alan Shearer's freedom of the city of Newcastle status entitles him to graze his cattle for free if he so desires. There, the police wait. They have cleared the street of Newcastle fans in anticipation of the arrival of 32 coaches carrying the bulk of the Sunderland following.

Newcastle owner Mike Ashley is in the Black Bull pub, mixing and singing with home fans. 'The southern based media paint a different picture, but we love the fact that he's a maverick, sits with us fans and has a pint in the Toon after a match,' one fan says. 'And he'd bought us with his own money.' Since 2006, both clubs have seen their previously unpopular owners replaced by new successors who have cleared the debts and invested in their new clubs.

The Sunderland coaches arrive in a giant convoy, the end of their 12-mile journey from the Wear to the north side of the Tyne. Fans brandish FTM stickers flicking V-signs to the Newcastle fans stood outside the pub. A police helicopter hovers above. *'Keano, he wanks his dog Keano!'* sing the Geordies, a play on the Mackems' *'There's only one Keano ...'*

Other Geordies wave their keys, a mickey take out of the Mackem accent and the way they say: 'Who's keys are these keys?' To anyone south of Darlington, it just sounds like a noise. The Geordie accent is slightly harsher, saying 'book', in contrast to the elongated Mackem 'boook'.

'We are the Sunderland haters,' continue the Geordies.

'What do you think of Sunderland?' asks a man in a black leather jacket. 'Shit' reply his mates. 'And what do you think of shit?' he continues. 'Sunderland.'

'Four-one, even Chopra scored,' they go on for the benefit of the new arrivals. £5 million striker Michael Chopra, now at Sunderland, scored just one goal in six years at Newcastle in an April 2006 derby which saw Sunderland humiliated. That was Alan Shearer's last game for Newcastle. Shearer, the Lion of Gosforth and hero of Newcastle, was surprisingly left on the bench by manager Ruud Gullit in a 1999 game which Sunderland won 2–1 at St James' Park. Gullit resigned days later.

The Sunderland fans kiss their shirts, while Newcastle fans sing songs mocking Sunderland's new association with Ireland – Irish owners, manager and sponsors. Hundreds of newly converted Irish Sunderland fans take football weekends in Sunderland, boosting the local economy.

Closer to the stadium, the police keep most Newcastle fans out of the vicinity. Known hooligans are told to leave or face arrest, but a mother and her four children are allowed to slip through, where they abuse the Sunderland fans. The family possesses six teeth between them and the mother has never troubled a catwalk with her presence, but that doesn't stop her screaming, 'Get a life, you ugly Mackem bastards!'

More police separate the two sets of fans as they make their way to the turnstiles in a tunnel under the vast main stand. There, the insults are amplified, with Sunderland fans called 'dirty Mackems' or 'The Great Unwashed', Newcastle fans simply as 'scum' or 'skunks' – a reference to Newcastle's black and white stripes. Sunderland sing: 'La, La, La, La, La, La, La;La La La La; La Sun-Lun,' to the Beatles *Hey Jude*. The Newcastle fans join in, replacing the final word with 'Geordies' but they're can't match the volume of the visitors, who are packed together on enemy territory.

Inside the stadium, a track-suited Kevin Keegan walks onto the pitch 40 minutes before kick-off, receiving a standing ovation as he works the adoring crowd. Suited, focused, intense, rival manager Roy Keane is not seen until the game starts.

'We know Keegan is flawed,' offers Martin, 'but he's genuine. He gives us belief. He's the best thing for our club.' Everyone from the tea lady to the most cynical fan loves him and when the Geordie standard of Dire Straits' *Local Hero* plays over the public address system, it could apply to Keegan. Conversely, Sunderland fans portray him as a clown-like figure and have a t-shirt showing Keegan with the slogan 'There's a circus in the town.'

'The news of Keegan's reappointment swept through the city,' says BBC Radio 5's John Murray, who grew up in the Tyne valley. 'People were beeping their horns and singing in the street. It's a cliché to say it, but this is a real football area. It's all-consuming in both Sunderland and Newcastle. When stories break associated with either club, everyone talks about them.'

The obsession is reflected in attendances. Newcastle, despite not winning the league for over 80 years, have the third highest average attendance (51,320) in England behind Manchester United and Arsenal. Sunderland (43,532) are fifth ahead of Manchester City, Everton, Aston Villa and capacity restricted clubs like Chelsea and Tottenham. Both North eastern clubs have plans to expand their stadiums further, yet the Mackems seemed doomed – with gates of 24,000 as recently as 2006, before Niall Quinn returned to their club as chairman and the public face of a consortium of Irish investors.

'The timing was perfect,' observes the *Independent's* Michael Walker, who has lived in the North East since 1984 and covers both clubs. 'Sunderland had a couple of bad lows that would suck the life out of any club, but they were resuscitated by Quinn and Keane followed, doing a great job. You can feel that there's something there. If Quinn hadn't come back, there would have been a vacuum. I think they would now be a third division club. Sunderland's identity relied more on the football club after the demise of the shipbuilding and coal industries. The football club is the flagship for the city and inspirational for the people.'

Shipyards and coal, two of the key industries on which Sunderland and Newcastle prospered, yet they sparked off a mutual loathing as long ago as the 1600s when King Charles I bestowed the East of England Coal Trade Rights to Newcastle, rendering the Wearside coal merchants redundant.

When the English Civil War started in 1642, Newcastle supported the Crown which had been so good to them, while Sunderland got behind the Parliamentarians. The division became a conflict between Sunderland's republicanism and Newcastle's loyalist self-interest.

These political differences culminated with the battle of Boldon Hill between the two towns in 1644 when a loyalist army from Newcastle and County Durham was defeated by the anti-monarchist Sunderland and Scots army. Newcastle lost and was colonised by the Scottish. It was subsequently used as a Parliamentarian military base for the rest of the war.

The rivalry continued during the Industrial Revolution as both centres had thriving shipyards, such as Swan Hunter on the Tyne. In 1840 Sunderland had 65 shipyards and by the boom years of the early 1900s these yards employed over 12,000 men, a third of the town's (Sunderland only became a city in 1992) adult population. Sunderland produced more than a quarter of the nation's total tonnage of merchant and naval ships for World War Two. Stories were rife of Wearsiders not being employed in Tyneside yards and vice versa. Sunderland's last shipyard closed in 1988 and the Swan Hunter cranes are being reassembled in India.

Industry has dictated supporting patterns to this day. The coal industry meant that Ashington, the pit village north of Newcastle famous for being the birthplace of Bobby and Jack Charlton, as well as Newcastle legend Jackie Milburn, attracted many Sunderland supporters who were miners in the Durham coalfields. And more recently, Newcastle people move to booming villages close to the giant Nissan factory in Washington, which, strictly speaking is in Sunderland. For the first time, that meant many fans came together in a working environment.

The focus remains the city centres. The regeneration, signalled by new art centres, flash apartments and the sleek millennium bridge that loom large on Tyneside reinforces Newcastle's standing as the regional centre and causes resentment in Sunderland, whose residents perceive a media bias towards Tyneside which further compounds their feeling of inequality.

'We pay taxes which get spent on developing Tyneside instead of our own city,' says Andy Fury, with justification.

It amuses Geordies that Sunderland people use Newcastle's airport and train station for major journeys or Newcastle's Arena to see any big concerts. The resentment is understandable. Sunderland's local authority contributed to a metro system, which didn't serve their city until recently.

'They have a reason to come here, we've got none to go there,' says Jensen. 'It's like asking a Mancunian what they would go to Bolton for.'

Despite the decline of its industries, Sunderland tries hard. The 48,000 capacity stadium, built on a former mine at Monkwearmouth, is the fourth biggest in England after Old Trafford, the Emirates and … St James' Park. Then there's the (struggling) but worthy National Glass Centre on the banks of the Wear, a booming student population and the North East's only Olympic sized swimming pool. Although not in the same league as the Tyne Bridge, the Wearmouth Bridge is elegant. It's not even fair to compare the virtues of the two city centres: Newcastle contains countless beautiful buildings, but Sunderland was bombed heavily during the war and rebuilt with the tenderness shown by a polar bear to a sea lion.

Sunderland is the 45th biggest urban area in England, a quarter the size of Newcastle's 879,000 population. For Sunderland to have such a well-supported club is incredible. Far bigger centres of population would love to boast a club with its profile and history. Founded in 1879, Sunderland were giants from the start; their 'team of all talents' became English champions four times between 1892 and 1902. The first Tyne–Wear derby took place in 1883, the first competitive fixture an FA Cup tie in 1888, with Newcastle winning the inaugural league meeting at Roker Park on Christmas Eve 1898. The rivalry developed during the 1900s, with the 1901 Good Friday meeting at St James' Park abandoned as up to 70,000 fans made their way into a ground which held less than half that. The cancellation prompted rioting.

Sunderland's two other titles followed in 1913 and 1936. Newcastle have won two fewer, and three of those four were between 1905 and 1909 – when the two sides dominated English football. The other was in 1927.

'We won our last title in the year that Brown Ale was invented,' says Martin, 'I don't think the two are entirely unconnected.' The blue star of the Newcastle Brown beer logo and the name of the Vaux brewery have adorned the Newcastle and Sunderland shirts respectively. Both were major employers which locals saw as icons of local pride, but both city centre breweries sadly closed.

Although without subsequent league success, both clubs had notable cup wins, Sunderland lifting the FA Cup in 1937 and 1973, Newcastle are five times cup winners, the last in 1955. Newcastle's last trophy was the 1976 League Cup. No club in the world is so well supported, yet consistently so unsuccessful; their recent honours board a list of runner's up, final and semi final appearances.

Newcastle did fare better in the always-contentious derby, as when local striker Peter Beardsley scored a hat-trick on New Year's Day, 1985. Beardsley works at Newcastle and claims that more people speak to him about that game than any other.

But Sunderland fans have their own cherished memories. Gary Rowell's hat-trick against Newcastle in 1979 was enough for him to be crowned the club's all time cult hero two decades later. In 1990, Newcastle finished third in the second division, Sunderland sixth. The pair met in a two-legged play off semi-final, the first match ending 0–0 at Roker Park. Sunderland strikers Marco Gabbiadini and Eric Gates etched their names in folklore with goals in the return leg, while Newcastle fans invaded the pitch in an attempt to get the result cancelled, holding the game up by 40 minutes.

The 1990s would go on to be good for both clubs. A new stadium was built for Sunderland to replace the cramped Roker Park, but not before away fans were banned at their former home in 1996 for safety and security reasons, provoking an angry response.

A last-minute agreement allowed 1,000 Newcastle supporters to attend the game but by then Newcastle had arranged for it to be broadcast at St James' Park and rejected the offer. Newcastle's then Chief Executive Freddie Fletcher suggested that the state of Roker Park was to blame and told fans: 'Don't blame Newcastle. Don't blame Northumbria Police. Blame Sunderland!' As a response, Newcastle banned Sunderland fans for the return game.

New regimes are in place now and relations between the clubs at board level are far better. At fan level, the enmity endures.

'It's the most important game of the season to both fans, with an inordinate amount of meaning and that feeling is growing, not receding,' says the *Independent's* Walker.

'The rivalry has become more bitter on their part because they're jealous of our relative success – filling an expanding stadium every week and consistently higher league positions than them,' adds Jensen.

Following a rousing rendition of *Blaydon Races* by a singer, the red and white shirts of Sunderland and the black and white of Newcastle take to the St James' Park turf. The home fans hold up black and white cards, paid for by a local radio company.

'*Stand up if you hate Sunderland,*' they sing as 49,000 people get up. '*You're just a small town in Durham.*' The Sunderland fans, 3,000 of them high on the third tier, respond with a cry of '*Sunderland 'till I die!*' They have banners taking the rise out of that famous Keegan outburst: 'We'd *love it* if we win. Love it.' Adjacent to them are the Toon Ultras – some of the younger fans in an otherwise ageing home crowd – at the back of the Leazes End stand behind a 'Bring The Noise' flag. It's Michael Owen who brings the noise, inspiring Newcastle's 2–0 victory against an injury hit Sunderland.

The Newcastle owner Mike Ashley wears a shirt with 'King Kev' on the back and dances a joyful but uncoordinated jig in his manager's technical area after the game. Later, he is spotted singing karaoke hits of Newcastle songs.

'Keegan's a bigger hero than Shearer,' says a delighted Jeff Cartwright from Wallsend. 'He's done it three times at this club, first as a player and now twice as a manager. It remains to be seen whether Keegan's return continues to satisfy his admirers, but for at least this week he has given Newcastle fans exactly what they want.

Life in the Glasgow Bubble

Rangers v Celtic, May 2008

Since 1888 Celtic and Rangers have been vying for supremacy in Glasgow. While Celtic became the champions of the Irish Catholic immigrants who flocked to the city, Rangers stood as the last staging post for native Scottish Protestants who feared the economic impact of this influx. The hatred still lives on to this day.

The Old Firm game doesn't attract the biggest derby crowds, nor is it between the world's biggest clubs. Other such matches boast better stadiums, better atmospheres and a superior standard of football. So why is this meeting of Glasgow rivals in the small pond of Scottish football seen as the ultimate derby?

'It should be about the football,' says former Celtic player John Hartson, 'but the Old Firm boils down to one thing: hatred. Pure and utter hatred between both sets of supporters. The thing is, Glasgow football thrives on that.'

'I played in many derbies: Arsenal v Tottenham, Luton v Watford, West Ham v Tottenham, Wimbledon v Palace, Coventry v Villa, West Brom v Wolves. I played in front of 75,000 for Wales v England. But trust me, you could add all those games together and it would be nothing like Celtic v Rangers. I mean that.'

'Unlike many other derbies, Old Firm matches normally have something at stake, usually a league title,' says Mark McGhee, a columnist for Glasgow's *Sunday Herald* who played in 18 Old Firm matches. 'In other British cities rival teams have their origins in different social and in some cases cultural backgrounds. None enjoy the added spice of religious difference as the main reason for supporting a particular team. Around the world, similar such conflicts of religious ideology have resulted in far worse things than two sets of football supporters who hate each others' guts.

'Local derbies are mostly relevant mainly just to those involved, and contrary to many fans' belief no-one else is really interested. That's not the case with Glasgow. All of this makes me think that the intensity, importance and the commitment by the fans to the continuation of the rivalry does make the Old Firm derby the greatest in football.'

Old Firm matches have taken place since 1888. Celtic became champions of the Irish Catholic immigrants who flocked to the city. Rangers stood as the standard bearers for the native Scottish Protestants who feared the impact of this influx. The complex clash of cultures was acted out in the riots and other trouble which marked many of these games, reflecting contemporary social and political frustrations during high periods of unemployment and deprivation. The religious affiliations between Glasgow Rangers and Glasgow Celtic became supercharged with tension because of the politics of Ulster. Rangers fans wave Ulster flags, in support of Protestantism and British Unionism. The tricolour of the Irish Republic flies wherever Celtic is supported, because of Celtic's historic association with the peoples of Ireland and Scots of Irish extraction, who are both predominantly Catholic.

On a wet Saturday spring morning in Glasgow, Scotland's biggest (and Britain's fifth largest) urban area of 1.7 million, not everyone is looking forward to the Old Firm game. Calls to the Scottish ambulance services soar 30 per cent on Old Firm match days. As you drive east from the hilly grid of the city centre north of the great River Clyde, with shining new offices, bars and outstanding architecture, the land-scape changes quickly, in striking contrast to the trendy Victorian suburbs of Glasgow's west end.

Emporio Armani and the bustling coffee bars of Merchant City soon give way to a tatty shop selling discount Celtic merchandise, pubs with boarded up windows, fast food takeaways, credit shops, community project offices and off-licences. Glasgow's east end is one of the most deprived urban areas in Europe; the average male life expectancy of 63 is 14 years lower than the British average, comparable with Iraq and several third-world countries.

The east end is Glasgow's Catholic heartland, save for a few scattered Protestant enclaves. A burly man in a Celtic shirt, wrapped in a Basque flag, smokes outside Bairds bar. The bars are full of men in Celtic kits, part of a contingent of 7,000 travelling fans who will make their way to Ibrox, the home of hated rivals Rangers, in an hour or two. Nearby 'Bar 67' is decorated with images of Celtic's Lisbon Lions, Jock Stein's greatest side, assembled from men born within a 30-mile radius of Glasgow, which became the first British side to lift the European Cup.

A caller on local radio dedicates a song to her best friend who is getting married. 'What's more important to you?' asks the presenter, who appears to have no interest in football, 'the wedding or the football match today?'

'The football,' replies the caller without hesitation. 'Come on the Hoops!'

The immense structure of Parkhead, its new steel stands hastily constructed in the 1990s to replace the vast terraces, rises out of a depopulated quarter of cheap retail parks, dominating the skyline and overshadowing the ominous looking tower blocks. There are signs of regeneration, such as a new national indoor sports arena and velodrome which will host several sports at the Glasgow 2014 Commonwealth games, similar to successful projects in Manchester's deprived east for the 2002 games.

On London Road, the only football shirts are Celtic's green and white hoops, but then the livery changes at Bridgeton Cross, an ultra loyalist enclave with Union flags and pubs whose names proudly demonstrate their British allegiances, such as one called 'The Londoner.'

In October 1996, 16-year-old Mark Scott walked through Bridgeton Cross on his way home from a Celtic game against Glasgow's third club Patrick Thistle. Scott, a Glasgow Academy pupil and son of a corporate lawyer, ran the gauntlet of hate from Rangers fans gathered outside a pub when Jason Campbell, 23, whose father and uncle were Protestant paramilitaries, sneaked up behind him, grabbed him and slashed his throat. Mark never saw his killer, who was jailed for life.

Cara Henderson, a school friend of Mark, subsequently set up 'Nil By Mouth' a charity aiming to challenge and eradicate sectarianism. Part of its mission statement reads: 'Abusive words perpetuate negative attitudes which lead to discrimination and abuse. Our work is about raising awareness, stimulating debate and encouraging people to think about sectarianism and what role they can play in challenging religious prejudice. The jokes and songs which may be regarded as harmless in reality help make sectarianism in Scotland, "just part of life." Nil by Mouth refuses to accept this and strives for positive change.'

In 1996, Celtic launched their Bhoys Against Bigotry campaign to 'educate the young on having … respect for all aspects of the community – all races, all colours, all creeds', according to then chief executive Ian McLeod. Within days, people had made spoof pin badges saying: 'Bhoys against bigotry, kiss a hun' (an offensive description of a Rangers fan).

'The worrying thing about sectarianism is that it bubbles under the surface in Glasgow and it permeates different levels of society,' says Stephen Pearman, the bright young sports editor of the *Sunday Herald*. Penman has no allegiance to either club, but knows the culture and acknowledges that the Old Firm is 'his bread and butter.'

'People on the Rangers' forums would have it that Nil By Mouth is a Catholic organisation,' says Penman. 'It is not. Cara would always say that sectarianism permeates all class levels in Glasgow. Middle-class doctors and lawyers will tell sectarian jokes around the dinner table. They will hold down perfectly responsible jobs, but when Saturday comes they will be singing the Sash [the Protestant Orange order's anthem] with the best of them. That is just as damaging – another indicator of how it is hardwired into the West of Scotland society. I love this city, but I hate sectarianism, hate it. It is the scourge of Glasgow. There have been murders very recently in Glasgow that have been committed on sectarian grounds. It's slowly getting better, thankfully, but it will take a lot of time.'

Penman frequently encounters sectarian sentiments. 'Michael Grant is our Chief Football Writer who has a column every week. We look at the comments on his articles. One week readers call him 'A dirty Orange bastard', the next 'a dirty Fenian bastard' [a pejorative term for a Celtic fan that stems from nineteenth century Irish nationalism]. Michael Grant is an Aberdeen supporter from the deepest darkest Highlands of Scotland. You will never change assumptions. People will say he is called Michael so ergo he is a Catholic and ergo he must be a Celtic fan. And that's the feedback in a quality newspaper.'

For the players, it can mean life in what Roy Keane referred to as 'the Glasgow bubble'. Some try to remain incognito, going to the supermarket with caps pulled low so that people can't see their faces clearly. The Celt Neil Lennon tried to lead a normal life and got into all kinds of scrapes. In Manchester, a city of a similar size, Wayne Rooney can generally still go out in the city, and though he is noticed, he will not be harassed. Most old firm players do not live in Glasgow when they retire. Most Manchester United players do.

It's two hours before kick-off. Spilling off the coaches close to BBC Scotland's sleek new glass office in the partly gentrified area of Govan on the banks of the Clyde, Rangers fans make their way past where the mighty shipyards, famous for their 'Clyde built' seal of quality, used to stand. Sectarianism was endemic there also.

'There was always a divide between Celtic and Rangers supporters, a real "them" and "us" mentality,' recalls the former Celtic midfielder Paddy Crerand, who worked at the shipyards while a junior player. 'If someone said that they supported Partick Thistle we thought that was just an excuse for being a Rangers fan. It was ridiculous. Men were working together, helping each other make the same ship, yet basically hating each other because they supported different teams. You never knew when an argument might get out of hand. I became a target for the Rangers followers because in their eyes Duntocher [the junior team he played for then] was just a junior Celtic team. In the yard, as at home, I had to be ready to hit back. It was a return to the law of the streets.'

But nothing is clear-cut in Glasgow. Crerand's brother, despite being born in the Celtic heartland of the Gorbals, was a Rangers fan. And one of Crerand's greatest friends was the Rangers legend Jim Baxter. The Celtic players used to watch the great Rangers teams of the 60s play in Europe – and support them. The formal showing of respect on Jim Baxter's death was observed perfectly by Celtic fans and the minute's silence for the former Celtic player Phil O'Donnell, who died tragically while playing for Motherwell in December 2007, by Rangers supporters.

Most of the east of the city is Catholic and Celtic, south and west of the city tends to be Protestant and Rangers, yet the support of both clubs extends way, way beyond Glasgow. Celtic are the club of the Irish Diaspora, Rangers big all over Scotland and in North America.

Both have substantial support in Ireland, with Rangers largely, but not exclusively in the north. One exception is the group handing out flyers by the exit to the Ibrox underground station. 'RANGERS FANS!'

it reads. 'DEFEND THE DUBLIN LOYAL RANGERS SUPPORTERS CLUB!' It is then explained that their banner, complete with the slogan 'Behind Enemy Lines' has been removed by Rangers at a game because it was deemed sectarian by a club on a mission to crack down on such sentiments.

'The banner had nothing to do with the Troubles,' reads the flyer, before stating that many of its Scottish-born members are 'married to Irish Catholics, etc – hardly a collection of Johnny Adair wannabes.'

Outside the Ibrox underground station, a Rangers fan selling the *Follow Follow* fanzine explains how he has seen just one Celtic fan all day, complete with a six-man police escort. A man walks past the scruffy, single-level 'Stadium' bar on Copland Road, vomits by the kerbside then shouts 'Fuck the Pope!' by way of clearing his throat. The sea of blue washes through the impoverished streets around Ibrox, many towards Edminston Drive where last night I attended a quiz night held by the Rangers Trust, a supporter shareholder group that seeks to give Rangers fans a greater say in how their club is run. The questions in the Wee Rangers pub may have been for the serious anoraks in Rangers' considerable support, but there was time to meet fans like Tommy Davids, who saw his first Old Firm game on New Year's Day 1939. 'There were 118,000 (Ibrox's record attendance) there,' he said. 'I was five and my sister was four. I was there when we beat them 8–1 in 1943 too. The rivalry hasn't changed and it never will. We hate them and they hate us.'

Among the Trust contingent were members from the 240 string Orkney True Blues, whose trip to a home game involves a two-hour boat to the mainland, then a three-hour coach trip to Inverness. A night there is followed by a four-hour trip to Glasgow; a journey they make six times a year. Celtic have a similar operation in the islands. 'We're a small community there so we have to get on with them,' says one of the fans. 'We pity them as they know no better.' Coaches leave for Glasgow from most Scottish and Irish towns every other week, frustrating fans in say, Aberdeen, who wonder why they don't support their local clubs. Fans of both Old Firm teams would argue that they, like Barcelona, are more than a club. Partick Thistle and Clyde, two other Glasgow clubs, hate both Rangers and Celtic and wear their loathing of the Old Firm as a badge of honour.

Inside the dressing rooms in the Ibrox main stand – Archibald Leitch's glorious red brick façade construction which can lay claim to being the finest stand in Britain – the teams get changed under the watchful eye of a black and white photo of Queen Elizabeth II. Outside, two police lines and an 80 metres buffer zone separate Rangers supporters from the Celtic fans arriving in the Broomloan Stand. The road behind it was known as 'wine alley', nearby Neptune Street as the Irish Channel. Celtic legend Kenny Dalglish grew up in the adjacent tower blocks, a Protestant Rangers fan who waited and waited for his childhood heroes to sign him. They never did. But Jock Stein, who was happy to sign players of either religion at a time when Rangers restricted themselves to Protestants, took him to Celtic.

Striker Maurice Johnston wasn't the first Catholic to sign for Rangers, although his signing in July 1989 caused huge controversy on both sides. Not only was he a Roman Catholic who had been a fan then a hero at Celtic before playing for Nantes in France, he had agreed to rejoin Celtic when Rangers boss Graeme Souness stepped in. Today, many of Rangers' heroes are Catholic, though mostly born outside Scotland.

Johnston was a key figure in the Rangers' revolution which began in 1986 under new chairman David Holmes. In the early 1980s, Rangers had averaged crowds of less than 20,000 in a re-modelled stadium. Holmes brought in Souness, who spent heavily on English players like England captain Terry Butcher. A first title in nine years followed in 1987 before David Murray, then a 37-year-old Edinburgh steel magnate, took over the club in 1988. Under manager Walter Smith, Rangers won nine titles on the trot, a run only interrupted by Celtic winning the Double in their 1987–88 Centenary Year.

As Rangers dominated, Celtic lolled in the doldrums. By 1990, they were £3.5 million in debt and light years behind Rangers in terms of playing and commercial success. Their Parkhead home was decaying, with gates poor. When Scots-born Canadian businessman Fergus McCann stepped in in 1994, the club was reputed to be only minutes from going bust. Parkhead was rebuilt, a first title in a decade followed in 1998 and Martin O'Neill became manager in 2000, winning his first Old Firm game 6–2, overturning the psychological advantage held by Rangers. Celtic have won six of the eight League titles since 2001.

'Celtic dominated,' says fan Larry McMahon, 'we were spending more money, we were buying better players, we had a better ground, we had a better manager, we had a better reputation, we were basically fucking them in every department. That's how it felt.'

There's an hour to kick off. The Celtic fans use a different network of streets, coaches and public transport, the vast majority of those going to the game kept apart until they reach the stadium. The Rangers fans sing '*Big Jock Knew.*' Others have pin badges with 'BJK' on them, or flags with the same message. In the early 1970s, young boys were abused by James Torbett, a youth coach at Celtic. The allegation is that manager Jock Stein knew about it and did nothing. Others say that Stein kicked Torbett out of the club, but that he wormed his way back in when Stein wasn't in a position of power. Stein, naturally, can't sue over the allegations since he passed away in 1985.

The song has become common currency on the terraces after both Celtic and Rangers clamped down on sectarianism, a way to wind opposition fans up when more openly sectarian songs have attracted sanctions. UEFA put its foot down over discriminatory chanting. Rangers were faced with a situation that if they didn't stop sectarian chants within the ground they could be fined and games would be staged behind closed doors.

Recently, both clubs have worked alongside the Scottish Parliament, church groups and community organisations to ban sectarian songs, inflammatory flag-waving, and troublesome supporters, using increased levels of policing and surveillance.

'You could argue that Rangers had a business imperative to try and stop overt sectarianism from the fans within Ibrox,' says Penman, 'but I genuinely believe that (Rangers chairman) David Murray finds the sectarian and bigoted element distasteful.'

'Because Rangers were a high-profile club who were fined by UEFA, Celtic fans pretend they are whiter than white. It simply isn't true. At times, Celtic Park and particularly the away support were rattling through the whole repertoire of republican anthems. The clubs will never eradicate a section of society who are by their nature bigoted and attach themselves to both clubs. Football is not the cause of sectarianism in the west of Scotland. Sectarian people will attach themselves to these clubs because of what they did and to a certain extent still stand for, but that doesn't cause sectarianism.'

There is still an element of the away support at both clubs domestically who continue to sing sectarian and bigoted songs, but the situation is improving. 'It has become far too sanitised,' one disillusioned Rangers fan says. 'You used to be able to go to football and let off a bit of steam and have a go at the Fenians.'

'The intensity is still there, how it manifests itself has changed,' says Celtic fan Larry McMahon. 'The all-seater stadium, increased policing and stewarding and fewer away fans creates a different experience. It's less foreboding. Compare that to the 1980 Scottish Cup Final where there was a mental riot on the pitch after the game. It was literally a pitched battle. The TV pictures and commentary captured the zeitgeist perfectly: the Celtic team with no numbers on the back of the shirts to spoil the hoops, punters with Status Quo barnets, denim jackets, scarves round the wrists, toe to toe scraps and the cops on horseback getting stuck in to the Celtic support (no surprise there). The commentator said in mock horror "Is this sport, is this football? It looks like outright war!" Which is what it was.'

UEFA have been satisfied with Rangers' actions and while both clubs are now regulars in the Champions League, attitudes to the two clubs differ internationally. Celtic's image is largely positive, Rangers isn't. The stereotypes have both been reinforced in recent seasons as both clubs reached (and lost) in UEFA cup finals. Celtic fans (around four million once some of their fans have used what Rangers fans call 'The Seville calculator') were lauded for their behaviour in southern Spain. In Manchester in 2008, the estimated 150,000 Rangers fans were all criticised for the drunken violence of a few. In the 2007–08 season, both the Old Firm played in Barcelona. Rangers took 21,000, the biggest ever following for a British club in Europe outside a final. The 12,000 who came to cheer on Celtic received positive media coverage, Rangers fans were heavily criticised, despite there being little discernible difference in their behaviour.

What changed is that Celtic fans benefited from Rangers' visit. The Catalan authorities were not ready for the huge number of Rangers supporters. Rangers fans were short changed by authorities happy to take their money, but unwilling to provide the infrastructure their presence required.

Rangers fans were castigated for urinating in the streets, Celtic fans weren't, because scores of portable toilets had been installed. Unsurprisingly, the numerous Irish bars in Barcelona either closed or employed heavy security for the visit of Rangers. For Celtic fans they issued commemorative t-shirts and stuck up posters of Jimmy Johnstone. A special fan zone was created for the Celtic contingent outside the city centre; Rangers fans faced lines of nervous police.

There were many ironic scenes, such as 'dangerous' Protestant Rangers fans singing sectarian songs in those Irish bars which did stay open, while 'friendly' Celtic fans loudly eulogised the IRA in those same bars months later – not that the Catalans, who view noisy inebriation as weakness and not a virtue, were aware of the nuances of fan culture. Well, apart from those who unfurled a giant Irish tricolour to agitate the Rangers fans.

The sheer size of the travelling support from both clubs was remarkable and well in excess of what Barça took to either Celtic Park or Ibrox – Barça needed only one plane to Glasgow; Rangers fans arrived on 97 flights for the return game in Catalonia. Their range of songs was comprehensive and flags from both sets of visiting Glaswegian fans were impressive. Given the sheer numbers of visiting supporters, both games passed with surprisingly few arrests and plenty of comic stories. Like the two Celtic fans negotiating with a Catalan tout for tickets. He cheekily asked for €200 a ticket; the alcohol fuelled pair thought about it and came back with their offer … €195.

The game is about to start and the whole of Ibrox is singing. Judged on noise level and passion alone, the spectacle far exceeds that of any other British derby. In the main stand, what seems like every single fan is singing: '*Oh Big Jock knew, oh Big Jock knew, oh Big Jock knew, oh Big Jock knew, oh Big Jock knew, oh Big Jock knew, oh Big Jock knew.*' They love it and glad-hand each other. Behind the goal, the Celtic fans are singing '*You'll Never Walk Alone.*'

Rangers are top of the league, with manager and club legend Walter Smith praised for turning the club around. Gordon Strachan, his counterpart at Celtic, who, despite winning the league two seasons on the trot and excelling in Europe, is under immense pressure from elements of the Celtic fan base who allege that he's 'not a Celtic man' – that is someone who doesn't believe that Celtic's fanbase is by far and away the best in the world. Strachan's honesty has to be admired, but not when he says that he doesn't listen to radio phone-ins because 'I can see the type of person who rings in, sat at home with a can of Kestrel lager with his dog by his side.' Martin O'Neill would have never said that about someone who pays his wages.

'Playing in an Old Firm match is one thing, playing well in one is something else altogether,' says Mark McGhee. 'For the players, particularly the indigenous ones, pressure builds as the match approaches. Anything that you ever thought about yourself will be tested in this fixture. Your bottle, your courage, your self-control. Many Old Firm matches have been threatened by the 'red mist', never mind any other sort of inclement weather. The present situation in the SPL is exactly the sort which fuels the rivalry. Once again the two Glasgow giants are runaway leaders in the championship. Times like these produce legends.'

Just before the goal, a can was thrown at Artur Borac, Celtic's Polish goalkeeper who crosses himself before kick off. In 2006, the authorities considered punishing Borac for 'inciting' Rangers fans. The Rangers fans respond in a mature manner and condemn the thrower until he is ejected: self policing at its finest. Celtic have the better of the first half, but it's Rangers who score on the stroke of half time, prompting an ear bursting rendition of '*We shall not be moved.*'

Half-time is an excuse for both fans to unfurl huge and carefully crafted flags. In the Celtic end, there's a giant depiction of Jock Stein with the European Cup (one trophy Rangers have never won) as his shadow. 'Is it cold in the shadow?' asks the flag. Others, in green and white and gold of the Irish tricolour, reference places like 'Port Glasgow', and players such as 'Aiden McGeady' – star of the current Celtic team. Rangers' flags come in different sizes and shades of red, white and blue, emblazoned with slogans like 'We are the people.' Others 'Bathgate RSC,' 'Glenrothes Loyal', 'Perth Loyal' and 'Charlton Loyal'.

Rangers hold on to victory in a fiercely contested game containing eight bookings. After the match, the presenter on Real Radio celebrates Rangers winning the league, arguing without doubt that the title is now a foregone conclusion. Prematurely, as it turned out. As Rangers' fixture backlog mounted up, Celtic powered on, winning seven games on the trot and defeating Rangers twice as three Old Firm matches were played out in the space of a month. Celtic won the league and completed a hat-trick of titles on the final day of the season and Strachan, in becoming the first Celtic manager since Stein to lift a hat-trick of titles, was able to raise the proverbial two fingers to his detractors.

The decision of the SFA not to ease Rangers' fixture problems created a furore. It added further fuel to the accusations of bias for one side or the other which litter the history of games between the two clubs and ensure that each subsequent derby is contested with a passion that shows no sign of decreasing.

Acknowledgments

This book would have been impossible without the help of a great number of individuals.

I'd like to thank all those I spoke to on my travels; strangers who willingly gave up their own time to meet me in bars, train stations or hotels. Many are quoted within, while others helped out in the background, like Neil Templeton and Mark Simpson, whose local knowledge proved invaluable in Belfast.

In Tel Aviv, Ouriel Daskal was exceptionally generous with his time. Jakob Storustovu knew everyone in the Faroes, and not just because he boasts the easiest phone number in the world, while Heri Simonsen's passion for life is unrivalled. In Wrexham, Irish was the man. Cheers.

In bustling Amsterdam, Longy watched, listened and cleared the ground with the rummest coves, while Erik van den Polder took a morning off work to help in Rotterdam.

Michael Martin did far more than he needed to in Newcastle, while in Liverpool I appreciated the assistance of Peter Hooton and Kevin Sampson; and John O'Shea. Phil Holt's contacts were invaluable for the Preston v Blackpool piece.

Everyone associated with Elgin City was a pleasure and I have happy memories of Robbie and the boys. But not of the ice.

Chris Todd's passion for Tenerife and football shone through, while Louise Smith took care of me when the sun went down.

FC Barcelona have always been efficient to deal with, thanks to people like Frances Orenes. Ditto Javier T at CF Real Madrid.

Andrea Landi smoothed everything in Rome, conjuring up an apartment by the Trevi fountain and a night out. In Glasgow, Mark Dingwall was spot on.

Agent Paul Morton was a guiding light, always full of suggestions and ideas. I told you United would win it. Thanks to everyone at *United We Stand*, especially Jim White and Adam Renton. Joyce Woolridge, as ever, was able to make an immense contribution – not least because of the love she gets from Sean and Andrew.

At HarperCollins, Tom Whiting, whose impetus and expertise pushed the project through, worked around a trip to see a real game in Moscow, Chris Stone was an assiduous reader and Dom Forbes designed a cracking cover.

All the lads (Gary, Louis, Matt, Hitesh and Nick) at *FourFourTwo* chipped in in various ways – and Hugh Sleight, a fine editor, has been a joy to work with for years. Thanks also to Martyn Jones and those fine pastries at Teddington.

Sincere thanks and love to Mum and Les, Dad and Jayne, Joz and Cathy, Hayley and Karl the blue, Sambrotta, Harry and the lovely Brazilian, Ba. We'll watch Gremio v Internacionale one day …

The Contributors

Louis Massarella is features editor of *FourFourTwo* magazine and author of several books on football.

Shahab Mossavat lives and works in Iran, where he is the presenter of *Four Corners*, a daily current affairs analysis programme on Press TV.

Kevin Buckley is based in Italy, from where he has covered Italian football for a variety of publications, including *Champions*, *The Observer*, *The Guardian* and *The Sunday Times*. He also contributes regularly to broadcasters including *Sky Sports*, *BBC Radio* and *TalkSport*.

Alex Olliver's journalistic credits include *The Daily Telegraph*, *Classic Rock*, *FourFourTwo* and numerous travel magazines, while his copy-writing has been used by companies as diverse as Canon, Pfizer and the Highways Agency.

Steve Morgan works on Manchester United's official publications and has written regularly for *FourFourTwo* and *When Saturday Comes*.

Steven Wells lives in Philadelphia where he annoys Americans by writing about English football, and baffles the British by writing about American soccer.

Celso De Campos Jr is a Sao Paolo-based journalist, writing mainly about football and music. He is *FourFourTwo*'s Brazilian correspondent.

Martin Mazur is a writer for *El Grafico*, Argentina's leading football magazine. From his home in Buenos Aires, he regularly enlightens *FourFourTwo* readers on the quirks of Argentinian football.

Si Hawkins is a freelance journalist living in London. He writes about football, music and comedy for *FourFourTwo*, *Metro* and *Guardian Unlimited*.

Steve Bryant is a British journalist who has been based in Turkey for many years. He was formerly BBC correspondent in Istanbul, and currently works for Bloomberg.

Dan Brennan, a regular contributor to *FourFourTwo*, and various other UK and foreign publications, runs Libero Language Lab, an editorial and translation agency specialising in football.

Mat Snow is unashamedly biased when it comes to the North London derby. He is a highly-respected music journalist and also the former editor of *Mojo* and *FourFourTwo*.

Daniel Neilson is a freelance writer and editor based in Buenos Aires. He has edited *Time Out Buenos Aires* and *Time Out Costa Rica* guidebooks, as well as contributing to *The Wire*, *The Observer* and *CNN Traveller* among others.

Neil Billingham spent seven years as a producer for the TV programme *Futbol Mundial*, travelling to more than 50 countries in five different continents. He is now a freelance writer and TV producer.

Robert Bright worked for *Empire, Q, Select* and *Top Gea*r magazines before moving to India to work as a freelance journalist. He now contributes to *The Guardian, The New York Times* and a plethora of magazines, focusing on travel, culture and sport.

Picture Credits

Page 1: Girl from Ipanema (PA Photos)

Page 2: River Plate Fans (PA Photos), Boca v River (PA Photos)

Page 3: Copa Libertadores (PA Photos), Gerrard and Anderson (PA Photos)

Page 4: Anfield Kop (PA Photos), Faroes' Derby (Andy Mitten), Dinamo Zagreb fans (FourFourTwo)

Page 5: Celtic fans (PA Photos), Arsenal players (PA Photos)

Page 6: Tel Aviv (FourFourTwo), Calcutta (FourFourTwo), Preston v Blackpool (FourFourTwo)

Page 7: Fenerbahce faces (PA Photos), Split lip (FourFourTwo), Elgin v East Stirlingshire (FourFourTwo)

Page 8: Tenerife banners (FourFourTwo), Barcelona fan (PA Photos), Essex Uniteds (FourFourTwo).